Fire Insurance Records for Family and Local Historians 1696 to 1920

David T Hawkings writes, lectures and broadcasts extensively on genealogical research, and is the originator of the television series 'Find Your Family'. He is the author of *Bound for Australia* (a reference work to the records of transported convicts), *Criminal Ancestors* (criminal records in England and Wales) and *Railway Ancestors* (historical records of the staff of English and Welsh railways).

100 Guineas
REWARD.

WHEREAS

Some Person or Persons did, in the Night of Saturday, the 17th of March Instant, maliciously SET

FIRE

to a RICK of WHEAT, standing in a Field called Little Reddings, at ST. LEONARDS, in the Parish of Aston Clinton, in the County of Buckingham, belonging to the Rev. E. Owen, whereby the said RICK was consumed,

A REWARD OF
100 GUINEAS

Is hereby offered to any Person or Persons who shall give such Evidence as shall lead to the Conviction of the said Offender or Offenders, and shall be paid on his or their Conviction, by me

EDWARD OWEN.

St. Leonards, March 18th, 1832.

Reward Poster, 1832

David T. Hawkings

Fire Insurance Records for Family and Local Historians 1696 to 1920

First published by Francis Boutle Publishers
272 Alexandra Park Road
London N22 7BG
Tel/Fax: (020) 8889 7744
Email: fire@francisboutle.demon.co.uk
www.francisboutle.demon.co.uk

ISBN 1 903427 14 2

Printed in Spain

Acknowledgements

I wish to thank the following without whose help this project would have been impossible: The archivists and librarians of all the record offices, libraries and universities throughout England, Scotland, Wales, the Isle of Man, Ireland and the Channel Islands for answering my questionnaires; the late David Hill and Martin Crewys, archivists of the Royal and Sun Alliance. Mrs Anna Stone and Mrs Sheree Leeds at AVIVA (formerly CGNU/Norwich Union), David Carter and Miss Clare Bunkham at the Prudential and Mrs Isabel Syed at Zurich; the staff of the Map Department of the British Library, the Print Department of the British Museum, the British Museum Newspaper Library at Colindale, and David Bromwich, librarian of the Somerset Local History Library at Taunton.

Miss Myrtle Mumford gave me details of the Sun trades indices which she continues to organise and direct. George Rigal kindly shared with me his detailed knowledge of the Sun Fire Office records and found some of the *famous people* given in Chapter 14.

Thanks must go to Miss Maureen Shettle who very kindly provided details of the Admiralty Registers which list firemen who were exempted from impressment into the Royal Navy and also gave me some entries from the Sun Fire Office Management meetings.

From Steven Freeth, Keeper of Manuscripts at the Guildhall Library, London and his staff there was continued help and support throughout this project over the last thirty years, and from Mrs Irene Pollock, Librarian of the Guildhall Library and her staff. Edwin Green and the late Hugh Cockerell (joint authors of *The British Insurance Business*) helped with detailed information as did Philip Abbott, librarian at the Royal Armouries, Leeds.

Thanks go to Brian Henham for writing the foreword to this book and to Roy Addis and David Hutchinson for so kindly supplying some of the illustrations from their collections.

I am especially grateful to Mrs Irene Coulson for preparing much of the text of this book on computer disk and so patiently coping with my endless alterations and amendments.

Contents

List of Illustrations

List of Figures and Tables

Abbreviations

Berks RO	Berkshire Record Office
Bucks RO	Buckinghamshire Record Office
Bury St Ed RO	Bury St Edmunds Record Office
Cambridge Uni Lib	Cambridge University Library
CIS	Co-operative Insurance Society
CRO	County Record Office
Cumb RO Kendal	Cumbria Record Office, Kendal
Cumb RO, Whit	Cumbria Record Office, Whitehaven
Derby RO	Derbyshire Record Office
Devon RO Ex	Devon Record Office, Exeter
E Sussex RO	East Sussex Record Office
Essex RO Chelms	Essex Record Office, Chelmsford
Essex RO Colch	Essex Record Office, Colchester
FO	Fire Office
Glasgow Uni Arch	Glasgow University Archives
GLDH	Guildhall Library, London
Gtr Man RO	Greater Manchester Record Office
Hants RO	Hampshire Record Office
Heref RO	Herefordshire Record Office
Herts Arch	Hertfordshire Archives and Local Studies
Hull Uni BJ Lib	Brynmor Jones Library at The University of Hull
Hunts CRO	Cambridgeshire County Record Office, Huntingdon
Lancs RO	Lancashire Record Office
Lib	Library
Lincs Arch Grims	North East Lincolnshire Archives, Grimsby
Lincs Arch Linc	Lincolnshire Archives, Lincoln
Mitch Lib Glasgow	Mitchell Library, Glasgow
N Devon RO	North Devon Record Office, Barnstaple
Nat Lib Scot	National Library of Scotland
Nat Arch Scot	National Archives of Scotland
Nat Lib Wales	National Library of Wales
Northants RO	Northamptonshire Record Office
Notts Arch	Nottinghamshire Archives
Nthbland RO	Northumberland Record Office
NU	Norwich Union
PRO	Public Record Office/National Archives, London
PRO N Ireland	Public Record Office of Northern Ireland
R&SA	Royal and Sun Alliance
RLM	Royal London Mutual Insurance Society
RO	Record Office

Shakespeare BT	Shakespeare Birthplace Trust Record Office
Surrey HC	Surrey History Centre
Uni	University
W Sussex RO	West Sussex Record Office
W York Arch Cald	West Yorkshire Archive Service, Calderdale
W York Arch Hud	West Yorkshire Archive Service, Huddersfield
W York Arch Kirk	West Yorkshire Archive Service, Kirkdale
W York Arch Lds	West Yorkshire Archive Service, Leeds
Waltham F Arch	Waltham Forest Archives
Warwick CRO	Warwick County Record Office
Westmr Arch	Westminster City Archives
Wilts RO	Wiltshire and Swindon Record Office
Wolv Arch	Wolverhampton Archives and Local Studies
Zurich	Zurich Financial Services

Foreword

Brian R G Henham

When I began my first job as an insurance fire surveyor almost forty years ago, I had no idea how much it would affect the rest of my life. It was not long, however, before I learnt that the post of insurance surveyor was first created as early as 1696, when the newly formed Hand in Hand Fire Office appointed Captain John Outing *"to attend Each Subscriber to survey the House Subscribed in order to take out Policyes"*. As I gazed at these words written with a quill pen in the Director's Minute Book, the ink still reasonably legible some 269 years later, I was overawed at the antiquity of the profession of which I had recently become a member. Numerous questions immediately formed in my mind. *What did the job of Surveyor entail, back in the days when William III was King of England and bewigged gentlemen exchanged gossip in the coffee houses of London, which was still recovering from the Great Fire of 1666? What were the people like who set up and ran those first insurance companies? Who and what did they insure?* The answers to these and many other questions were, I was sure, contained in those dusty old books hidden away in the depths of the Guildhall Library, London and various other libraries and record offices scattered throughout the UK. I was hooked! I needed to know more.

Sadly, as I was about to find out, many of the old insurance records had already been destroyed; some by the ravages of time; some at the time of acquisition by another company; some by fire; and others by act of War. But what, I asked myself, was left of the old insurance records? Where were they? What could I learn from them? Where on earth should I start to look?

Now, half a lifetime later, after years of research for several books, I have found the answers to many of my questions. How much more simple, however, my journey through the records would have been, had I had access to a comprehensive book such as the one that you are about to read.

During the period when I was using insurance records for the purposes of research into the history of fire insurance and fire fighting, David Hawkings was using the same records in his study of family history. We both ended up in many blind alleys and dead ends but if the information was there, by and large by trial and error we eventually found it. Now, drawing on his vast knowledge of insurance records, David has painstakingly put together the ultimate work of reference that has for so long been needed. Reading through the manuscript for the book, I have found myself saying over and over again, *"I wish I had known that several years ago!"*

Throughout the book, all document references are quoted where necessary.

There is much original research, such as the broad-brush analysis of 17 towns in the Introduction and the explanation of the notation and format of early fire policies in Chapter 2. The latter will prove to be of enormous value to those unfamiliar with these records. The author has illustrated each chapter with ample examples drawn from the records, including some superb cameos such as the Sun Fire Office policy taken out by William Deacon in 1831 covering 28 Portsmouth Public Houses, with all the tenants mentioned by name.

Even when consulting original records, it is easy to make simple mistakes. One such example quoted in the book is the renumbering of houses that occurred in the early 20th century, which means that the house now numbered 20 High Street may well have had a different number in the 19th century. Finally, the Appendices contain a wealth of factual information, tabulated for ease of reference, much being original work that will not be found elsewhere.

For the genealogist, the surviving insurance records predate the first useful population census of 1841 and therefore form a most valuable source of information. There is a vast amount of social, economic and family history hidden in the surviving records of the British fire insurance industry and this book will help you to track it down much faster and more accurately than was possible when I first started to use insurance records for research purposes.

Brian Henham is an Associate of the Chartered Insurance Institute (ACII) and Vice President of the Fire Mark Circle of Great Britain.

Preface

Sooner or later every family and local historian refers to newspapers in an attempt to gain some understanding of the day to day events in a district at an earlier period. Many of the inhabitants will be found recorded for posterity, even if merely in the birth and marriage columns or in an obituary notice. Other more dramatic events often reveal information about people.

In pursuit of detail for my own family history I turned to the Wellington (Somerset) newspapers. An article in *The Wellington Times* for 14 April 1870 reads: 'Fire. On Saturday last, soon after one o'clock in the day, a fire occured at *The Kings Arms Inn*, which might have been attended with serious results. It appears that during the morning the chimney of Mr Hawkins's sitting room had been on fire, and had been put out. Some of the burning soot, however, fell down the adjoining bedroom chimney, and set on fire a bundle of straw which had been pushed up the chimney to stop the draft during winter. The burning straw fell into the room, setting fire to the carpet, and thence to the valance, and before anyone knew of it the whole room was in a blaze. Mr Hawkins's niece was the first to raise the alarm as she found the sitting room full of smoke. Mr Hawkins went to ascertain the cause and found the room a fire as we have stated. Help was speedily obtained and the burning bed clothes were thrown out of the window and the fire extinguished. The damage is estimated at £30. The premises are insured in the Sun Fire Office.'

An enquiry to the archivist of the Sun Alliance confirmed that the Sun Fire Office was indeed the original name of that company. Policies and other records, I was told, have been preserved and are held at the Guildhall Library, London. Claims were recorded in the minutes of the Committee of Town Insurances. It was not difficult to locate Mr Hawkins' claim. The minutes of that committee for the 10 May 1870 read:

'Wellington .1975835, Michael Hawkins * of Wellington, Som. Inn. £32.9.0.'

* Subsequent research has shown that Michael Hawkins is not related to the author.

The number 1975835 is the policy number which was located in the Sun policy register reference Ms 11937/520 for the Country Department. See page 107.

The Wellington Times, and its rival *The Wellington Weekly News* were both established in 1869. No newspaper was printed in Wellington before this date. *The Taunton Courier* was a much earlier newspaper and spread its coverage over West Somerset. A search through this revealed that a fire had broken out at Rockwell Green, Wellington on Friday 2 February 1827, but the names of those persons suffering losses from this fire were not stated. I had established that my family was living at Rockwell Green at that time; had any member of my fami-

The Fire Brigade – Scaling Ladders, Hoses etc. c.1849. From Illustrated London News

ly been involved, I wondered? A search through the loss registers of the Sun soon identified Thomas Cornelius, a tailor, (one of my ancestors) as a claimant. A further search revealed that Thomas Cornelius had also made a claim in 1810 (see page 51). Unfortunately the early claims registers do not record the policy numbers of the claimants. Searching backwards from 1810 (the date of the earliest claim found for him) his policy was found in 1805. A further search backwards from this date located another policy in 1801. Other policies under his name have been found in 1816, 1821 and 1822. No policy has been found before 1801 but his father Samuel Cornelius is named as a tenant in 1796, in a house in South Street, Wellington, owned and insured by Peter Southey, a farmer of West Buckland.

Thomas Cornelius, who died in 1829, made no mention in his will of his daughter Elizabeth or her husband Robert Hawkings. It had been assumed that both Elizabeth and Robert Hawkings were, for some reason, out of favour. A study of the insurance policies, however, proved this assumption far from the truth. In fact Robert Hawkings had become the owner of five houses previously owned by Thomas Cornelius some years before Thomas Cornelius died (see page 104). Four policies have been found for this Robert Hawkings together with two policy endorsements and a joint policy for his sons John and Thomas Hawkings. Another policy was found for John Hawkings and two for his sister Elizabeth Hawkings.

Some years ago after giving a lecture on fire insurance records a member of the audience mentioned to me that she was trying to trace the family of John Boon, of Lyme Regis, Dorset. He lived there in the early 19th century. An insurance policy was later found for Henry Stanton and John Boon of Lyme Regis. This policy referred to 'John Boon's house and offices adjoining at Ilminster Somerset'. Research in Ilminster parish registers revealed some of John Boon's family.

Another enquirer asked if I had any knowledge of the origins of Samuel Swinnerton of *The White Hart Inn* in Colnbrook, only a few miles from where I was living at that time. Samuel Swinnerton lived in Colnbrook in the early 18th century, but where did he come from? Insurance policies were found for Samuel Swinnerton of Colnbrook for the years 1792, 1798 and 1806. An earlier policy dated 1791 (see page 98) recorded him at the *The Rose* in Monkwell Street, London and also referred to *The White Hart* at Colnbrook, Middlesex. Another policy for 1785 recorded him as: 'of Monkwell Street, London'.

Such information is indeed of great value to both local and family historians. After many years of research much has been learned about the historic records of fire insurance companies and is given in this book.

David T. Hawkings

Introduction

The loss of property by fire has always been of great concern, particularly in the days when many buildings were more vulnerable when built of timber and roofed with thatch.The only likely means of financial compensation was through the charity of the parishioners of the established church, usually organised by the clergy or local magistrates. Collections were made for local victims of fire. The following is taken from *Somerset and Dorset Notes and Queries*, volume 1, dated 1890, and refers to a conflagration in Yeovil, Somerset on 28 July 1640. (The origin and location of the document is not given.)

A Protecion for losses by fire graunted unto the
Inhabitants of Yeovill in the County of Somersett

Charles by the grace of God King of England Scotland ffrance and Ireland defender of the faith. TO ALL and singular Archbishops, Bishops, Archdeacons, Deanes and their officialls, Parsons, Vicars, Curats and to all spirituall persons. And also to all Justices of Peace, maiors, Sheriffs, Bailiffs, Constables, Churchwardens and head boroughes. And to all Officers of Citties, Boroughes and Townes corporate, And to all other our officers, ministers and subjects whatsoever they will be as well within liberties as without to whom these presents shall come greeting. WHEREAS We are credibly given to understand as well by the humble supplicacion and peticion of our poore distressed subjects the Inhabitants of Yeovell in our County of Somersett as also by a certificate made at the general quarter sessions of the peace holden at Bridgwater for the said County the sixth day of October last past 1640 under the hands of our trusty and well beloved subjects Sir William Portman, Baronett, Thomas Luttrell, Thomas Smith, William Every, John Harrington, George Paulett, Robert Harbyn, Robert Hunt and William Bull Esquires Justices of the Peace for the said county. That within or uppon the eight and twentieth day of July last past 1640 about one of the Clock in the afternoone of the same day there happened to our said Towne of Yeovell being an ancient market Towne a suddayne and grevious misfortune of fire begyning in the house of Walter Whitcombe which by reason of the dryness of the season, the winde being strong and high, and the irrestable, vehement and terrible flames thereof, did in a short space utterly consume waste and burne downe fourescore and three dwelling houses besides many other outhouses wherein lived twoe hundred families conteyning in them six hundred persons at the least of men women and children besides very many barnes, stables, staules and other buildings and outhouses to the number of twoe hundred together with corne, hay, wood, coale, householdstuffe and other wares and goodes, they having housed most of theire hay and made provision of coale, wood and other necessaries for the whole year following for themselves, families and cattell, which were all burnt, wasted and consumed by the saide fire amounting in all to the value of Twelve Thousand pounds, a great part of which people receiveth reliefe and not able to subsist without the same and are about the number of three hundred persons and a great part of them Trades men whoe had only their houses and trades by which they formerly lived in good sort and sett many people on work and relieved many but are now themselves destitute of houses or any means to relieve themselves and theire families as appeareth to our foresaid Justices uppon the oathes of John Jennings gentleman, John Laver gentleman, Christopher Allambridge and Thomas Rocke able and sufficient Inhabitants of the saide Towne verifying likewise that by this untimely accident our saide poore Subjects are greatly impoverished and utterly undone, left in great distresse and misery, who have humbly besought us of our aboundant and gracious goodnes and clemency. We would be pleased to provide some convenient meanes for theire reliefe and mayntenance by granting them licence and power to aske and receive the charities of weldisposed people for theire support and livelihood unto whose request as also upon the certificate of our foresaide Justices. We most willingly have condiscended and esteemed noe one thing to be more necessary then the re-edifying of decayed Townes and the relieving of the poore distressed people thereof, have thought good to commend the same charitable consideracion of all our loving Subjects within the said County of Somersett and of the other Counties and places hereafter mencioned. Not doubting but that all good Christians rightly and duly considering the premisses will be ready and willing to extend their liberall contribucionns in soe good, soe necessary and so charitable a deede. KNOWE ye therefore that of our especiall grace and princely compassion We have given and granted and by these our Letters Patent under our great Seale of England doe give and grant unto the Inhabitants of Yeovell in our County of Somersett aforesaid and to their Deputy and Deputies the bearer or bearers thereof, full power, licence and authority to aske, gather, receive and take the almes and charitable benevolence of all our loving Subjects whatsoever inhabiting within the Counties, Shires, Citties and priviledged places throughout the whole kingdom of England and Domynion of Wales (except the Counties of Leicester, Nottingham, Derby, Lancaster, Yorke, Northumberland, Cumberland, Westmerland and Durham) for and toward the recovery of their said losses and the releife and mayntenance of such and soe many as are fitt to partake of this Collecion, according to the directions hereafter expressed. WHEREFORE We will and command you and every of you that at such tyme and tymes as the Inhabitants of Yeovell aforesaid their Deputy or Deputies the bearer or bearers hereof shall come and repair to any your Churches, Chappells or other places to aske and receive the gratuities and charitable benevolence of our said subjects quietly to permit and suffer them soe to doe without any manner your lett or contradicions. And you the said Parsons, Vicars and Curats for the better stirring upp of a charitable devocion deliberately to publish and declare the tenor of these Letters Patent or the Coppy or Briefe hereof unto our said subjects upon some Sunday shortly after the same shall be tendred unto you and before the expiration of the date hereof. Earnestly exhorting and perswading them to extend their liberall contributions in soe good and charitable a deed. AND you the Churchwardens of every parish where such collecion is to be made as aforesaid to collect and gather the almes and charitable benevolence of all our loving Subjects as well strangers as others. AND what shalbe by you soe gathered to be by the minister and yourselves endorsed on the backside of

these our Letters Patent or the Coppy or Briefe hereof in words at length and
not in figures. And the some and somes of money soe gathered and endorsed
Our Will and pleasure is shalbe delivered to the bearer or bearers of these
Letters Patent warranted and allowed to receive the same and to no other person when as thereunto you shal be required. AND LASTLY Our will and pleasure is for the more assurance of faithful and equall dealing in the receipt
accompt and distribution of the moneys collected by virtue of these our Letters
Patent, that noe man shall receive any of the moneys soe collected but such as
shalbe appoynted thereunto by Deputacion under the hands and seales of
Edward Philips and Robert Harbyn Esquires and that the moneys collected and
raised by virtue hereof, shalbe distributed amongst such of those dampnified by
the saide fire, only as neede the same and are fitt to be relieved by publique
charity and by such proporcions as shalbe thought fitt and sett downe in writing under the hands of the persons last named, at such tymes and places of their
meeting as by them shal be from tyme to tyme appoynted for that purpose. It
being not our intencions that any of those whoe are otherwise of ability and in
the judgement of the persons last named not thought fitt to be relieved by this
collecion, should be made partakers of it, And they in like manner to appoynt
in whose hands the moneys collected are to be kept untill the same shalbe distributed and how the accompt thereof shalbe ordered according to the true
intent and meaning of our royall will and pleasure herein declared any Statute,
law, ordinance or provision heretofore made to the contrary in anywise notwith-
standing. IN WITNESS whereof We have caused these our letters to be made
Patent to continue for the space of one whole yeare next after the date thereof
and not longer.

WITNES ourselfe at Westmynster the seaventeenth day of
November in the sixteenth yeare of our Raigne.

Such collections were often carried out, and records of them were entered in
parish registers or other parish documents. They often include collections for
parishes many miles away and in other counties. The following entries were
found in the parish register for Aston Samford in Buckinghamshire.[1]

Jan'ry ye 20th 1705
Collected then for the use of the Sufferers by fire at Merriden in the
County of Warwick the sum of one shilling and two pence.

May ye 5th 1706
Collected in the parish Church of Aston Sampforde for the relief of
the sufferers by fire in ye Town of Bradmore in the County of
Nottingham the sum of one shilling and two pence.

Until the end of the 17th century fire insurance did not exist.The Great Fire of
London in 1666 devastated the City and resulted in many thousands of people
becoming homeless.Tradesmen who lost workshops and tools of trade had no
means of earning a living and many became destitute. It was not until 1680 that
fire insurance first became available when *The Fire Office* was established. This
was re-named *The Phenix Office* in 1705. This company was wound up in 1722.
No records of this organisation are known to have survived. In 1683 *The Society
for Insuring Houses from Loss by Fire* was established and was later re-named *The*

*'The Times'. A depiction of fire extinguishing, showing the Union Fire Office
fire engine. William Hogarth, 1762*

Friendly Society. This appears to have been wound up some time after 1740 and
no records have been located though some fire marks survive.

In 1696 *The Contributors for Insuring Houses, Chambers or Rooms from Loss by
Fire, by Amicable Contributions* was founded. (This was re-named *The Hand-in-
Hand Fire Office* in 1713.) Initially cover was given only to houses in London but
from 1806 fire insurance by this fire office was available for all property
throughout Great Britain. Policy records survive from its foundation. (See
Appendix 2.) The policy layout and notation is given in Chapter 1. The next fire
insurance company, *The Sun Fire Office*, was formed in 1710. This company
issued cover for the whole of Great Britain from its beginning and policy
records survive from this date. Policy layout and notation is given in Chapter 2.
Other companies appeared soon after, notably *The Union Fire Office* (1714), *The
Westminster Fire Office* (1717), *The Bristol Crown Fire Office* (1718), *The Edinburgh
Friendly Society* (1720) and *The Friendly Society of Glasgow* (1720), but these gave
only cover for property in their immediate locality.

The London Assurance Corporation and *The Royal Exchange Assurance* (both
formed in 1720; see Chapter 2), were the first after the *Sun* to offer cover nationally and policy records for both these organisations survive. Many more local
insurance companies were set up after the *London* and *Royal Exchange* but it was
not until 1782 that *The New Fire Office* was formed and gave cover throughout
Great Britain. (*The New Fire Office* was re-named *The Phoenix Fire Office* in
1785.) Although no company policy registers are known there are many agency
policy registers for the *Phoenix* held at Cambridge University Library. (See

Merryweather and Son's patent fire engine c. 1862.
From Illustrated London News

Appendix 5.) *The British Fire Office* (formed in 1799) also offered cover through-out Great Britain but this company lasted only five years; it amalgamated with the *Sun Fire Office* in 1804. (No records are known to survive for *The British Fire Office*.) The next company to offer fire cover throughout Great Britain was *The Globe Insurance Company* founded in 1803, and some agents' policy records survive. See Appendix 2.

The Royal Kalendar, which was first published in 1767, gives the following 'Offices of Insurance for Houses and Goods', and lists their officers and directors:

    Hand-in-Hand Fire Office
    London Assurance
    Royal Exchange
    Sun Fire Office
    Union Fire Office
    Westminster Fire Office

If the *British Fire Office* (1799–1804) is ignored, the following are the only insurance companies which gave national coverage before 1800:

	Established	Company Policy Registers
Sun Fire Office	1710	1710–1863 (small gaps)
London Assurance Corporation	1720	1721–1729, 1733–1809, 1821–1881
Royal Exchange	1720	1753–1759; 1773–1883

New Fire Office	1782	no known company policy registers,
(Phoenix)		but many agents' policy registers
		commencing soon after formation

The *Sun* provided by far the greatest proportion of national fire insurance cover. *The New Fire Office* (*Phoenix*) was formed by owners of London sugar refineries, primarily to provide cover for industrial premises. Initially its cover for domestic property was small. It can therefore be concluded that a large proportion of insurance policies covering domestic property and small businesses survive for the period before 1800. The records after this date are even fuller.

In the year 1716 the *Sun* recorded that its insurance had grown by 25% and in that year houses and shops accounted for 67% of the policies issued, 10% were for inns, 9% for warehouses, 5% for farms, barns and malthouses, and only 1% for mills, factories and workshops of all kinds. Shopkeepers, tradesmen and craftsmen formed 30% of the total number insured. By 1790 houses and shops still formed 67% of policies, inns were only 4% and farms had risen to 10%. Warehouses were then 8% and mills, workshops and factories a further 8%. By September 1863 the *Sun* had issued over twenty and a quarter million policies, and transcripts of most of these survive in the policy registers at the Guildhall Library.[2] (The last policy in the last register known to survive is policy number 2026800, issued to Edward Upton, a labourer, on two cottages at numbers 1 and 2 Salem Cottages, Southborough, Kent, dated 23 September 1863.[3])

An analysis of policy holders for 17 towns throughout England for the late 18th century is given in Tables 1 to 4. (At this time insurance cover in Wales and Scotland was very sparse. These countries have therefore been omitted.) The numbers of policies in the *Sun* and *Royal Exchange* are taken from the microfiche indices which cover the period 1775 to 1787. The numbers of gentry (men and women), professional men (lawyers, physicians, clergy, etc.), tradesmen and innkeepers are taken from the Universal Directories of England and Wales which range in date from 1791 to 1798. Unfortunately there are no national directories for the period covered by the microfiche indices. Many of those persons found in these indices are also found in the Universal Directories. Because of the date differences between the indices and the directories this analysis cannot be precise but is close enough to give a fair indication of the proportion of gentry, professionals, tradesmen and innkeepers who were insured in late 18th century England.

The national average of gentry with property fire insurance computes to approximately 36% (see table 1). The national average for professionals is 22% (see table 2). This analysis does not include those covered by the *New Fire Office* as no company policy records are available, neither does it include the many local insurance companies, though it is known that the total value of national cover given by all these companies was less than 10%. If a researcher is looking for details of a particular gentleman in England in the late 18th century there is about a one in three chance that a record will be found in the *Sun* or *Royal Exchange* indices. The figure for professional men is about 22%, or approximately 1 in 5. The combined figure for both professionals and gentry is 41%.

A similar analysis for the same period for inns and tradesmen is given in Tables 3 and 4. The national average for inns covered by insurance computes to 20%, or 1 in 5. That for tradesmen is 28%, approximately 1 in 4. In addition to the above there are numerous policies for householders, most of whom do not appear in the trade directories at this period. Very few farmers appear to have had property insurance in the 18th century. It should be noted, however, that many farmers were tenants of landowners. It was usual for the landowner (not his tenants) to take out insurance on tenanted property. See chapter 8.

Agents for insurance companies were usually local shopkeepers or businessmen. They sold insurance cover on behalf of the company. The *Sun*'s agents received 5% of each premium with a commission of 6d for each new policy sold. Premiums were paid to head office by a *bill of exchange*. The agent passed full details of the insured property to the head office where these were entered into ledgers. It is these ledgers which survive for the *Sun Fire Office*, the *London Assurance Corporation* and the *Royal Exchange Assurance*, and some other companies. The agent also kept full details of policies he had issued for his own reference. Some agents' records also survive (most in local records offices.) All known company and agents' policy records are given in Appendices 2, 3, 4 and 5.

The policies for all companies were written into ledgers at head office in numeric order of policy number. Blocks of numbers were issued to local agents and ¢ policies were issued their details were returned to head office. Some companies used several ledgers for a particular date span. Thus a gap in the numbering in one ledger was filled by the missing block of numbered policies in another ledger covering the same dates.

Contrary to popular belief, Lloyds of London was not the sole insurer of ships. Many ships were insured with other companies and industrial premises, banks, gaols, union workhouses, churches, etc., and even privately owned bridges, were insured from the 18th century. The landed gentry often recorded all their property in great detail, naming each tenant with his trade and place of abode, naming the cottage, farm or workshop. The owners of single houses or workshops took out insurance cover on buildings rented out, and tenants were often named in the policies together with their trades. The applied premium rate varied somewhat depending on the trade carried out in a building. A blacksmith and any other tradesman using forging or other heating methods was a higher risk than a printer or weaver. Buildings with heating pipes carried a higher premium and thatched buildings were clearly of greater risk than those roofed with tiles or slates.

Occasionally the risk was considered too great and insurance was refused as appears against some insurance policy entries. *Sun Fire Office* policy number 971444[4] dated 29 September 1820, in the name of Patty Browne of Bristol, lists her property in Wiveliscombe, Somerset and in Clayhidon, Devonshire with a total value of £950. This insurance was refused. Another policy, number 984413[5] in her name dated 13 October 1821 was not refused. The total value was then £700. A detailed comparison of the two policies shows that some of the buildings in the first policy are not included in the second. The insured values of each building in the second policy vary somewhat; some up, some down. The major difference is that the applied premium rate for a corn mill and smith's shop was increased from 15 shillings to 18 shillings per £100.

It was obviously in the interest of insurance companies to ensure that fire fighting equipment was readily available in all towns and cities. Such equipment was often given, or money donated by the insurance companies towards the purchase of buckets, fire engines, etc.

Sun Fire Office
General Committee[6]

21 Oct. 1732   Ordered that two Dozen of Buckets be sent to the Town of Wellington in Somersetshire to be under the care of the Agent there.

Sun Fire Office
Committee of Management[7]

29 Jan. 1778   That £25 be paid to the Town of Wellington in Somersetshire towards their purchasing an Engine.

Records of claims against loss by fire give the cost of repair or replacement but these early policies do not include cover for damage or loss by other incidents such as flood, storm or burglary. Some records are very detailed giving the name of the policy holder, the address and description of his property, together with the value of the loss. In addition to the claims registers references to claims are to be found in the minutes of board and other committee meetings.

Sun Fire Office
Committee of Management[8]

11 Ap. 1839
The Secretary read a Letter dated Boulogne 27 Feby 1839, from Mr Charles Wright on the part of Mr Taylor of Calais, giving Notice of his being interested in the House called *Bagatelle* at Bath, insured by Mrs Anna Long for £400 Pr P[y] No. 1,280,229 & which was injured by Fire on the 26 Dec[r] last.

16 June 1839
That the Claim of Mrs Anna Long P P[y] No. 1,280,229 amounting to £400 for Loss on *Bagatelle House*, Bath be discharged, provided such a receipt be supplied as shall be satisfactory to the Legal Advisor of the Office, particularly with reference to the Notice from Mr Taylor, the Mortgager.

Some records of losses and claims are less detailed and record only briefly the location of the property with the value of the loss. The following is an example:

Manchester Assurance Company
Committee Book[9]

Thursday 24th October 1901 Losses Advised

Branch	Description and Situation of Risk	Net Loss
Bristol	Dwelling, Wellington	£188
London	"	£250
Glasgow	"	£70

The Canterbury Volunteer Fire Service c.1872. From The Graphic

It was not until the 19th century that insurance cover was granted for farming stock and produce:

Essex and Suffolk Equitable Insurance Society[10]
Board Minutes

14th day of October 1816 This being a Special Meeting to take into consideration the propriety of receiving Insurances on Farming Stock in the aggregate.

It was Resolved: That the Society will in future insure Farming Stock & Produce in one Sum but that the same shall extend to the Stock and Produce on one attached occupation only; and this Regulation shall include the Policies already granted.

Claims for losses were applied for through the agents. Claims records were kept at the company's head office. (See Chapter 4.) The company directors showed surprising compassion towards their clients and sometimes paid for loss or damage even when the policy renewal premium had not been paid:

Sun Fire Office
Management Committee[11]

6 June 1839
The sum of £15 be presented to Alex[r] Thompson of Edinburgh towards the Loss he sustained on the 10 May 1839 estimated at £41-5 he having omitted to renew Policy No. 1,270,543 which expired at Xmas last, though frequently applied to by Messrs Allan.

Worcester.

Names of Agents | Names and Additions of Sureties Dates of Bonds Penalties

Edward Squire — Edward Squire of the City of Worcester / Philip Rufford of the same place Gent / Francis Wilson of the same place Mercer — 26th March 1783 — £500

Francis Wilson — Francis Wilson of the City of Worcester Gent / Edward Squire of the same place Gent / Robt. Vaughan Brooke of Cheapside Stationer — 28 May 1788 — £600
this Bond ....

John Morris — John Morris of the City of Worcester Draper / Francis Wilson of Kempsey Co Worcester Gent / Robert Brook of Hurcott D. D. — 1 Octr. 1803 — £600
(th alive 24 July 1805)

John Morris — John Morris of the City of Worcester Gent / Edwd. Squire of the same City Esq / Francis Wilson of Kempsey Co Worcester Esq — 10 June 1806 — £600
Appointed 5 May 1803 J.M. dead

John Sev. Ballard — John Severn Ballard Worcester Grocer / The Rev. Fred. Stafford of Kniverton Wor. / John Lane of Hanley Castle Wor. Farmer — 21 July 1814 — £600
Appointed 28 April 1814

Jn. Sev. Ballard — John Severn Ballard, of the City of Worcester, Grocer; / John Dent, of Worcester aforesaid, Esquire, ... / John Lane, of Hanley Castle, Worcester, yeoman; ..... — 7 Mar. 1833 — £600

Thomas Arundell Venables — Thomas Arundell Venables, of the City of Worcester, Grocer / Rich. Stribourn Senior, of Finsbury place, Tea Dealer / John Dent, of the said City, Merchant, ... — 13 Nov. 1833 — £600

Sun Fire Office. A page from an Agent's Bond Book

Royal Exchange Assurance
Fire Committee[12]

March 26th 1856
Letters were read from the Company's Agent at Bishops Stortford stating that the House belonging to Ann Watts at Hallingbury, in the County of Essex, and assured to Lady day 1855 by Policy No. 608286 for £50 and the Furniture therein for £25, had been destroyed by fire, with the exception of a portion of the Furniture, and that her reduced circumstances were the cause of the Policy not being renewed as usual at Lady day 1855. That the Assured in consequence of the calamity is plunged into deep distress, and that her case having excited a strong feeling of Sympathy in the neighbourhood, he (the Agent) was induced to submit these particulars to the company in the hope that they would be pleased to allow her some portion of the loss she had sustained, which is estimated at about £47.10/-

The Committee having maturely considered all the circumstances attending the case, particularly that the Property destroyed having been insured with the Company upwards of 30 years, were of opinion to present Mrs Watts with £50, and it was Resolved to recommend to the Court of Directors, to authorise that sum being presented accordingly.

Dramatic action was sometimes taken by the firemen in order to prevent a fire spreading:

Sun Fire Office
Committee of Management[13]

8 June 1826
Resolved that Ten Guineas be presented to Mrs Fry of Wellington [Somerset] in consequence of the roof of her house having been taken off (which was not insured) in order to stop the progress of the fire in an adjoining Building.

Fraudulent claims were not uncommon. It was sometimes the case that a building was over-insured and arguments ensued in the event of a claim. To overcome this it became necessary for the property to be surveyed before the insurance was accepted and very often a surveyor's report was required after a fire to confirm that the value of the claim was not excessive. Sometimes, rather than pay the claimant for his claim the insurance company paid a builder directly for the repair or re-building of the property.

There appears to have been particular trouble in London in areas where poor Jewish people lived:

Sun Fire Office
Committee of Management[14]

12 Oct. 1786
Read the Surveyor's report, stating that upon Examining the Accounts of losses claimed by the Inhabitants of Dukes Place, Three

Herring Court, New Court and Sugar Baker Yard in consequence of a Fire which happen'd in the night of 2nd Sept last, they find the amount thereof to be 22 in Number, to be upwards of £1612. Although goods could be only destroyed by Fire in the House of Judith Isaacs, the upper story of which was burnt and the next story somewhat Damaged, so that the claims were in general made for goods stolen during the Fire. That from every appearance of the persons and Habitations of many of the claimants they had the greatest reason to suspect their Account to be false or Fraudulent. And they further report that from the narrowness of the passages in said Courts & Yard and the number of Timber erections behind them they conceive that Insurances on the Buildings or Goods therein to be extremely Hazardous.

Resolved that it be recommended to the General Quarterly Meeting, That no Jew shall hereafter be insured without a report from a Survey having been made to Mr Winston and by him to a Committee or to the Secretary for Approbation and that no premiums are to be received for Policies now existing without the concurrence of a Committee or of the Secretary, And that an Account of all policies belonging to the lower order of Jews which expire at Christmas next be made out also a similar Account for the Lady Day, Midsummer & Michaelmas Quarters. And that Mr Norris or Mr Gubbins do report to this Committee any places the Residence of the lower Order of Jews which may appear to them extremely hazardous.

2 Nov. 1786
Read Mr Norris's Report of Streets, Lanes & Courts, the residence of the lower order of Jews, which appears extremely hazardous.

Resolved that no Insurance shall hereafter be made on Goods or Stock or Apparel in Houses situated in any of the above places & that no premiums are to be received in any policies now Existing for Stock in Trade, Goods or Apparel. And that no Buildings situated in either Streets, Lanes or Courts reported extremely Hazardous in Mr Norris's Report shall hereafter be insured without any Approbation of a Committee or the Secretary.

This became known as the *Jews Clause* which can be found written against some policies.

It was clearly advantageous for the insurance companies to pay a reward to people who successfully prevented a fire from spreading or were able to extinguish the fire. On the 5 September 1839 the Sun Fire Office Management Committee[15] authorised the following: 'That the Sum of £20 be presented to Mr Saml Winmill of Alderbrook, Essex insured P P^y N° 1145263 for his exertions in arresting the Fire (in a hay stack occasioned by natural heating) by which it was prevented from extending to the Farm Buildings & other Farming Stock'.

Rewards were also offered for information which would lead to the arrest and conviction of arsonists (often recorded as incendiaries):

The total Sums assured on Farming Stock in
the Quarters ending Midsummer 1839 & 1840

	1839	1840
London	2,900	4,200
Westminster	200	1,200
Agents	439,630	489,133
	442,730	494,533
		442,730

Increase on the Quarter £ 51,803

Duties paid in the Years ending Midsummer 1839 & 1840

	1839	1840	Increase	Decrease
London	19071.17. 8	19255. 1. 5	183. 3. 9	—.—.—
Westminster	6856. 3. 6	7233.10. —	377. 6. 6	—.—.—
Agents	41650.12. 2	42978. 5. 7	1327.13. 5	—.—.—
	67578.13. 4	69466.17. —	1888. 3. 8	—.—.—
		67578.13. 4		

Increase on the Year — £ 1888. 3. 8

Farming Stock in the Years ending Mids: 1839 & 1840

1839		1840	
Michas 1838	647,681	Michas 1839	569,378
Xmas "	1,907,419	Xmas "	1,871,390
Lady V 1839	1,553,713	Lady 1840	1,471,171
Mids: "	442,730	Mids: "	494,533
	4,551,543		4,406,472
			4,551,543

Decrease in Year ending Mids: 1840 £ 145,071

adjourned

Royal Exchange Assurance. Fire Committe minute Book giving sums assured on farming stock 1839 and 1840

Essex and Suffolk Equitable Insurance Society
Board Minutes[16]

15 April 1817
The Directors having met to consider of a letter received by Mr
Cha. Malden the Agent to the Phoenix Office offering a reward of
£100 for the apprehension and conviction of the person or persons
who set fire to the premises at Abbotts Hall in Great Wigborough,
occupied by Mess[rs] Lungley & Brewer and insured in that Office.
The Directors present are unanimously of opinion that this Society
sho[d], in conjuction with the Sun Fire Office, & Royal Exchange
Office, bear an equal proportion in offering a further Sum of £100,
for the above purpose, and a handbill is hereby ordered accordingly to that effect, the Agents to the Sun Fire & Royal Exchange
Offices having obtained the consent of their respective Directors
thereto.

The pursuit and trial of arsonists was of continuing concern. The following was
recorded by the Sun Fire Office Committee of Management[17] on 23 September
1824: 'The Secretary reported that Robt. Ball of No. 97 Strand had been brought
to Trial at the Old Bailey on a charge of Arson and had been convicted'. The Old
Bailey Court records[18] show that Robert Ball was tried at the Seventh Sessions,
20 September 1824. His case, number 1381 before Justice Gaselee, states that
'Robert Ball was indicted for that he on the 14th August, at St Clement Danes,
unlawfully did set fire to a certain house, there situate, then being in the pos-
session of John Fearn, with intent thereby to injure and defraud Charles Pole
then and there being, one of the subjects of His Majesty, and then being the
Treasurer for the time being, under the name of the Sun Fire Office Company,
against the statute &c.' Evidence was given by several witnesses and Ball was
found guilty and his sentence 'Reserved for the consideration of the Twelve
Judges'. No judgement has been found in the Old Bailey records.

The Newgate Prison Register[19] records Robert Ball as aged 26 years, 5' 6" tall
with fresh complexion, brown hair and hazel eyes, 'stoutish', born at Plymouth
and by trade a carpenter. He was 'brought into custody' on 23 August and committed by Sir R. Birnie. He was found guilty and sentenced to death but the
judgement was 'respited'. On 8 March [1825] he was sent to the Prison Hulk
York at Gosport. He was given a sentence of 'transportation for life' and trans-
ferred to the *Sesostris* on 16 November 1825. She sailed for New South Wales on
23 November 1825, arriving at Sydney on 21 March 1826.

It was important for the insurance companies to be aware of property at risk
of fire or explosion. Some warehouses, refineries and factories were particularly vulnerable. The following was recorded by the Royal Exchange Assurance 'At
a Special Committee for the Fire Business'[20] on 15 June 1829: 'Mr Ward laid
before the Committee the following Statement of the Fires in Sugar Houses
[refineries] in and about the Metropolis from Dec[r] 1805 to the present time'.
There follows a list of 77 Occupiers of Sugar Houses each with the date of the
fire and the address. Forty-eight of these are recorded as 'damaged' and 29
'destroyed'. It is interesting to note that many foreign names appear as occupiers (Schlincker, Hahn, Bajsans, Du Croz, Steinmetz, Kruggs, Cootmeyer,
etc.).

32

BATH FIRE-OFFICE.

ABSTRACT of the Clause in the Act of Parliament of the Sixth Year of QUEEN ANN, with Respect to SERVANTS carelessly setting Fire to Houses.

WHEREAS Fires often happen by the Negligence and Carelessness of Servants; therefore, if any menial or other Servant or Servants, through Negligence, or Carelessness, shall fire, or caused to be fired, any Dwelling-house, Out-house, or Houses, such Servant or Servants, being thereof lawfully convicted, by the Oath of one or more credible Witnesses, made before two or more Justices of the Peace, shall forfeit and pay the Sum of ONE HUNDRED POUNDS to the Churchwardens of such Parish where such Fire shall happen, to be distributed among the Sufferers by such Fire, in such Proportions as to the said Churchwardens shall seem just: And in Case of Default or Refusal to pay the same immediately after such Conviction, the same being lawfully demanded by the said Churchwardens, that then, and in such Case, such Servant or Servants shall, by Warrant under the Hand of two or more Justices of the Peace, be committed to some Workhouse, or House of Correction, as the said Justices shall think fit, for the Space of *Eighteen Months*, there to be kept to hard Labour.

☞ *You are desired to put this up in some public Part of the House.*

Courtesy of the Somerset Record Office T/PH/sg

Bath Fire Office.
Warning to servants about the risk of fire through their carelessness

Policy holders were obliged to report any special circumstances which might affect the risk of fire:

Nottinghamshire and Derbyshire Fire
and Life Assurance Company
Board Minutes – Chesterfield Directors[21]

4 October 1858
At a meeting held this morning a complaint having been made to Mr Robinson (agent) by Mr A. Vickery of Horsley Gate, an insurer, that the Game Keeper of the Duke of Rutland in his neighbourhood is in the habit of firing rocketts over Mr Vickery's land to frighten off the Game & which Mr Vickery considers dangerous to the Stacks &c.

Ordered that Mr Robinson report the same to Mr Wood, Secretary.

The introduction of steam traction engines for agricultural purposes brought with it the inevitable hazards of sparks from the fire boxes. There was much concern voiced about these 'lumbering giants' and fire insurance companies were well aware of the increased risks from such machines. *The Farmers and General Fire, Life and Hail Insurance Company* kept records of them.[22] A transcript from one letter they received is given here:

Sun Fire Office
Threadneedle Street
30th March 1880

Dear Sir,

Pardon my negligence in not having sent an earlier reply to your letter of 20th inst.

You ask "Will this decision be applicable to the destruction of property on farms, caused by the use of Steam Engines, which are not the property of the Insured."

"We lately took opinion of Mr Cohen Q.C. and Mr Mancell Jones in a somewhat analogous case in which we were advised with respect to the case of a tenant farmer who had hired an engine to do work on his farm as follows:

If the tenant knew that the engine which would be sent according to his orders was improperly constructed and dangerous, and the engine so sent was worked without negligence, he could not maintain any action against the owner of the engine, but if he simply gave directions to the Defendants to send a Steam Plough with a man to work it, then he could, in our opinion recover from the Defendants (the owners of the engine) an amount equal to the sum required for repairing the damage caused by a fire ignited by the Engine."

"The second of the hypothetical cases here is that which of course always happens in practise; farmers don't know whether Engines are properly or improperly constructed; they know nothing about the construction of Engines; all they know is that they want work to be done and send for an Engine, in which case you see, Counsel are of opinion that the man hiring the Engine can recover for damage done by it.

I think as the law now stands the liability of the owners of Engines is made pretty clear. All we should do, is to take care to enforce the liability; we do so whenever occasion occurs.

I think the passage I have quoted answers the questions you put to me."

Yours Truly
Fred[k] H. Norman

Stamp duty was introduced on fire insurance in 1782 when one shilling and six-pence was payable on every £100 of property insured. This rose to two shillings in 1797, two shillings and six pence in 1804, three shillings in 1815 and then reduced to one shilling and six pence in 1865. In 1869 stamp duty on fire insurance was abolished:

Royal Exchange Assurance
Special Fire Committee[23]

10 November 1826
A letter from the Secretary of the Stamp Office dated the 17th Inst. was read directing that in future the Quarterly returns of Fire Duty are to be made up in strict conformity with the Act of Parliament.

Resolved that Mr Browne be requested to obtain an interview if possible with the Commissioners of Stamp Duties in order to explain the manner in which the Account rendered by this Company is arranged and obtain their sanction for the same form being continued, the only deviation from the Rules prescribed by the Act being the omission of the name and address of the Assured against the renewal Policy numbers.

Stamp duty was payable on each policy and this, together with the premiums, was collected by the agents. The names of the agents are often recorded in the minutes of the company meetings. With the increase in demand for fire insurance more agents were appointed. One agent originally covering a large district, in time had this sub-divided and this district was then covered by several more agents.

The earliest policies were usually very brief but gradually over the next half century fuller descriptions of the insured property were recorded. By the end of the 18th century the policies were much more descriptive. Examples are given in Chapters 7 to 14. Some early policies on domestic property occasionally did give much detail; the Hand-in-Hand Fire Office even recorded the dimensions of buildings and rooms. See Figure 1 (page 44) and page 194.

Although many companies have no known surviving policy registers details of some policies can be found in the minutes of the various companies' meetings. The following is an example:

Monarch Fire and Life Assurance Company
Board Minutes[24]

2nd April 1839 —— the Fire Risks of the week amounting to £14600 were read & confirmed.
£2000 Fire Ins[ce] on *The Catherine Wheel* in the Borough to be brought before the next Board previous to its being concluded.
£1500 on Mr Grose's fixtures & Stock in Tooley St. (a wooden building) agreed to be taken.

9th April 1839 £2000 fire Ins[ce] on *The Catherine Wheel* in the Borough was withdrawn.

The myth that up to the 19th century few working people and tradesmen moved from their native place is dispelled by many of these policies. Policies have been found which record *small* owners of property living in one place and insuring property a great distance away. Some with property in Ireland also insured buildings in England. Examples are given in Chapter 12. Many policies have been found linking policy holders who lived abroad with property in Great Britain and Ireland. Examples are given in Chapter 13. A policy linking a person with two places is indeed of great value to the genealogist as this may be the only surviving document which records the link. Such policies survive from long before the 1851 population census; the earliest census to record places of birth.

The landed gentry usually listed their farms and other property in great detail giving the names of each farm, together with the names and occupations of the tenants, and the location and description of the tenants' houses, cottages, farms, and workshops. Examples are given in Chapter 8. Even on a small rented house, the owner was named and the tenant was usually recorded, together with his trade or occupation. (The trade of a person is of interest because trades were not regularly entered into parish registers until 1813.)

The name of an inn or farm is usually given in the policy document. Details of the exact location of domestic property are not likely to be found, though in towns the name of the street is usually stated. Policies should be used in conjuction with Land Tax Returns which usually give names of owners and occupiers. Land Tax Returns exist for many counties[25] from the last half of the 18th century. Some exist for an earlier period. A dwelling or workshop is often known by a previous owner's name. Tithe maps help to identify and locate a particular property; these were drawn up in the 1830s and 1840s.[26]

Advice on how to locate a particular person's policy is given in Chapter 6.

Amendments to policies were recorded by *Endorsements*. These survive for some companies, including the Sun Fire Office. Many endorsements are included in Chapters 7, 9, 10 and 12 and more are given in Chapter 3. Endorsements record change of ownership, modifications to buildings, change of use, the addition of heating stoves, the addition of contents to the policy, etc. Mortgaged property was identified in the original policy naming the mortgager and the mortgagee. When the mortgager died such details were written into an endorsement, often naming the executor of the will of the deceased.

No specific registers for any company have been found which record the recruitment of staff although some staff records do survive. See Chapter 5.

Reference to staffing matters including local agents may often be found in the
minutes of various company meetings. From the time of Queen Anne some firemen were exempt from impressment into the Royal Navy. Such men are found
recorded in the Admiralty Office *Registers of Protection from being Impressed*
(PRO reference ADM 7/363 to 390, covering the years 1702 to 1828). There are
also many references to immunity from impressment in company minutes.
Some examples from the Admiralty registers are given in Chapter 5.

References to individual staff are to be found throughout the minutes of the
various committees and the next of kin of those staff who had died were often
given financial assistance as shown in the following:

Sun Fire Office
Management Committee [27]

10 Nov. 1785
That Four Guineas be paid to Elizabeth Wright, widow of Thomas
Wright, late porter to this Office in consideration of her being left
in great distress with a family of five children.

Staff who had suffered injury whilst on duty were often given medical
treatment:

Sun Fire Office
General Committee [28]

6 June 1723. 'That Mr Ward pay Mr Vicaridge ten shillings and sixpence for attending Stafford, the Waterman hurt by the fire in
Bishopgate Street, and that it be recommended to the next Gen[l]
Meeting to appoint some one surgeon to attend the cure of their
hurt and wounded men'.
19 June 1723. Mr Ward pay Jonathan Stafford £3-3s as a Bounty to
being hurt at the Fire in Cammomile Street.

When a policy was issued the property owner, on paying the premium also pur-
chased a *fire mark*. This was a metal plaque in the form of the emblem of the
insurance company.[29] Some insurance companies included on the fire mark the
policy number relating to the particular building being insured. The fire mark
was affixed high up on the front of the insured building. It indicated that the
building was insured with a particular insurance office. Without a fire mark,
the company's firemen were unlikely to attempt to extinguish a fire. Many fire
marks are still to be found on buildings around the country both in Britain and
abroad. The policy for an existing building with a numbered fire mark can eas-
ily be located if the register containing that policy survives.

Policies have been found for official buildings such as union workhouses,
county gaols, court houses and churches. Examples are given in Chapter 9.
Many railway stations and surrounding buildings and workshops were insured
with the Sun Fire Office. See Chapter 10. Lloyds of London was not the only
insurer of ships. The records of several insurance companies include policies
for ships. See Chapter 11. Many famous people and early established national
companies appear in profusion amongst these records. Some examples are

given in Chapter 14. Fire insurance plans often give in great detail the construction and location of insured property. Details are given in Chapter 15.

Appendix 1. This lists companies which gave fire insurance cover. It does not include life or other insurance companies. The companies are arranged by date of their formation and changes of name are also recorded.

The places each company covered are given. An indication of whether or not historical records are known to survive is noted, with a separate reference to policy registers. The current location of the records is shown, together with references to the appendices in which the records are listed. (Appendices 2, 3, 4 and 5). Appendices 2, 3, 4 and 5 have been given numerical sub-divisions to enable the exact location within these appendices.

Appendix 2. This lists the records held at the Guildhall Library, London, which are likely to be of most interest to family and local historians. Material such as shareholders' records and accounts are not usually included unless these are the only records for a particular company.

Appendix 3. This lists insurance records held by county record offices and other local archives and is arranged in four sections:
3.1   England
3.2   Wales
3.3   Scotland
3.4   Ireland

This was compiled from questionnaires sent to each record office. It does not include references to the numerous individual policies held in many record offices.

It should be noted that no insurance records were located in the Republic of Ireland. Many fire insurance companies were established in the Channel Islands, the first being *La Société de St. Sauveur*, Guernsey in 1800 followed by the *Guernsey and Jersey Fire Insurance Company* in 1808. No records of these or any other insurance company have been located either in Guernsey or Jersey. There are no insurance records held at the Isle of Man Public Record Office.

Appendix 4. This gives eleven insurance companies with details of the records still in their keeping.

Appendix 5. This lists fire insurance records held at Cambridge University Library.

Appendix 6. A group of volunteers has, for many years, been indexing many tradesmen in the Sun Fire Office policy registers for various years from 1710 to 1840 (see Appendix 6 for full details).There are 634 trades which are listed alphabetically in this appendix. The index is arranged in four sections and deposited at :
1.   The Museum of London
2.   The National Maritime Museum, Greenwich
3.   The Royal Armouries, Leeds
4.   The Victoria and Albert Museum, London.

Appendix 7. This gives details of the monetary system in use in Britain up to the introduction of decimal currency.

Because of company takeovers it has been difficult to locate the whereabouts of some records. Some records listed in *The British Insurance Business* have not been located. The archivist of one company admitted that certain documents were 'no longer available'. Other records, known to have been deposited in a particular record office 'cannot be found'. In 1998 General Accident merged with the Commercial Union to form CGU and in 2000 CGU merged with Norwich Union to form CGNU. On 1 July 2002 CGNU became AVIVA. The archivists of AVIVA are currently cataloguing the mass of records which have been brought together as a result of these mergers.

Amongst the London Assurance and the Sun Fire Office archives are to be found records of wills and probates. These have not been explored in any great detail but are likely to be only for those persons with financial interests in these companies. References to these wills and probates are given in Appendix 2.

A brief survey of the records of life insurances for the 19th century indicate that these appear to be for the middle and upper classes only. It is hoped that a separate study of Life Insurance will be undertaken in the near future.

To date fire insurance records have been little used by historians yet they contain all manner of interesting and useful information for 'house detectives' and local and family historians. It is of particular interest to note that policy records exist not only for Great Britain but include a large number for the Isle of Man, the Channel Islands and Ireland.

The combined insurance policy records create what might be described as a huge directory of the country. They give the names and addresses of much of the population from labourers to the landed gentry, and cover a period starting over 300 years ago and 140 years before the first useful population census. It is hoped that the 18th century records of the larger insurance companies (in particular the Sun Fire Office, the Royal Exchange Assurance and the Hand-in-Hand Fire Office) will be filmed and fully indexed so that they will be more readily accessible to all family and local historians.

It has been noted that the calculations of the premiums and stamp duties for some policies do not always appear to be correct. The sums shown in the examples given in this book are as in the original documents. Care has been taken with the transcription of documents; the random use of capital letters and abbreviations, and the peculiarities in spelling are as in the originals. Punctuation has been added to many of the transcripts to make for easier reading.

Notes

1. Bucks RO PR9/1/1
2. About 6% missing.
3. GLDH Ms 11937/527
4. GLDH Ms 11937/130
5. GLDH Ms 11937/137
6. GLDH Ms 11931/4
7. GLDH Ms 11932/11
8. GLDH Ms 11932/25
9. GLDH Ms 16227/1
10. GLDH Ms 16206/1
11. GLDH Ms 11932/25

12. GLDH Ms 16237/5
13. GLDH Ms 11932/21
14. GLDH Ms 11932/13
15. GLDH Ms 11932/25
16. GLDH Ms 16206/1
17. GLDH Ms 11932/20
18. Records held at the Guildhall Library, London
19. PRO PCOM 2/197
20. GLDH Ms 16237/1
21. GLDH Ms 18311
22. GLDH Ms 14999
23. GLDH Ms 16237/1
24. GLDH Ms 11661/1
25. *Land Tax Assessments c 1690 to c 1950*; J. Gibson and D. Mills, Federation of Family History Societies
26. Tithe Maps are held in most county record offices and duplicates are held at the Public Record Office, London.
27. GLDH Ms 11932/13
28. GLDH Ms 11931/3
29. The Hand in Hand, Sun, London Assurance, Royal Exchange, Phoenix and many local fire offices had policy numbers cast or stamped on their fire marks. See *The British Fire Mark* by B.W. Wright.

Table 1   Analysis of Gentlemen with Fire Insurance, c1775 to c1798 *Sun* and *Royal Exchange* (England only)

Town	County	Number in directory	Number Insured		Total Insured	
			Sun	*Royal*	*No.*	*%*
Boston	Lincolnshire	*8	12	0	12	100
Burton on Trent	Staffordshire	16	3	0	3	19
Chelmsford	Essex	14	3	8	11	79
Chester	Cheshire	224	43	4	47	20
Chichester	Sussex	35	6	8	14	40
Evesham	Worcestershire	5	1	0	1	20
Faversham	Kent	55	2	0	2	15
Kendal	Westmorland	28	2	0	2	7
Leominster	Herefordshire	24	4	0	4	16
Morpeth	Northumberland	6	2	1	3	50
Oakham	Rutland	11	1	0	1	9
Padstow	Cornwall	8	0	1	1	12
Reading	Berkshire	38	24	7	31	81
Wellington	Somersetshire	5	5	0	5	100
Whitby	Yorkshire	*2	7	0	7	100
Whitehaven	Cumberland	42	7	0	7	16
Yarmouth	Norfolk	73	56	7	63	86
		Total **594**			Total **214**	

The average number of gentlemen with their property insured computes to 36%

*Less number in the directory than number insured

Table 2   Analysis of Professional Men with Fire Insurance, c1775 to c1798. *Sun* and *Royal Exchange* (England only)

Town	County	Number in directory	Number Insured		Total Insured	
			Sun	*Royal*	*No.*	*%*
Boston	Lincolnshire	24	13	0	13	54
Burton on Trent	Staffordshire	11	1	1	2	18
Chelmsford	Essex	16	4	8	12	75
Chester	Cheshire	95	11	0	11	11
Chichester	Sussex	35	5	1	6	17
Evesham	Worcestershire	23	1	0	1	4
Faversham	Kent	13	2	0	2	15
Kendal	Westmorland	27	1	1	2	7
Leominster	Herefordshire	27	0	2	2	7
Morpeth	Northumberland	26	0	0	0	0
Oakham	Rutland	12	0	1	1	8
Padstow	Cornwall	2	0	0	0	0

Reading	Berkshire	35	12	2	14	40
Wellington	Somersetshire	16	3	0	3	18
Whitby	Yorkshire	12	6	0	6	50
Whitehaven	Cumberland	20	1	0	1	5
Yarmouth	Norfolk	40	14	5	19	4
		Total **434**			Total **95**	

The average number of professional men with their property insured computes to 22%

Table 3   Analysis of Insured Inns, c1775 to c1798
Sun and *Royal Exchange* (England only)

Town	County	Number in directory	Number Insured		Total Insured	
			Sun	*Royal*	*No.*	*%*
Boston	Lincolnshire	37	5	0	5	13
Burton on Trent	Staffordshire	17	1	2	3	17
Chelmsford	Essex	29	2	16	18	62
Chester	Cheshire	83	3	2	5	6
Chichester	Sussex	2	0	2	2	100
Evesham	Worcestershire	27	1	0	1	3
Faversham	Kent	16	6	0	6	37
Kendal	Westmorland	39	1	0	1	2
Leominster	Herefordshire	21	0	0	0	0
Morpeth	Northumberland	32	0	0	0	0
Oakham	Rutland	8	2	1	3	37
Padstow	Cornwall	4	0	0	0	0
Reading	Berkshire	*12	14	0	14	100
Wellington	Somersetshire	13	8	0	8	61
Whitby	Yorkshire	*7	8	0	8	100
Whitehaven	Cumberland	56	1	0	1	1
Yarmouth	Norfolk	10	9	0	9	90
			Total **413**		Total **84**	

The average number of inns insured computes to 20%

*Less number in the directory than number insured.

Table 4   Analysis of Tradesmen with Fire Insurance c1775 to c1798
                Sun and *Royal Exchange* (England only)

Town	County	Number in directory	Number Insured		Total Insured	
			Sun	*Royal*	*No.*	*%*
Boston	Lincolnshire	225	54	2	56	24
Burton on Trent	Staffordshire	154	7	28	35	22
Chelmsford	Essex	143	18	116	134	93
Chester	Cheshire	717	62	10	72	10
Chichester	Sussex	172	23	30	53	30
Evesham	Worcestershire	198	2	1	3	2
Faversham	Kent	188	25	0	25	13
Kendal	Westmorland	277	17	1	18	6
Leominster	Herefordshire	205	17	7	24	11
Morpeth	Northumberland	190	2	1	3	2
Oakham	Rutland	91	12	0	12	13
Padstow	Cornwall	30	7	1	8	26
Reading	Berkshire	170	117	7	124	72
Wellington	Somersetshire	73	47	0	47	64
Whitby	Yorkshire	152	107	0	107	70
Whitehaven	Cumberland	204	15	0	15	7
Yarmouth	Norfolk	252	233	7	240	95
		Total **3,441**			Total **976**	

The average number of Tradesmen with their property insured
computes to 28%.

Chapter 1

The Earliest Fire Insurance Organisations

The Fire Office

The first organisation to insure property against loss by fire was *The Fire Office* which was established in London in 1680. It was also known as *The Insurance Office for Houses*. In 1705 it was re-named *The Phenix Office*. There are no known surviving company records of *The Fire Office* though some individual policies are deposited at the Guildhall Library, London and in other record offices. *The Phenix* stopped offering insurance in 1713 and was wound up in 1722. No fire marks are known to survive. Their fire mark depicted a Phoenix above a fire.

The Friendly Society

The Society for Insuring Houses from Loss by Fire was formed in 1683. Later the name was changed to *The Friendly Society* and is believed to have been wound up in 1729. No known records have been located although there are a number of surviving fire marks.

The Hand-in-Hand Fire Office

In 1696 *The Contributors for Insuring Houses, Chambers or Rooms from Loss by Fire, by Amicable Contributors* was formed. It was re-named *The Hand-in-Hand Fire Office* in 1713 and in 1836 became *The Hand-in-Hand Fire and Life Insurance Society*. For a long period the *Hand-in-Hand* insured only houses and appartments in London. It was not until 1806 that cover began to spread to the rest of Great Britain.

Policy registers survive for the period 1696 to 1865 (with some gaps) at the Guildhall Library, London, manuscript references Ms 8674 to Ms 8677, and most have name indices. (See Appendix 2). No policy endorsement records are known for the *Hand-in-Hand Fire Office*.

The format and notation of entries in the policy registers is shown in Figure 1 on the following page.

Figure 1. *Hand-in-Hand Fire Office* – Format and Notation of Entries in Policy Registers

GLDH Ms 8674/8

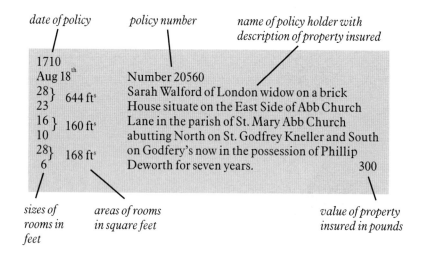

Note: There is no reference to the amount of the premium paid

Claims against loss are recorded in the minutes of Directors' Meetings, 1697 to 1833, GLDH Ms 8666. The following is an example:

GLDH Ms 8666/3

> Tuesday 23 January 1710
> Ordered that John Walton pay Thomas Saville Esq, One pound seventeen shill[s] and 6[d] for a damage sustained the 19th instant at his house in Broad Street, St. James the Policy No. 4933 and Thomas Owen Esq, Ten shill[s] for a damage in Chapel Street & Orchard Street the 9th Jan[y] the Policy No. 7,686 take Acq[ies] [sic] and Endorse ye sd. Sumes upon ye sd Policyes.

A Hand in Hand Fire Office fire mark.
This design was used from c.1840 to c.1870

Chapter 2

The First Three Fire Insurance Companies with National Coverage: Policies, Endorsements and Claims

Although many insurance companies had been established in the 18th century, until 1781 only three companies offered fire insurance nationally throughout Great Britain and policy records survive for each of these.

1. The Sun Fire Office, founded in 1710
The Sun initially issued cover for London only but within a few years had spread to much of England and later to Wales, Scotland, Ireland and the Channel Islands. By 1792 the growth of work in the many country agencies was so great that in 1793 a separate department, *The Country Department*, was established to deal with all work outside London. The original department, named *The Town Department*, continued to deal only with London policies.

Policy registers exist in three series:

Old Series; Town Department	1710 to 1864 (8% missing)	*GLDH Ms 11936*
	(London only from1793)	
Craig's Court (London)	1726 to 1732	*GLDH Ms 11936A*
Country Department	1793 to 1863 (3% missing)	*GLDH Ms 11937*

The Sun is one of very few companies to have any surviving policy endorsement records and its is the most comprehensive:

Endorsement Books	1728 to 1865 (some gaps)	*GLDH Ms 12160*
New Policy Endorsement Books	1819 to 1861 (some gaps)	*GLDH Ms 12161*

The Sun is also the only known company to have a comprehensive series of Registers of Losses

Country Losses	1803 to 1864	*GLDH Ms 11937A*
Town Losses	1851 to 1866	*GLDH Ms 11934B*

CONFIDENTIAL.—*This Book is the property of the Office, and is for the use of the Agent only.*

SUN INSURANCE OFFICE LIMITED

LONDON, E.C. 2.

Agents' Instructions *re* Fire Business

The Directors naturally expect Agents to do their utmost to extend the Office connection, but they rely upon their exercising great care in the selection of risks, and submitting only such proposals as from their knowledge of the character and standing of the Proposers they are able confidently to recommend to the Office to accept. The systematic distribution of the Office Prospectuses in likely quarters is strongly recommended.

RATES.—A Table of Rates for various ordinary risks is supplied for the use of Agents.

PROPOSALS.—Proposals received should be promptly forwarded to the Office. When desired in risk of ordinary hazard and amount, a portion of the premium may be received, and a Deposit Receipt issued on a form which can be obtained on application to the Office.

A separate sum must be placed upon each detached building, and on each of several buildings which adjoin but do not communicate with one another. A range of buildings communicating internally may however be insured in one sum. This rule applies similarly to the contents of such buildings.

In every case the precise situation, the construction and covering, and the trade (if any) carried on must be given, and any process of manufacture or special method of heating or lighting should be stated.

Household Furniture must be separately valued from Stock in Trade.

Rent (payable or receivable) may be insured for a specific sum.

Farming Stock must be insured under separate policy. A special form of proposals is supplied for such.

A new policy is itself a Receipt for the first premium paid.

A new policy if not taken up in reasonable time should be returned to the Office.

The Office should be immediately advised of the receipt of a renewal premium hitherto paid through another channel.

(G. Gall 720.)

BOOK KEEPING.—On receipt of a new policy it should be entered in this Book under the respective headings of—

(a) New Policies, the new policy (or first) premium being entered here.

(b) Renewals, under the Quarter at which the policy becomes due, the annual renewal premium being of course entered.

The space allowed for "Property Insured" will suffice for an abbreviated description, *e.g.*, "Hd. Gds. £100, Stock £200, Building £300, Rent £30."

ACCOUNTS.—It is most important that the prescribed dates for rendering Accounts given in the Renewal List supplied for each Quarter should be scrupulously observed.

The Renewal List and Notices for the ensuing Quarter, together with Receipts, should be supplied in good time, provided that the previous Quarter's Account has been rendered. The Notices should be despatched to the Assured by the Agent about ten days before Quarter Day. For this purpose the Quarter Day are allowed for renewal from the Quarter Day. For premiums of £2 and upwards the Renewal Receipt must bear a month after each Quarter Day. A statement of new policies issued to date is sent about fifteen days of grace, provided no fire has happened, and must be dated the actual day of issue. Remittances should be made payable to the "Sun Insurances Office Ld." (and crossed to the "A/c. of Payees.")

ENDORSEMENTS.—Agents are authorised to make endorsements on policies allowing Removal or Change of Interest, &c., in cases where there is no increase in the Fire Risk, a copy of the same to be

In the case of any Lapsed Policy the reason for discontinuance should be stated against the entry in the Renewal List. A Lapsed Policy can only be revived (assuming no fire has occurred) by payment of the premium from the date of expiry. Otherwise the issue of a new policy is necessary.

transmitted to the Office within a week on the form supplied for the purpose. Such form will be found to contain examples of the wording to be followed in ordinary cases.

CLAIMS.—Agent should report losses immediately giving Insured's name, policy number, and the item or items under which a claim will arise. Pending receipt of instructions from the Office the Insured should take all proper steps to protect salvage from further injury. Without delay, and within fifteen days after fire, the Insured should furnish, at his own cost, a detailed estimate of the loss, giving quantities, prices, &c., due regard being given to the condition of the property at the time of the fire and the value of any salvage. The Agent must not assist in the preparation of the account. In forwarding the claim to the Office the Agent should state his own opinion as to its accuracy, and add any further comments likely to assist in the consideration of the case.

After the payment of a partial loss the policy remains in force for the balance of the sum Insured by the item or items affected during the remainder of the current term, but after the policy becomes valid again for the full amounts as fixed. If desired the Insurance may be at once restored to its original amount by a revision of the policy.

CONDITION OF AVERAGE.—This mainly applies to the exceptional cases in which it is desired to insure two or more separate risks under one sum. In such cases the condition has no effect whatever when the property is insured up to its full value and only becomes operative in the event of under insurance, *e.g.*, for property insured for only half its value only half the loss is recoverable.

In all ordinary policies (*i.e.*, not subject to the average condition) the full value of the property destroyed is recoverable up to the sum insured.

CORRESPONDENCE.—It is particularly desired that the Agent will correspond on separate sheets relative to—

1. Proposals, Revisions and Endorsements.
2. Accounts.
3. Fires and Claims.
4. Other matters.

Sun Fire Office. First page of Instructions in an Agents' Renewal Book

The *Sun Fire Office* records are held at the Guildhall Library, London. (See Appendix 2.)

The following indices exist for the policy registers:

1. 1711–1712 and 1714–1715   *GLDH Ms 17816*
2. 1714–1731   Card Index (by Alan Redstone)   *GLDH Ms 17817*
                  Alphabetical name index
                  arranged by county (England
                  only, excluding London)
3. 1714–1731   Printed index of 'Somerset Insurance Policy Holders'
                  published by the *Bristol and Avon Family History Society*
4. 1775–1787   Microfiche
                  a. Alphabetical index of surnames
                  b. Place name index
                  c. Index of Trades
                  d. Valuations (Policies arranged by value)
                  e. Policy List (Policies arranged in numeric order)

Copies of these microfiche indices are available in most record offices throughout England and Wales, the Guildhall Library, London and The Society of Genealogists, London.

5. Numerical Indices of Policies, (1723 to 1846) *GLDH Ms 21595* and *Ms 21596*

6. Index and abstracts of craftsmens' and traders' policies (634 trades).

   Town Department   1710 to 1840 ⋆ (incomplete)
   Country Department   1793 to 1840 ⋆ (incomplete)

For fuller details of years covered and trades included see Appendix 6.

⋆This indexing has been carried out by a group of volunteers who have to date covered about 50% of the Town Department and 10% of the Country Department. It is intended to continue working through the whole of the policy registers for both *Town* and *Country Departments*. At the time of going to press it was learnt that the London Archive Users Forum had received a Heritage Lottery award to index a further 30 Sun Fire Office policy registers.

7. In 1998 The Surrey Local History Council began indexing all the Sun Fire Office policies relating to the historic county of Surrey from 1788 to 1793. This is a place name index.

Figure 2.   *Sun Fire Office* – Format and Notation of Entries in Policy Registers (Fictitious policy to show various notations at different times)

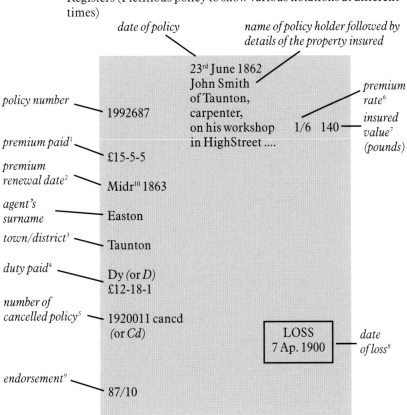

Notes
1. Fifteen pounds, five shillings and five pence.
2. Midsummer 1863 (sometimes the actual date is given).
3. This was not given until 1832.
4. Twelve pounds, eighteen shillings and one penny. This was not entered until 1831. Duty was introduced in 1782 and abolished in 1869.
5. From 1854 the number of the previous policy relating to the property is shown as cancelled.
6. One shilling and six pence per £100. This did not appear until 1815.
7. One hundred and forty pounds.
8. From about 1895 onwards when a claim was made the policy was stamped with the date of the loss.
9. A two-part number is sometimes found written at the end of a policy. This refers to an endorsement to the policy. The example shown means endorsement volume 87, page 10, where details of the endorsement will be given in full. (Endorsement volume Ms 12160/87). Some of the early policy volumes record these entries more fully, eg. Ind. 87 page 10 or 87* 10.
10. Midsummer

A Sun Fire Office fire mark with policy number.
This design was used from 1710 to c.1735

Endorsements to Policies

Changes to existing policies are recorded in *Indorsement Books*. These cover the period 1728 to 1865; GLDH Ms 12160. Reference to an endorsement is given in code at the end of a policy. See Figure 2.

The following is an example which shows the number of the policy to which it refers as policy number 1091961. (See also Chapter 3.)

GLDH Ms 12160/107 page 268

1091961	1846	Memo. The interest in this policy is now
Robert Hawkins	May 15th	the property of George Knight of Ninehead
		in the County of Somerset Painter and
173*		Glazier as Mortgagee of the premises here
		insured
		Entd in the Office Book W.D. Horsey
		this 15th day of May 1846 Agent, Wellington

* This is the volume number which contains the policy to which this endorsement refers e.g. Ms 11937/173

Claims against Loss

There are name indices of claimants covering the period 1804 to 1864 (in 5 volumes) These are known as 'Country Losses'; GLDH Ms 11937A. These give the date of the claim, name of the claimant, place of the loss, agent's name and the amount of the claim. Example:

GLDH Ms 11937A/1A

12 July 1810, Thomas Cornelius, Rockwell green, Jones, £85

GLDH Ms 11937A/1A

12 July 1810, Thomas Cornelius, Rockwell Green, Jones, £85

Claims are also recorded in the minutes of the Committee of Management (1725 to 1802), GLDH Ms 11932. Example:

GLDH Ms 11932/17

12 July 1810
£85-0-0 Thomas Cornelius of Rockwell Green, Wellington, Taylor, eighty five pounds

Further references to claims are also found in the minutes of the Committee of Town Insurance (1730 to 1896), GLDH Ms 11934. Example:

GLDH Ms 11934/10

12 July 1810 Thomas Cornelius of Rockwell Green, Tailor. £85

Other claims are recorded in Register of Town Losses (1851 to 1866) GLDH Ms 11934B. This is a name index arranged by first letter of surname of claimant.

A collection of over 300 original claims documents for the period 1770 to 1788 is held by the Society of Genealogists, London, and are listed in the *Genealosgists Magazine* for December 1975.

---

2. The London Assurance Corporation (founded in 1720)

This company was originally formed to give marine cover, though it soon spread its insurance to domestic buildings throughout England, Wales, Ireland and the Channel Islands. Policy registers survive for the following years: 1722 to 1727, 1760 to 1761, 1821 to 1826, 1863 to 1884, GLDH Ms 8747 and 1856 to 1898 (Jersey only), GLDH Ms 8747A.

There are no registers of losses or claims. Claims against loss are found in the Minutes of the Fire Committee, 1725 to 1924, GLDH Ms 8735. See Appendix 2. No policy endorsement records have been found. The format and notation of entries in the policy registers is shown in Figure 3. No indices exist for these registers.

Figure 3.   *London Assurance Corporation* – Format and Notation of Entries in Policy Registers

GLDH Ms 8747/3

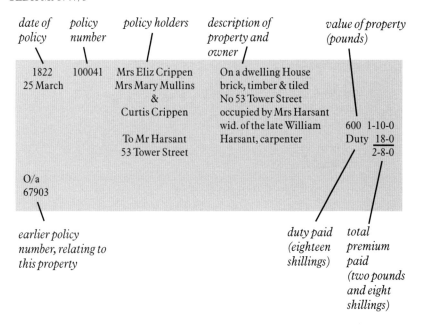

date of policy	policy number	policy holders	description of property and owner	value of property (pounds)
1822 25 March	100041	Mrs Eliz Crippen Mrs Mary Mullins & Curtis Crippen	On a dwelling House brick, timber & tiled No 53 Tower Street occupied by Mrs Harsant wid. of the late William Harsant, carpenter	600 1-10-0
		To Mr Harsant 53 Tower Street		Duty 18-0
				2-8-0
O/a 67903				

earlier policy number, relating to this property

duty paid (eighteen shillings)

total premium paid (two pounds and eight shillings)

Losses and Claims

Claims against loss are recorded in the Minutes of the Meetings of the Fire Committee (1725 to 1924). Example:

Offices of Union Assurance in Cornhill, 1830, by Geo. Scharf

GLDH Ms 8735/5

Friday the 23d Septemr 1785
Mr Peter Besley Demanded £30-5-0 for Loss & Damage by Fire in
Fetter Lane to his Wearing Apparel, Household Goods & Goods in
Trust Assured by this Corporation in Policy No. 42545
The Committee on Examining the Papers produced adjusted the
same at £13-7-6.

Resolved that it is the Opinion of this Committee that a Warrant
be made out to Mr Peter Besley for Thirteen Pounds seven shillings
& sixpence in full for Loss & Damage by Fire in Fetter Lane to his
Wearing Apparel, Household Goods, & Goods in Trust, Assured by
this Corporation in Policy No. 42545.

A London Assurance Corporation fire mark with policy number.
This design was used from 1722 to 1723

Courtesy of Roy Addis

3. The Royal Exchange Assurance (founded in 1720)
This company gave cover for the whole of England from its formation although it issued far less policies than the Sun Fire Office. The earliest surviving policy register dates from 1753. There are four series of registers:-

Fire Policy Registers 1st Series	1753 to 1759	GLDH Ms 7252
Fire Policy Registers 2nd Series	1773 to 1833	GLDH Ms 7253
Fire Insurance Registers	1803 to 1883	GLDH Ms 7254
Supplementary Agents Series	1809 to 1870	GLDH Ms 7255

There are no registers of losses or claims but claims are recorded in the Minutes of the Fire Committee GLDH Ms 16237 (1825 to 1888). Indices exist to the policy registers for the period 1775 to 1787 on microfiche:

a. Alphabetical index of surnames
b. Place name index
c. Index of trades
d. Valuations (Policies arranged by value)
e. Policy List (Policies arranged in numeric order)

Copies of these indices are available in many record offices in England and Wales and at the Guildhall Library, London and The Society of Genealogists, London.

Figure 4.   *Royal Exchange Assurance* – Format and Notation of Entries in Policy Registers

GLDH Ms 7252/2

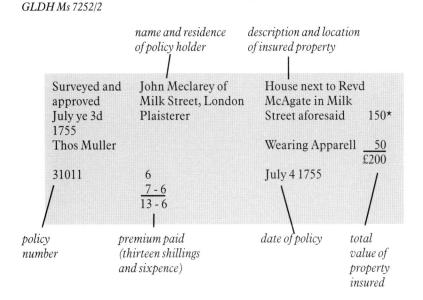

---

*   Later policies have the premium rate following the value of each part of the property. e.g. 250 2/- means value £250 @ 2 shillings per £100. This premium would compute to 5 shillings.

Claims Against Losses

Claims against losses are recorded in the Minutes of the Special Fire Committee (1825 to 1888), GLDH Ms 16237. Each volume has a place name index at the front but the places of claims are not included. Example:

GLDH Ms 16237/5

> 25 March 1857
> Reigate   Richard Cannock, Policy No. 695650. Stock and uten-
>   sils in his Farm called *Crutchfield* situate at Horley, in
>   the County of Surrey. £361-8-6

There are no policy endorsement registers for the Royal Exchange but it should be noted that endorsements are entered and interspersed in policy registers. The number for an endorsement is the same as the policy number.

*A Royal Exchange Assurance fire mark with policy number.
This design was issued in 1721*

58

Sun Fire Office. A page from a Policy Endorsement Register

Chapter 3

Endorsements to Policies

During the life of a policy any alterations to the insured property, or changes in the circumstances of the owner or occupier, were usually recorded in an endorsement. Such circumstances included the building of an extension to the insured property, the erection of additional outbuildings, the removal, addition to, or inclusion of the contents of the building, the addition of heating systems and forges, the change of ownership, change of named tenants, or the death of the owner.

Many endorsements have been included with their related policies in Chapters 7, 9, 10, 12 and 14. Further endorsements of particular interest are given in this chapter.

Sun Fire Office

GLDH Ms 11260/6 page 251

97898	Richard Prosser, King Street, St Gyles. Removed to his Brick
	dwelling house over against the Playhouse Passage on the East
68 *323	Side of Drury Lane. Two Hundred and forty pounds. And into his
	Brick Still house in the Yard behind & belonging to his said house.
	sixty pounds 24 March 1748 *C Q*

Sun Fire Office

GLDH Ms 12160/6 page 251

46888	George Cowdry, Midd^x, now John Hatchett of Bedfont in the
	County aforesaid Farmer left him by the last will & Testament of the
28 * 87	said George Cowdery deceased. 4 Apr 1748 *C Q*

Sun Fire Office

GLDH Ms 12160/6 page 251

75981	John Wilson, King Street, Covent Garden, now Catherine Wilson,
	Relict & Ex^x of the last Will and Testament of the said John
49 * 438	Wilson. 28 March 1748 *CQ*

Sun Fire Office

GLDH Ms 12160/48 page 286

	27 September 1796
630209	John Foster, Fetter Lane, Removed one Hundred pounds Household Goods, all his Wearing Apparel & one Hundred & Fifty Pounds
398	Utensils & Stock from Nº. 118 Fetter Lane to a Brick House in his own tenure Nº. 8 Lifsham Green, Paddington, Where the same Continue &c

Sun Fire Office

GLDH Ms 12160/48 page 388

	15 February 1797
571579	Matᵂ Craven, Gracechurch Street. Matthew Craven having quitted Partnership with John Burtton Lucas, The Interest in this Policy as
369	far as Relates to the Utensils & Stock is now the property of the said John Burtton Lucas & Francis Proctor, the latter being admitted into partnership. *JR*

Sun Fire Office

GLDH Ms 12160/60 page 530

838436	Edward Smalwood. An Iron Stove having lately been Erected in the Shop of the house Insured by this Policy and it being done in a
90	Substantial & Secure Manner is hereby allowed without Prejudice to this Policy.
	NB The Stock in this Shop is Insured by the Royal Exchange Office Who have allowed this Stove
	John Bingham Janʸ 4 1816

Sun Fire Office

GLDH Ms 12160/87 page 81

1229780	1838, 5 July
John Craig	Robert Kinneburgh, pewterer in Edinburgh has now an
229	interest in the within Policy to the extent of one half, the said
Scotland	John Craig Esq having conveyed to him the undivided half of the property within mentioned.

Sun Fire Office

GLDH Ms 12160/87 page 245

1288884	1838, 10 Dec.
	Be it remembered that the insurance by the within policy
Jas Steel	will expire on the 26ᵗʰ May 1839, not on the 20 January 1839 as
251	within stated, having commenced on the 26ᵗʰ November 1838 for
Quarterly	Six Months; not on the 20ᵗʰ July as within stated.

Phoenix Fire Office

Cam Uni PX 960

25 March 1843

Policy nº 753131 The Afs^d (aforesaid) having rem^d (removed) from the within

Name   Levy   ment^d (mentioned) D Ho (dwelling house) it is hereby
agreed that the within desc^d (described) moveable prop^y
(property) shall henceforth be ins^d (insured) as follows.
Viz. On Lin (linen), P B^s (printed books) PJr^s (printed journals) & prints dep^d (deposited) in the D Ho of Mr Judah Hart,
Goldsmith, sit (situate) Nº 31 Bevis Marks. Bk & T^r bt (brick

and timber built)	£400	3/-
On Jewellery th.(therein)	£200	5/-
On H^d Furn^e (hard? furniture) dep^d (deposited)		
in the Wareho. of Messrs Horsey & Co. Packers,		
bk bt (brick built) having a Steam Engine		
th.(therein) as per the Office Surv^s (surveyor's)		
Rep^t (report) *I* 747 sit No 33 Camomile S^t	£570	7/6
On ch Gl (china, glass) & LG Plates		
(large? glass? plates) th. (therein)	£80	7/6
And on Lin (linen) W Ap^l (wearing apparel)		
wat^s (whatsoever) & Trin^ts (trinkets) in the		
Afsds (aforesaid's) now D.Ho. bk.bt.		
pri (private) sit. Nº 7 South S^t, Finsbury	£150	2/-
Total sum insd as before A (annual) Prem	£5-9	

Recd the sum of £1-1 ado^l (additional) Prem to Michs next

Law Union and Rock Insurance Company

GLDH Ms 21271/1

Policy number 7396   It is declared that the within named Robert Dicken is
now residing at Peper Harrow near Goldaming in the
county of Surrey. And that the five cottages aforesaid
are now occupied by:–
1. Robert Bonchill
2. [*blank*] Chafer
3. Patrick Brannan
4. [*blank*] Dyke
5. Frederick Roby

Dated this 25th day of March 1858   A.S. Field Agent at Leamington

Sun Fire Office

GLDH Ms 12160/158 page 203

1887377	John Heelas,
	John Heelas Jnr 11 March 1861
485	& Danl Heelas

Memorandum.   A Gas Stove in the front Shop on the Ground Floor of
                     the within mentioned premises, well secured, allowed
                     in addition to the two stoves within mentioned
                     Entered at Reading 11 March 1861
                          J.T. Blandy, agent
          See Secy's letter of 9th March 1861

County Fire Office

GLDH Ms 18817

Policy No. 984647
Quarter when Renewal falls dew   Midsr
Name of Insured   *~~Thomas~~ Ann Green
Copy of Endorsement   The interest in this policy is now
                                        become the property of the Executor by
                                        Executorship
                                        James Cox   agent
                                        Stow on the Wold   12 July 1886

          *Thomas has been crossed through

County Fire Office

GLDH Ms 18817

Policy No. 927187
Quarter when Renewal falls due   Michas
Name of Insured   Rich
Copy of Endorsement   The amount hereby insured is now
                                        reduced to £900 viz. £700 on the Dead
                                        Stock and £200 on the Live Stock at the
                                        future Annual Premium of £2-5-0
                                        instead of as states within
                                        James Cox   Agent
                                        Stow on the Wold   22 Octr 1886

Sent to Bristol Office 25 Nov 1886
Reduction
Amount taken off   £1000
(Farming and stock only)
Premium taken off   £2-10-0
Amount Remaining Insured   £900
Future Annual Premium   £2-5-0

Chapter 4

Losses and Claims

Many fire insurance companies recorded losses and claims at their various committee meetings. *The Sun Fire Office* additionally kept Loss Registers:

1. Country Losses 1803 to 1864   GLDH Ms 11937A (5 volumes) (names arranged alphabetically)
2. Town Losses 1851 to 1866   GLDH Ms 11934B (names arranged alphabetically).
3. There are also Miscellaneous Claims 1771 to 1788 GLDH Ms 21075, indexed by Ms 15742

The following are some examples of losses and claims from the *Sun Fire Office*, the *Hand-in-Hand Fire Office*, the *Church of England Assurance Institution*, the *Royal Exchange Assurance*, the *Essex and Suffolk Fire Office*, the *British General Insurance Company* and the *London Assurance Corporation*.

Hand-in-Hand Fire Office

GLDH Ms 8666/10

At a meeting of the Directors of the Amicable Contributors at the Office in Angell Court on Snowhill, Tuesday ye 1st April 1729

Bradley's damage to be repaired by S. Howard

Mr Haddon from ye Committee for surveying Mrs Bradley's dam[a] in W[te] hart Court in Bermon Street reports that he has agreed with Mr Sam[l] Howard to repair ye same for five Guineas.

Ordered that W. Taylor pay Mr Howard 5 Guin[s] in full thereof upon his finishing ye same to ye satisfaction of ye sufferer

Sun Fire Office. A page from the register of Country Losses relating to claimants with surnames beginning with the letter P

Sun Fire Office

GLDH Ms 12019/1

General Cash Book

Examples:

27 Jan 1758

Samuel Wymkan	for his loss	£163 - 5 - 1
Thomas Freeman	" " "	38 - 18 - 6
James Smith	" " "	25 - 9 - 6
" "	" " "	35 - 4 - 3
John Morgan	" " "	26 - 0 - 2
John Rose	" " "	71 - 7 - 0
Thomas Banks	" " "	81 - 14 - 0
John Walters	" " "	16 - 17 - 1
John Brooke	" " "	7 - 1 - 6
Samual Winnis	" " "	5 - 0 - 0

Sun Fire Office

GLDH Ms 21075

Miscellaneous Claims

Robert Armitage and William Roper in Bishopsgate within, Stationers and
Paperhanging Makers, make Oath and say. That on or about the Fifthteenth
Day of November 1771 an accidental Fire happened in their Manufacturing
House in Flying Horse Stable Yard in Houndsditch, by which Fire they sustained the loss and Damage of their Utensils and Stock, Which Damages are
contained and Specified in an Inventory taken of the same and hereto
annexed.

And these Deponents further say, that said Inventory to the Best of their
Knowledge and Belief contains a true, full and faithfull Account of the
Damages done to their said Utensils and Stock, Which were these Deponent's
own proper Goods and Chattells and deposited in the aforesaid
Manufacturing House only at the Time said Fire happened, and all which
were burned, lost or damaged by said Fire.

And Lastly these Deponents further say, That said Utensils and Stock in the
Manufacturing House before mentioned were not insured in any other Office
at the Time said Fire happened – and that their real and just Loss occasioned
thereby amounts to the Sum of;
One Hundred Sixty three Pounds three Shillings & 6

Sworn at London the 24th Decr 1771 before me } Willm Roper
                                                                Robt Armitage
Wm Nash
Mayor

The Minister, Church Wardens and other Inhabitants of the Parish of St.
Botolph, Bishopsgate, Do hereby certifie That on or about the Fifteenth Day
of November 1771 an accidental Fire happened in the Manufacturing House

NORWICH UNION SOCIETY,

INSTITUTED 1797.

Detail of Losses,

(IRISH DISTRICT.)

1818.	£	s.	d.	1819.	£	s.	d.	1820.	£	s.	d.	1821.	£	s.	d.
Whalley	36	18	10	E. G. Mason	180	6	1	Hunt and Co.	141	17	4	Ann Anderson	3	14	8
Cunningham, Bell, and Co.	2577	13	0	Moore and Fisher	1	0	10	W. and T. Wise	630	0	5	Francis Arthur	21	0	0
John Ryan	29	9	0	J. P. M'Kee	1	5	0	Nugent	15	0	0	Anthony Wills	4	4	0
John Bow	16	3	11	Wheeler and Co.	1931	3	0	John Hickey	600	12	4	Andrew Jameson	500	0	0
West Darby	15	19	11	T. Boswell	2000	0	0					John Hickey	354	13	9
Mackenzie and Co.	20	0	0												
William Allman	2773	1	6												
Peter Tivey	18	0	0												
H. P. Swayne	323	1	6												
W. Watson	1383	17	3												
N. Sloane	30	11	1												
	7343	9	11		4113	14	11		1387	10	1		883	12	5

Examined,

PHILIP JAMES KNIGHTS,
GEORGE STACY,

Auditors.

Norwich Union. Details of Losses, 1818–1821

of the within named Messrs Robert Armitage and William Roper, situated in Flying Horse Stable Yard, in Houndsditch, By which Fire they sustained the Loss and Damage of their Utensils and Stock. And We do know, or verily believe, That the said Messrs Robert Armitage and William Roper are Persons of good Repute and that they realy and by Misfortune without any Fraud or evil Practice have sustained by said Fire a Loss to the Amount of the Sum mentioned in the within affidavit.

John Waring — Min[r]
B. W. Morrison ⎫
Mich[l] Hayward ⎭ — Church Wardens
Joshua Malcher
Robert Ray
Cha[s] Cornwell
W[m] Peters
John Miles
William Ayres

Courtesy of AVIVA

Sun Fire Office

GLDH Ms 11935/7

Committee for Country Insurance

20 Aug. 1775

Examined the following small Losses to which we recommend to be paid [includes the following]

John Pittman in Dorchester	Gent	£3 - 1 - 0
Robert Elliott "	Labourer	£3 - 15 - 2
Joseph Lovelace "	Victualler	£10 - 13 - 8
Mary Bartlett "	Spinster	£6 - 16 - 9
John Tapp "	Cooper	£7 - 14 - 2
Catherine Mansfield "	Malster	£8 - 0 - 2
Samual Hillard "	Victualler	£4 - 11 - 4
Edward Ensor "	Butcher	£3 - 1 - 2
Robert Lock "	do	£4 - 15 - 6
Mary Greening "	Widow	£4 - 14 - 0
Eliz. Reed "	Haberdasher	£7 - 9 - 6
Samuel Corpe "	Cabinet Maker	£3 - 7 - 0
Samuel Slade "	Gent	£6 - 4 - 3
Isaiah Roberts "	do	£9 - 17 - 0

Surveyor's Charge for adjusting all Losses in said Town   £16 - 4

Agent's Expenses in Journeys to & at said Town during the
Fire & Settlement of said Losses.   £13 - 15

Note: No reference to Dorchester has been found around this date in the minutes of the Country Insurance Committee ref Ms 11935/6

The next meeting dated 13 September 1775 includes the following:

Thos. Pouncey of Dewlish [*sic*] in Dorset, yeoman
for his Loss at Dorchester   £360

Robert Strickland	in Dorchester	Gent	£330 -12
James Bailey	in Dorchester	Clothier	£60
John Holmes	in ditto	Innholder	£53 - 9 - 4
Joseph Bennett	in ditto	Victualler	£50
John Chapman	in ditto	Baker	£32 - 6
Wm Banks	in ditto	Cheesemonger	£26 -18 - 2

This fire at Dorchester is also referred to at the Committee of Management on 31 August 1775:

GLDH Ms 11932/10

Committee of Management
31 August 1775

12-12-6   To Isaac Sparks of Dorchester in Dorset Malster, Twelve Pounds twelve shillings and sixpence for his loss

~~3-8-6~~*   To Ann Strickland in ditto spinster, three pounds eight shillings and sixpence for her loss

* Crossed through in original

Discharged & £4-8-6 ord. in lieu thereof. vide Com of 28 Sept.

4 - 17 - 8	To Martha Strickland in ditto widow
3 - 1 - 0	To John Pitman, Gent
3 - 15 - 2	Robert Elliott
10 - 13 - 8	Joseph Lovelace
6 - 16 - 9	Mary Bartlett
7 - 14 - 2	John Tapp
	etc., etc.

Also:

17-0-0 To John Carter seventeen pounds for casting 1000 marks

Hand-in-Hand Fire Office

GLDH Ms 8666/25

Directors' Meeting
July 13th 1784

Alexʳ Crickett   Ordered that Alexander Crickett be paid for the damage
damage £39-8-0 by fire to his house in the Butcher Row, No.28552   £39-8-0

date ditto   Mr Brinnell from the Committee for surveying the damage
Report of the   by a fire in the Strand, reported that a house insured by
Comᵉ in the   Robert Birch in a Policy No. 21674 for £300 is dimolished &
Strand   cannot be Rebuilt for less than £600. And that a house
                   insured by George Hampton in a Policy No. 89407 for £500 is
                   also dimolished & cannot be Rebuilt for less than £800. To
                   which the Board agreed & ordered that Robert Birch be paid
                   for the loss of his house, No. 21674 £300 and that George
                   Hampton be paid for the loss of his house, No. 89407 £500 at
                   the usual time, being the whole sums insured thereon.

London Assurance Corporation

GLDH Ms 8735/5

Committee of Fire

Friday 23ᵈ Septemʳ 1785

Mr Peter Besley Demanded £30-5-0 for Loss & Damage by Fire in Fetter Lane to his Wearing Apparel, Household Goods & Goods in Trust Assured by this Corporation in Policy No. 42545.

The Committe on Examining the Papers produced, adjusted the same at £13-7-6.

Resolved, that it the Opinion of this Committe that a Warrant be made out to Mr Peter Besley for Thirteen Pounds seven shillings & sixpence in full for Loss & damage by Fire in Fetter Lane to his Wearing Apparel, Household Goods & Goods in Trust, Assured by this Corporation in Policy No. 42545.

Sun Fire Office

GLDH MS 11932/18

Committee of Management
12th July 1810

Includes the following:-

20 - 4	The Rt Hon[ble] Lord Harrow for loss in Grosvenor Square	Twenty pds 4/-
84 -13	The Rt Hon[ble] Lord Limerick for loss in Mansfield Street	Eighty Pounds [*sic*] 13/-
100	Widow of John Clues for loss on 3 Houses in Rockwell Green	One Hundred Pounds
40	Grace Hill of Rockwell Green, Wellington, Widow	Forty Pounds
85	Thomas Cornelius of same Place, Taylor	Eighty Five Pounds
130	Widow Stradling of D°	One Hundred & Thirty Pounds
84 -17	John Wright of Tiverton, C° Devon, Yeoman	Eighty Four Pounds 17/-
35 -13- 2	Ambrose Weslake of St Thomas Apostle, Devon, Vict[r]	Thirty Five Pounds 13/2
6 -15- 3	W[m] Wills of same Place, Gent	Six Pounds 15/3
346 -14- 6	Mary Langdon of Chard, Widow	Three Hundred &Forty Six pds 14/6
114- 7- 9	Christ[r] Vickary of Liverpool, Pawnbroker	One Hundred & Fourteen pds 7/9

Essex and Suffolk Equitable Insurance Society

GLDH Ms 16206/1

Directors' Meetings

2 July 1821	That Mr John Sewell be allowed 16/- for assistance at a small fire upon his premises.

That the consideration of Mr Steel's loss by fire to property insured by Pol[y] 4385 be deferred till the particulars are stated.

Hand-in-Hand Fire Office

GLDH Ms 8686

Surveyors Estimate Book
February 25, 1822
Robert Ray of Montague Place, Russell Square, and Frank Sotheran.
A Damage to No. 99775 being to Houses in Old Street known by No's 128, 129, 130, 131, & 132 the damage is to No 128
Mr Long to repair
Surveyed Feb[y] 26th, 1882   Estimate [£]11-7-0
Will[m] Jupp
Agreed with Mr Long to repair

Royal Exchange Assurance

GLDH Ms 16237/1

A Special Fire Committee

19th February 1827

Ordered that Mr John Stevens, the Company's Surveyor be desired to endeavour to ascertain in what way the late fire in Sir Henry Blackwood's house, No 7 Cornwall Terrace, Regents Park was caused by the Warm Air Stove

March 12, 1827

In conformity to the Minutes of this Committee of the 19th February last Mr Stevens the Company's Surveyor made the following report on the late fire at Sir Henry Blackwood's House viz
"The Stove is in a Passage on the Basement for warming the Hall and Stair Case; there are two apertures for the heated air; the smoke is conveyed by a flue about 7 feet long to a regular Chimney formerly intended to warm the Hall, the flue which ascends within the thickness of the Party Wall. The fire was caused by the flue from the Stove having been cut into the wall too near to the ground floor joists, or a wooden brick connected therewith, which were ignited."

Sun Fire Office

GLDH Ms 11932/22

Committee of Management

12 Ap. 1832

The Secretary [also] stated to the Committee the circumstances attending a suspicious Fire in a Public House at Bradford, Wilts, the Building was insured by Policy N°. 1085086 for £300, the Stock and Utensils in which were insured in the Salamander Office for £800.

Resolved.

That in the event of the Landlord being bound over to prosecute, this Office will pay its proportion with the Salamander Office, of the surplus Expenses of the Trial beyond the Allowance received from the County.

Sun Fire Office

GLDH Ms 11934/12

Committee of Town Insurance
13 October 1835

(Paid)

The Norwich Union Fire Office for this Offices proportion of the Reinstatement of house at Froxfield, Wilts insured in this Office Py no: 1126377   £127-5

Note: It is unusual to find a policy number given against a claim as early as this.

Church of England Life and Fire Assurance Trust and Annuity Institution

GLDH Ms 12160D/1

Directors' Meetings

Friday 6th June 1845   The Secretary reported that the surveyor had effected a settlement of Mr James French's claim (assured by Policy N° 1697 for £250 viz House £150, Outbuildings £100) for £67-10-0 of which the Board approved and directed a Cheque to be drawn for the amount

Sun Fire Office

GLDH Ms 12019/27

General Cash Book [*sample page*]

1862	By Claims (contd)	
May	Bro^t forward	
		£1368 - 12 - 10
347	Edm^d Law	84 - 10 - 2
348	Ja^s Elston & an	70 - 0 - 0
"	Donaldson & Hume	24 - 17 - 9
"	Elizth L. Dunlop & an	31 - 16 - 3
341	Saml Pearson	65 - 0 - 0
346	G. E. Lallemande	16 - 7 - 6
339	Amelia S. Strickland	10 - 0 - 0
348	Fra^{is} H. Dickenson	14 - 17 - 6
345	Willm Page	16 - 17 - 0
349	do	6 - 18 - 0
"	Willm Bate	13 - 0 - 0
"	Richd Jaggers	60 - 0 - 0
341	Fred^k Dadswell	75 - 0 - 0
349	Thos Perfect	30 - 0 - 0
348	Fred^k Smart	16 - 0 - 0
"	John Blin	13 - 0 - 0
"	Willm Durell	25 - 0 - 0
"	Edwd Marshall	6 - 1 - 0
346	Willm Low	65 - 0 - 0
347	Willm Finch	450 - 0 0
348	Arthur Pickering	31 - 7 - 5
346	Raikes Currie & ors	400 - 0 - 0
348	Charles Jeffcoat	19 - 0 - 0
347	Willm Hy Bedding	500 - 0 - 0
348	Willm Bracher	265 - 2 - 9
"	Edwd Pulleyn	6 - 0 - 0
50	Mr Relton on a/c of Small Losses	150
	Carr^d forw^d	£4114 - 2 - 0

British General Insurance Company
GLDH Ms 23684

Total Losses (Marine)
Names of Ships (indexed at front) with newspaper cuttings

Example:

BONNY
Policy.   L'pool SH 27/7
        Line   500
        R/I   £375
        12 mos @ 1-7-27
"London. Apr. 12. [1928] The Owners of the Steamer *Bonny* advise *Bonny* ashore one mile east Cape Palmas. Tug and pumps from Lagos have been cabled for and steamer *Jekri* is standing by."

The owners of the steamer *Bonny*, London for West Africa, advise. "We have received a cable from our Agent at Monrovia, dated April 11 stating that the *Bonny* is ashore about one mile east of Cape Palmas No.1 hold full of water, steamer *Jekri* standing by"
    We have also received a cable from Lagos dated Apr. 11 stating Monrovia request tug pumps to assist *Bonny*, Cape Palmas. Propose sending marine tug *Rollicker* arranging best terms possible, can leave tomorrow morning (Apr.12).

Monrovia Apr. 12 – British Steamer *Bonny* grounded mile east of Cape Palmas, damage, if any, not known at present. British steamer *Jekri* reported to be standing by.

Chapter 5

Staff and Agents

There are no known continuous series of registers of staff for any fire insurance company though some staff records do survive. There are, however, many references to staff in the minutes of companies' meetings. The enrolment of agents was conducted by the boards of directors and recorded in the minutes of their meetings. Payments to others who assisted at fires have also been found. The following are examples:

Hand-in-Hand Fire Office

GLDH Ms 8666/4

At a meeting of the Directors of the Amicable Contributors
at the Office in Angell Court on Snow Hill on 11th Aug. 1713
Whereas the order for suspending Jn° Hankinson being now read a Third time it is now unanimously agreed that the said Jn° Hankinson be suspended & is hereby suspended.

Whereas it appears to this Board that Jn° Hankinson hath embezzled sev[el] considerable sums of money belonging to this Society & absconded from the Service of the said Office. Ordered and Agreed nomine contradirente that the said Jn° Hankinson be discharged from the Service of the Society & hereby Discharged from all Employment whatsoever in the said office this being the first time of reading.

Ordered that Mr Jn° Hughes be Desired to audit the Late clerk Jn° Hankinsons acc[ts] wth all expedicion & that he accept of such reward as the Board of Directors shall think fitt for the service.

Directors Meeting on Tuesday 4th May 1714

Sam Hill Samuel Hill being nominated to be the messenger to this Society was upon the question agreed to, and that this be the first reading & that it be mentioned in the next Summons to require a majority

John Legg A motion being made in Charity to John Legg and his wife and children to enable them to Subsist he being discharged from his place & salary. The Board in compassion to his hard circumstances and to save the Society the wages of thirty nine pounds to a person incapable of doing the Society any Service were pleased to order him fifteen pounds & that he & his family do remove out of the house betwixt this & midsummer next; at the time of his removal he is to have the sd money pd him by John Hughes.★˙

★ *A note crossed through refers to, 'his incapacity of discharging the duty of his place of messenger ——'*

Hand-in-Hand Fire Office

GLDH Ms 8666/10

Directors Meeting on Tuesday ye 1ˢᵗ Aprill 1729
Ordered that W. Taylor pay Geo. Harrington the following alarms. Viz

0-1-0	March 25	at Mr Yalden's in Hart Street 1 man
0-4-0	27	at Mr Bell's Brewhouse in Water Lane 3 men each 1[s] inq. 1[s]
0-9-0	28	at Mr Browning's in Southwᵏ 9 men each 1[s]
0-5-6	30	at Mr Pelling's in Cicell Street 3 men work'g an hour each 18ᵈ inq. 1[s]
0-4-0		– at Mr Smith's St Olave Street 3 men each 1[s] inquiry 1[s]
0-1-6		– at Capt Jones's one man an hour 18d
[£] 1-5-0		

Note: [s] represents shilling

Sun Fire Office

GLDH Ms 11935/7

Committee of Country Insurance

21 Feb 1777   We recommend that Eleven Pounds four shillings & five pence be paid to Mr John Scriven, Agent to the Office at Bristol for Repairs to the Office Engine under his Care at that Place.

20 June 1777 List of Agents who have sent up their accounts to Lady 1777

Henry Biggin	Ware	£260
Eliz. Dagnall	Aylesbury	58 - 19 - 0
John Drury	Evesham	52 - 1 - 6
Saml Gray	Chelmsford	104 - 4 - 1
Thos Hide's Executr	Cambridge	356 - 13 - 2
William Nicoll	Aberdeen	42 - 5 - 4
Danl Norton	Uxbridge	133 - 9 -11
Richd Stone	Thame	25 - 12 - 1
Geo. Tompson	Northampton	68 - 13 - 6
Thos. Walker	Buntingford	145 - 18 - 9
		43 - 12 - 0
		£1291 - 9 - 7

12 May 1780   Mr Abraham Chapman the Agent at Stony Stratford, having been a Long Time in Arrear in paying the Ballancesof his Accounts, not having made any Remittances of Late, This Committee do recommend, that he be discharged from that Agency, and another appointed.

A List of the Agents who have sent up their
Accounts from Midsummer 1748 to Michaelmas 1748

James	Ashley	Lincoln	33. 17. 8
George	Calverley	Newbury	147. 10. 7
David	Dwerell	Poll	71. 13. 3
Dwerell	Dagnell	Aylesbury	25. 1. 10
Samuel	Daniel	Colchester	25. 6. 8
John	Green	Buntingford	54. 16. 7
William	Jackson	Marlborough	185. 9. 7
Daniel	Jones	Twickenham	47. 9. 10
John	Maynard	Northampton	132. 8. 9
Richard	Marchant	Bath	33. 18. 1
Cuthbert	Ogle	Newcastle	45. 7. 3
John	Press	Norwich	218. 18. 11
John	Pottell	Oxford	69. 16. 6
Thomas	Partridge	Nottingham	100. 13. 4
Thomas	Richardson	Ipswich	84. 10. 2
John	Scott	Lynn	90. 13. 11
William	Smith	Peterborough	52. 8. 4
Thomas	Steel	Chichester	40. 6. —
Benjamin	Todd	Cowes	16. 13. 5
Richard	Willis	Andover	142. —. 9
Joseph	Woollams	Buckingham	18. 14. —
			1637. 15. 5

A List of the Agents who have not sent up their Accounts

Alex	Aberdeen	Aberdeen	Midr 1746
David	Alexander	Chester	Xmas 1747
William	Bentley	Leicester	Mid 1748
David	Baird	Edinburgh	Xmas 1747
Philip	Dauncey	Woolph	Xmas 1747
Thomas	Fowler	Yarmouth	Mich 1747
William	Greenall	Banbury	Lday 1748
Thomas	Hopper	Durham	Midr 1747
John	Hickin	Stafford	Mich 1746

Sun Fire Office. A page from a list of agents from a
Country Committee Minute Book, 1748

Hand-in-Hand Fire Office
GLDH Ms 8666/25

Directors Meeting, December 20ᵗʰ 1785

Thomas Smith appeared at the Board & resigned his place of a Fireman to this Society.

Janʸ 3ʳᵈ 1786
Ordered that Mr John Nicholls be paid £5-5-0 for his extraordinary trouble in making an estimate of the damage to the house of John Alexander Gresse Esq. In Tottenham Court Road

Essex and Suffolk Equitable
Insurance Society
GLDH Ms 16206/1

Board Minutes
The following is written near the back of the volume covering the years 1802 to 1821:

Agents

Jas. Butler	Chelmsford
Geo. Becham	Rayleigh
Wᵐ L. Barnes	Saff. Walden
John Barnard Jun.	Harlow
Benja. Chapman	Harwick
Edwᵈ Chapman	Mendlesham
Alfred May	Malden
Richᵈ G. Dupont	Sudbury
Tho. Eddison	Romford
Tho. & R. Joslin	Braintree
Samˡ Jesup	Halsted
John King	C. Hedingham
Bethia Matthews	Coggeshall
Geo. Oliver	Bury
Jos. Y. Oliver	Ipswich
Wᵐ Rolph	Billericay
Tho. Scrivener	Manningtree
Jos. Sewell	G. Dunmow
Jas. Seaman	Thorp
Benja. Salmon	Gt. Oakley
Jas. Wild	Woodbridge
Frans Wilson	Gr. Clacton
Phil. Youngman	Witham
John Rudlin	Brightlingsea

Sun Fire Office

GLDH Ms 11932/18

Committee of Management (Extract)

12th July 1810

That the following Payments be made

600	Managers' Salaries	Six Hundred Pounds
75	Secretary'do	Seventy Five Pounds
45	Committee of Cash	Forty Five Pounds
37 -10	Auditors' Salaries	Thirty Seven Pounds 10/-
13 - 2 -6	Solicitors' Salaries	Thirteen Pounds 2/6
206 - 5	Inspectors' Salaries	Two Hundred & Six Pounds 5/-
25	Treasurer's Salaries	Twenty Five Pounds
100	Secretary in lieu of Coals Candles & Office Expenses	One Hundred P[ds]
37 -10	Contingent Expenses of Craigs Court	Thirty Seven Pounds 10/-
15 -15	P. Bewicke Esq for making up y[e] Duty Account	Fifteen P[ds] 15/-
125	H. Watts Esq for ¼ Annuity to Mids [*Midsummer*]	One Hundred & Twenty five P[ds]
112 -10	Job Marks for ¼ Pension to D°	One Hundred & Twelve P[ds] 10/-
25	Jonathan Crowther for D° to D°	Twenty Five Pounds
7 -10	Thomas Simson for D° to D°	Seven Pounds 10/-
15	John Headworth for D° to D°	Fifteen Pounds
25	John S. Turner for D° to D°	Twenty Five P[ds]
15	James Bradley for D° to D°	Fifteen P[ds]
7 -10	as Robinson for D° to D°	Seven P[ds] 10/-
5	Jos White for D° to D°	Five Pounds
3 -15	John Cross for D° to D°	Three P[ds] 15/-
15	Thos Fowler for D° to D°	Fifteen P[ds]
13 -13	John Masters for 13 Weeks @ £1-1 Per Week	Thirteen P[ds] 13/-
7 -10	W[m] Ward in lieu of Fires	Seven Pounds 10/-
6 - 5	John Scholey for D°	Six Pounds 5/-
4 -10	John Outridge for ¼ Pension to Mids [*Midsummer*]	Seven Pounds 10/-
5	James Broughton for ¼ Pension to Mids	Five Pounds
5 - 5	W[m] Costellow for making returns of Fires to D°	Five Pounds 5/-
381 - 7- 6	Firemen & Porters for attending Fires ¼ to Mids [*Midsummer*]	Three Hundred & Eighty one Pounds 7/6
26 -12-6	D° for Alarms ¼ to Mids [*Midsummer*]	Twenty Six Pounds 12/6

continued

| 86 -19 | Fire Patrol for ¼ Attendance to D° | Eighty Six Pounds 19/- |
| 49 - 5 | 1000 Policies to be stamped to N° 846050 | Forty nine P^{ds} 5/- |

Essex and Suffolk Equitable Insurance Society

GLDH Ms 16206/1

Board Minutes

Fourth Day of November 1816

That Mr Edwd Ind of Romford, a member of the Society and a large Insurer be written to, informing him of the negligence & inattention of Mr Tho.Eddison the Society's Agent there, and particularly of his neglect in not answering letters sent to him by the Secretary, and not paying his balance £67-19-4 due at Christmas last, & requesting the favor of Mr Ind to recommend a proper person as agent to the Society, in lieu of Mr Eddison.

Sun Fire Office

GLDH Ms 11932/21

Management Committee

23 Feb. 1826   The Secretary reported that John Hawkins, one of the Pensioners of this Society, died on the 11th of Feb

Royal Exchange Assurance

GLDH Ms 16237/1

Fire Committee

26 Feb. 1827 Mr Bird informed the Committee that in conformity with the directions of the Chairman, J.Thomson, the late driver of the Company's Engine at Wapping Station has delivered his clothes to the Foreman.
Ordered that they be returned to him after taking off the buttons.

Royal Exchange Assurance

GLDH Ms 16237/1

Fire Committee

August 6, 1827

A letter from Mr Lochner the Company's Surveyor was read informing the Committee that the Engine house in Jeffries Square is complete. Resolved that the Engine on the Southwark Station be removed to the new Engine house aforesaid to take the duties allotted to her by the regulations made in Decr 1826, and that the Engine on the Wapping Station be removed to the Engine house on the Southwark Station and be allowed to attend fires on the Surrey side of the River till further orders.

Resolved also that John Flower late Engineer to the Wapping Engine do take care of the Engine in Jeffries Square and be allowed to live in the Rooms over the Engine house at a Rent of £8 p. annum, subject to the approval of the Governor.

March 15, 1830
A letter was read from Emanuel Pester Davy of Beaminster in the County of
Dorset, ironmonger, offering himself as Agent to the Company for that Town in
the room of John Colman resigned. A satisfactory account of Mr Davy rec^d thro'
Mr T.G.Read of Dorchester.

Royal Exchange Assurance

GLDH Ms 16237/1

Fire Committee Minutes

Augt 11, 1828
Ordered that the Agent at Colyton be directed to retain the best of the 2 Engines
belonging to the Company in that Town and have the same painted, and to dis-
pose of the other to the best advantage.

   Letters from Mr Ward were read inclosing applications from the following
Persons to become Agents to the Company viz.

Wm Macquire, draper & auctioneer   Northampton
Thos Cleaver, auctioneer   Wellingborough, Co. Northampton
John Oldham, watch & clock maker   Southam, Co. Warwick
Ja^s Thompson, shopkeeper   Solihul, Co. Warwick

Resolved to recommend to the Court of Directors to appoint the said W^m
Macquire, Thos Cleaver, Jn° Oldham & Ja^s Thompson Agents accordingly & that
the usual Security from the three former be dispensed with for the present.

Sun Fire Office

GLDH Ms 11934/12

Committee of Town Insurance

9 April 1833
Frederick Robertson a Candidate to be admitted as a Lad into this Office,
having appeared this day before the Committee, and answered all such
enquiries, as the Committee thought proper to put to him, are of opinion that
he is a proper person to be recommended to the Committee of Management,
for admission as a Lad on Trial.

Globe Insurance Company

GLDH Ms 11685

Register of Agents' Securities (Place-name index at front)

Example :   Huddersfield
                                   Charles Turner
                                   £200
                                   28 March 1850

                                   Jos^h Turner of Huddersfield, woolstapler

                                   Josiah Berry of Lockwood near Huddersfield
                                   woollen manufacturer and merchant
                                   3 Nov. '53

Norwich Union. Two pages from an Agent's Policy Book, 1825, showing a rare example of a sketch of an insured property

the UNION FIRE-OFFICE, NORWICH.

How built and covered.	Occupier's Name and Business.	Where situate.	Sum insured.	Rate per Cent.	Annual Payment.
	Himself	Knowlidge	250		6
Do.	John Harberton	Do.	150		
			60..3'		12
				£ 18/	
brick stone & tile	occupied by William Stannard Clothier	Knowlidge brickton Norfolk 10/6	1000		
—	—	— 10/6	100		
Do.	Do.	— 10/6	50		
		— 10/6	125		12 6
brick & slate	Do.	— 3/-	25	3/	9
brick & slate	Do.	— 3/-	175	7/6	13 1½
Do.	Do.	2/-	50	1/6	9
Do.	Do.	2/-	50	1/6	9
Do.	Do.	3/-	25		1 3
			1600		

Royal Farmers and General Fire,
Life and Hail Insurance

GLDH Ms 14998

List of Agents
(Arranged by County and then by [town] Agency)

Example: Somerset
             Wellington
             To be addressed to Mr Voisey, Painter &c Wellington, Somerset
                                                              10/1/99

             Mr John Voisey, Plumber, Painter &c   28/1/73
             Mr I.W. Bell Messr Fox Fowler & Co's Bank
             corresponded for Hail only, agent to
             Bristol Branch   14/1/95

             Taunton
             Mr Samuel Fisher, 8 & 9 Fore Street,
             Ironmonger   14/4/68

             Wiveliscombe
             ~~Mr William John Broughton Knight, High Street, Chemist~~*
             Mrs Sophia Knight (Chemist) Market Place   9/6/74

*Crossed through in original

Norwich Union Fire Insurance Society

NU 38/4/1

Clerks Attendance Book
Monday July 17/76 [1876]

Name	Arrived	Departed
Geo. Clark	9 - 4	
W. White	9 - 15	7 - 30
W.E.H.	9 - 15	4 - 12
H.W.C.	9 - 21	4 - 2
C.H.	9 - 22	4 - 25
T.L.Y.	9 - 23	4 -
D.W.	9 - 25	4 - 7
H.I.A.C.	9 - 26	4 - 2
H.B.	9 - 28	4 - 10
W. Finch	9 - 30	4 - 2
G.S.S.	9 - 30	4 - 1

Tuesday July 18/76 [1876]

Geo. Clark	9 -	[blank]
H.F. Butler	9 - 15	4 - 3
H.W.C.	9 - 23	4 - 5
G.S.S.	9 - 24	4
D.W.	9 - 24	4 - 5
W.F.	9 - 25	4 - 5

T.S.S.	9 - 27	4 - 5
H.I.A.C.	9 - 28	4 - 5
W.E.H.	9 - 29	[blank]
W.W.	9 - 30	6 -15
C.H.	9 - 36	5 -15

Norwich Union. Caricature of female staff by W.E. Oliver, 1921

Norwich Union Fire Insurance Society

NU 38/6/1

Life and Fire Office Staff Lists
'This list has not been kept up so far as entering new
Fire Office births since May 1877'

List of Clerks in the Norwich Union Life and Fire Offices

Name		Date of Entry	Remarks	Office
Corsbie	Joseph	1810	Died Sept[r] 15th 1861	Fire
Sowels	William		Died 1856	"
Clark	John		Died June 24th 1864	"
Starling	Thomas		Died 1843	Life
Walker	W[m] T.		Died Feby 6th 1863	Fire
Wilson	Lewis		Retired. Died Nov 1878	"
Brundell	Cha[r]		Died 1854	Life
Corsbie	D. T	1821 June 25	Retired May 17th 1874 Died April 7th 1876	"
Leman	Robert		Died March 18th 1863	Fire
Ibrook	R.		Retired March 25th 1857 Died 1877	"
Clark	James	1829	Pensioned June 24th 1873 Died Nov 20th 1876	"

continued

Clark	Samuel		Died June 27[th]1868	
Booth	George		Died June 27th 1862	"
Winter	Jno Green		Died May 14th 1864	"
Rushmere	W[m]		Retired 1853. Died 1872	"
Todd	William	1833	Paralysed Dec[r] 26th 1870 Pensioned June 1871 Died Oct[r] 13th 1873	Life
Holmes	Geo. P.	1834 Mar	Appointed Cashier Jan[y] 6th 73 as Chief Clerk Sep[r] 1874 Superannuated Oct[r] 1880 Died Dec[r] 9th 1899	"
Studball	Paul		Died	Fire
Starling	Robert		Died 1851	"
Cook	James	1835 June 5th	Died March 7th 1867	"
Driver	William		Died Aug[st] 29th 1876	"
Fountain	Thos		Discharged Nov[r]1861 Died	"
Bunyon	Geo.		Accepted the Dublin Agency Afterwards appointed to Bristol Agency Died Jan[y] 26 1900	"
Sharp	Fred[k]		Accepted the Dublin Agency died 1861	"
Wodehouse	Geo.B		Retired March 1890	"
Sowels Jr	William	1846	Retired Dec[r] 31st 1893 Died Sept[r] 1st 1902	"
Walker	Fred[ke]		Left 1850 [?]	"
Starling	Thos L.	1845 Jan 1	Died Dec[r] 22[nd]1878	Life
White	William	1847 Feb[y]	Resigned Jan[y] 2nd 1882 Pensioned from Dec[r] 31 1881 Died	"
Clark	Geo. O	1848 Mar 27	Retired 31st 1905	Fire
Corsbie	Hy W	1852	Left Jan[y] 1st 1865	"
Perowne	Rob[t]	1852	Left Feb[y] 26th 1882 Appointed District Manager to FO at Birmingham Died 23 July 1886	"
Button	Edward		Absent several Mo[s]. Place filled by Jn[o] De Caux May 30th 1864 Died 1865	"
Leman	Chas		Left September 29th 1855	Life
Sowter	William	1852	Retired – Died April 1903	Fire
Corsbie	Horace W	1853 Feb[y] 8	Superannuated Decr 31st 1891 Died Oct 27th 1904	Life
Rudd	E.I.G.	1853	Left Mar 25th 1869 (Ill health) Died August 3rd 1870	Fire
Corsbie	H.I.A.	1854 May 2	Appointed Inspector of Agents for S. Eastern District Oct 1885 for eastern Counties Jan[y] 1894	Life

Norwich Union Fire Insurance Society

NU 38/6/1

Register of Staff Birthdays

1878

N.U.F. Office

Names		Date	Remarks
Woodhouse	B.G.	10th Dec[r]	
Sowels	W[m]	6th Feb[y]	
Clark	Geo. O	18th Oct[r]	
Perowne	R[t]	20th Aug[t]	Birmingham June 1882 Dead
Sowter	A.	5 Jan[y]	
Grinling	H.B.	3rd Ap[l]	
De Caux	Lucas	12th Ap[l]	
Page	Rt	18th Aug[t]	
Blazeby	H.E.	4th July	
Lowne	W.C.D.	24 Dec[r]	
Bailey	J.C.I.	12 July	
Gissing	R.H.	4 Feb[y]	
White	A.E.	9 May	
Casman	S.I.	6 Sept[r]	Dead
De Caux	John	6 Ap[l]	
Jay	G.B.	18 Oct[r]	Dead
Abel	W[m]	15 Nov[r]	
Gissing	J.E.	17 Jan[y]	
Perowne	Jon[n]	24 Mar	
Del	W.H.	12 May	Left 1881
Oury	W.	22 Ap[l]	
Large	Cha[s]	9 Nov[r]	
Clark	W[m]	13 March	
Niverre	C.E.	3 March	
Armstrong	–	12 Nov[r]	
Elmer	E.J.	7 June	
Clark	Frank	7 March	
Irls	R.H.	18 Oc	Left 1/1/78
Starkey	J.H.	27 Jan[y]	Dead
Lamb	S.	18 July	
Brown	T.	29 Oct	Died 4th Nov[r] 1886
Nockolds	J.	11 May	
Mallett	R.F	7 Jan[y]	
Hitchman	A.E.	13 Sept[r]	
Mallett	Robert	2 Dec	
Palmer	R	26 Dec[r]	Left 1880
Sowels	F	28 May	Died 24th Oct[r] 1887
Drane	W.J.	9 Dec[r]	
Nockolde		15 April	
Edwards	E.	11 Ap	
Carman	F.	19 Ap	Left
Bokenham		4 May	

continued

Wilde		[blank]	
Bellman		7 May	
Wilde	S.	18 Aug^t	
Duge	Herbert	1 March	
Barker	C.	10 Oct	
Hardy		23 Sep	
Messent		18 Aug	
Grand		8 July	Left gone to Gurney's [Bank]
Scott	W.H	20 Sept^r	Dead
Sidell	A.	16th Jan^y	
Brown	John	11 Ap^l	
Hart		9 Aug^t	
Bailey Jr		[blank]	
Kent		[blank]	
Holmes		[blank]	
Quinton		22 Oct^r	
Linay		10 Septr 91-21	
Troughton	H.	12 Jan^y	

Law Fire Insurance Society

GLDH Ms 15018

Salaries 1883 to 1914

Examples:

Age	Name	Department	Commt of Service	Salary Xmas/88	Date of Last Increase	
64	Shaw R.J.	Principal Clerk Agency Dept	Sept 45	450	Xmas	86
61	Wells F.S	Principal Clerk Town Dept	L'day 54	400	"	"
65	Sanders A.	Agency Ledger Keeper	Feb 48	350	Xmas	81
39	Beal E.W.R.	Town Dep	Aug 68	350	Xmas	87
35	Sanders E.T.	Agency Dept	Xmas 66	250	Xmas	84
35	Wood H.S.	Town Dept	Mids 69	250	"	"
35	Smith G.G.	Principal Clerk Accountants Dept	Xmas 69	300	"	87
32	Garwood A.E.	Agency Accounts	Nov 72	200	"	85
40	Francis B.	Agency Dept	Dec 72	200	– – – –	
32	Oldham H.	" "	Nov 74	180	Xmas	87
31	Bagnald W.L.	First Renewal Clerk	June 72	190★	"	85
34	Paine E.	Town Dept	Dec 75	180★	"	86
31	Harwood C.W.	Town Dept & Petty Cash Keeper	Dec 75	180★	"	85
30	Snell T.E.	Town Dept	Dec75	180★	"	"

29	James H.	Fire Loss Clerk	Feb 76	200	"	86
27	Clabon C.C.	Town Dept	Mar 78	160	"	87
28	Creasy L.E.	" "	" "	160	"	87
26	Curtis A.L.	Agency Dept	June 79	140*		

*£10 annually to £200

Law Union and Crown Insurance Company

GLDH Ms 21276

Register of Salaries

Dublin Branch

Name	C. Webb
Amount	£20
Appointed	9th May 1899
Commenced Work	17th May 1899

Increased to £30 p.a. from 1st July 1900

Name	T.M. O'Callaghan
Amount	£100

Appointed District Agent at Cork under agreement.
6 July 1900 commenced work

Name	J. Short
[£] 110	from 1 April 1896
120	from 1 March 1897
130	from 1 January 1898
150	from 1 January 1899
160	from 1 January 1900

Atlas Assurance Company

GLDH Ms 16176/1

Agency Appointments [page 114]

Branch or Depot	Bristol
Name	Ernest Richard Davies
Occupation	Solicitor
Locality	Ross
County	Hereford
Agency Cancelled	See Davies & Harris

Submitted to Court 12th Dec. 1899

Sun Fire Office

GLDH Ms 11932/47

Committee of Management

20 January 1902
Clerkships
Submitted results of the City of London College Examination on 15th Inst and Resolved.

That Vernon Harry Webber (184 marks) having passed the usual medical examination be appointed a Junior on the usual months probation, to fill the 3rd vacancy for additional Clerks, declared by the Committee on the 2nd inst.

Also that the following gentlemen having passed the medical examination be appointed supernumaries in lieu of the three members of staff still away at the War.
Norman Beaumont Foster (179 marks)
Francis Ramsay Fraser Biscoe (169 marks)
Herbert John Basket (167 marks)

Law Union Fire and Life
Insurance Company

GLDH Ms 21278/1

Staff Register

page 8   Head Office Staff
      Name   Vyvyan Ward Dougherty
      Salary   £90
      Date of Appointment   29 Jan 1909
      Agency Assistant
      3rd Class Railway & other expenses
      Direct Life Acc. And Burglary Business
      Transferred to Accountants Dept. 8/09
      Formerly a member of the Investment Dept   See page 23 [*following*]

page 23 Head Office Clerical Staff
      V. W. Dougherty   born 27 Nov 1886
      Date of Appointment   27 March 1905
      Salary   £40 (Includes £10 for shorthand)
      Increased on   1 April 1906 to £50
                                  1 April 1907 to £60
                                  1 April 1908 to £70
      Duties   General Manager's and Departmental correspondence. Make out Diary daily lists of matters to be attended to. Make out cases for declined loans. See that inclosures advised in departmental letters were put in their envelopes. Shorthand and typing. Assist generally in work of department.
          Mr Dougherty on the resignation of Mr Parsons took over his duties as detailed above and shows promise of soon being proficient therein.
          Mr Dougherty is also a very promising junior.

GLDH Ms 21278/2 page 16
Accountants Department

V.W. Dougherty   D.O.B. 27-11-86   Appt.   27/3/05
    1914   £130
    1915   £140 1/1/15
    1916   On Service
    1917   On Service
    1918   On Service
    1919   170 13/4/19

Note: There are many men here recorded as 'Killed in Action'

page 28
Fire Department

V.W. Dogherty
Date of Birth   27-11-86
Date of Appointment 27-3-05
    1920   £300   7/20
    1921   £320   1/21
    1922   £320

Note: From Accountant's Department 1919

page 42
Fire Department

V.W. Dogherty 3 Onslow Avenue Mansions, Richmond
Date of Birth   27-11-86
Date of Appointment   27-3-05
Date and Amount of last Increase prior to 1932
        [£]20   1/21
    1923   £320
    1924   £320
    1925   £320
    1926   £320
    1927   £330   1/1/27
    1928   £340   1/1/28
    1929   £350   1/1/29
    1930   £360   1/1/30
    1931   £360

Watermen who were employed as firemen, and others, such as fishermen, merchant seamen employed in the coastal trade shipping coals and other fuels and servants to Royalty and the Government were exempt from impressment into the Royal Navy and these men were recorded by the Admiralty Office. Each was issued with a *Certificate of Immunity from Impressment.*

The following are some examples of firemen from the Admiralty registers:

PRO ADM 7/390

A List of Firemen employed by the Albion Fire & Life Insurance Company 23 Feb 1812

Name	Address	Age	Height	Complexion	Hair
Peter Croxford[1]	Green Bank, Tooley St	53	5' 7"	Dark	Dark Brown
Jon[a] Crookland	Morgans Lane, Tooley St	29	5' 7"	Sallow	Dark Brown
Nathl. Hudson	Legge Alley, L------	36	5' 7"	Dark	Dark Brown
Robt. Pettey	Bell Court, Bell Street	35	5' 5½	Fair	Dark Brown
Thos. Holland	Queen St.	37	5' 9½	Fair	Sandy
Jos. Wade	Maid Lane, Bankside	34	5' 6"	Fair	Sandy
Jn° May	Bedfd Bury Court Garden	29	5' 6"	Dark	Dark Brown
Peter Croxford Jun[r]		26	5' 6"	Dark	Dark Brown
Jn° Colcomb	Trinity Upper Thas. St.	46	5' 5"	Dark	Dark Brown
Edwd. Eglintine	Cheqrs. Court Soutwark	35	5' 7"	Fair	Red
Thos. King	Houghton St., Clare Market	34	5' 6½	Dark	Dark Brown
Richd. Mitchell	New Court, St. Catherines	33	5' 8"	Dark	Dark Brown
Henry Milne	Robin Court, Tooley St.	35	5' 7½	Dark	Dark Brown
Phil. Martin	Castle St. Southwark	27	5' 6"	Fair	Light
Jos. Babington	Vine Yd. Tooley St.	24	5' 6"	Fair	Light Brown
Jas. Winton Brown	Freemans Lane, Horsleydn	25	5' 6½	Fair	Light
Jn° Miller	John St. Horselydn	38	5' 6"	Sallow	Dark Brown
Wm Blinco	Castle St. Southwark	23	5' 6"	Fair	Light Brown
Robt. Barrow	Cupers Bridge, Southwark	23	5' 6"	Dark	Dark Brown
Edwd. Hamilton	Bankside, Southwark	23	5' 8"	Dark	Dark Brown
Fras. Godfrey	Wilds Passage Drury Lane	25	5' 5"	Dark	Dark Brown
Thos. Humphreys	19 Star Ct, Nightingale Lane	25	5'5½	Dark	Dark Brown
Jas. Upton	Three Cup Alley, Shadwell	36	5' 8"	Fair	Light Brown
Hy. Fairman	Ryals Ct, Horslydn[2]	21	5' 6"	Fair	Light Brown

1. Another list dated 7 Feb. 1827 in the same register lists Peter Croxford now aged 67 and living at 15, Southwark Square, Bridge St, Southwark. His height has reduced to 5' 5½ and his hair now grey.
2. Horsleydown, Southwark, Surrey

The Admiralty Registers, PRO reference ADM 7/363 to 390 cover the years 1702 to 1828.

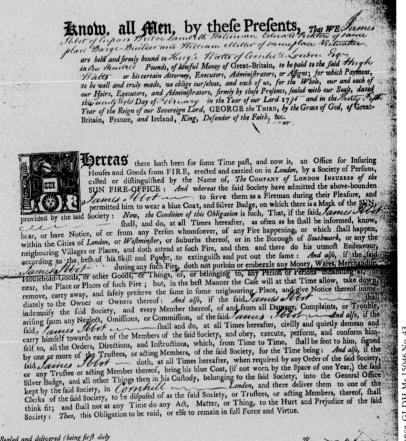

Know, all Men, by these Presents, That WE *James Ibbot of Upper Bridoe Lambeth Waterman, Edward Pickton of same place Barge-Builder and William Miller of same place Victualler*

are held and firmly bound to *Hugh Watts of Cornhill London Esqr.* in One hundred Pounds, of lawful Money of Great-Britain, to be paid to the said *Hugh Watts* or his certain Attorney, Executors, Administrators, or Assigns; for which Payment, to be well and truly made, we oblige ourselves, and each of us, for the Whole, our and each of our Heirs, Executors, and Administrators, firmly by these Presents, sealed with our Seals, dated this *Twenty eight* Day of *February* in the Year of our Lord 179*4* and in the *Thirty Fifth* Year of the Reign of our Sovereign Lord, GEORGE the Third, by the Grace of God, of Great-Britain, France, and Ireland, King, Defender of the Faith, &c.

Whereas there hath been for some Time past, and now is, an Office for Insuring Houses and Goods from FIRE, erected and carried on in London, by a Society of Persons, called or distinguished by the Name of, The COMPANY OF LONDON INSURERS of the SUN FIRE-OFFICE : And whereas the said Society have admitted the above-bounden *James Ibbot* to serve them as a Fireman during their Pleasure, and permitted him to wear a blue Coat, and Silver Badge, on which there is a Mark of the SUN, provided by the said Society : Now, the Condition of this Obligation is such, That, if the said *James Ibbot* shall, and do, at all Times hereafter, as often as he shall be informed, know, hear, or have Notice, of or from any Person whomsoever, of any Fire happening, or which shall happen, within the Cities of London, or Westminster, or Suburbs thereof, or in the Borough of Southwark, or any the neigbouring Villages or Places, and doth attend at such Fire, and then and there do his utmost Endeavour, according to the best of his Skill and Power, to extinguish and put out the same : And also, if the said *James Ibbot* during any such Fire, doth not purloin or embezzle any Money, Wares, Merchandise, Household-Goods, or other Goods, or Things, of, or belonging to, any Person or Persons inhabiting at, or near, the Place or Places of such Fire ; but, in the best Manner the Case will at that Time allow, take down, remove, carry away, and safely preserve the same in some neigbouring Place, and give Notice thereof immediately to the Owner or Owners thereof : And also, if the said *James Ibbot* shall indemnify the said Society, and every Member thereof, of and from all Damage, Complaints, or Trouble, arising from any Neglect, Omissions, or Commission, of the said *James Ibbot* And also, if the said, *James Ibbot* shall and do, at all Times hereafter, civilly and quietly demean and carry himself towards each of the Members of the said Society, and obey, execute, perform, and conform himself to, all the Orders, Directions, and Instructions, which, from Time to Time, shall be sent to him, signed by one or more of the Trustees, or acting Members, of the said Society, for the Time being : And also, if the said *James Ibbot* doth, at all Times hereafter, when required by any Order of the said Society, or any Trustee or acting Member thereof, bring his blue Coat, (if not worn by the Space of one Year,) the said Silver Badge, and all other Things then in his Custody, belonging to the said Society, into the General Office kept by the said Society, in *Cornhill* London, and there deliver them to one of the Clerks of the said Society, to be disposed of as the said Society, or Trustees, or acting Members, thereof, shall think fit ; and shall not at any Time do any Act, Matter, or Thing, to the Hurt and Prejudice of the said Society : Then, this Obligation to be void, or else to remain in full Force and Virtue.

Sealed and delivered (being first duly stamped) in the Presence of

Barclay Jr.

The Mark of James Ibbot

Edwd. Pickton

Wm. Miller

Sun Fire Office. A Fireman's Bond for James Ibbot

A List of the Thirty Firemen belonging to the Hand in Hand Fire Office with the Places of their abode.

Chas: Gould Foreman	Christ Church Surry
Jno: Manning Deputy	St Margaret Westminster
Wm Harrington Engineer	St Bridget London
Wm Gurney Deputy	St Sepulchre Do
Jas Crees	St Bridget Do
Welfare Killick	St Saviours Southwark
Wm Richman	St Saviours Southwark
John Ferrier	Christ Church Surry
Richd Aaron	St Bridget London
Geo. Phelps	St Catherines by the Tower
Jno Melham	St Mary White Chapel
Jonathan Bell	St Mary Lambeth
Jno Holloman	St Ann Blackfryers
Jos. Bull	St Catherines by the Tower
Jos: Latham	Whitefryars
Danl: Robinson	St Saviour's Southwark
John Fisher	St Sepulchre London
Jerem Mildmay	St John Wapping
Jno Hilliard	St Mary Lambeth
Robt Marshall	St John Horsleydown
Robt Brown	St George in the East
Phil. Gough	St Bennet Paul's Wharf
Jno Powell Edward Nicholls	Christ Church Surry Jonathan Sharp
Thos Halsey	St Botolph Aldgate
Wm Webb	St George in the East
Hen. Cochram	St John's Southwark
Jno Dawson	St John's Do
Robt Cawood	St Martin in the Fields
Jno Somes	St George's Middlesex
Wm Powell	Christ Church Surry

The usual Certificate dated the 1st Feby 1755 is on the other side.

Hand in Hand Fire Office. List of Firemen with their addresses

Chapter 6

Locating a Policy for a Particular Person

As has already been stated, some insurance company policy registers have name indices. The *Hand in Hand Fire Office* policy registers have a name index entered in each register. Some indices also exist for the *Sun Fire Office* and the *Royal Exchange*. (See Chapter 2 and Appendix 2.) Initial searches should be carried out in these indices. Most other insurance company policy registers are not indexed, however, and with these it is necessary to search the whole of a register to try and locate a particular policy holder.

There are a few guidelines which may shorten the time of a search. Newspapers should not be overlooked. A fire was a notable event and was usually recorded in the local newspaper. Householders and tradesmen suffering losses by fire were often recorded by name and in many instances the name of the fire insurance company covering these losses was given, sometimes with the value of each claim.

In the case of the Sun Fire Office there is a series of Registers of Losses (see Chapter 4 and Appendix 2). The names of claimants are recorded alphabetically, so it is a quick procedure to locate someone who had a loss and made a claim. As these registers do not usually record the related policy numbers it is necessary to search the policy registers backwards from the date of the claim to find the related policy.

Policy premiums appear to have been paid annually except in unusual circumstances. The exceptions often included ships whose insurance premiums whilst in dock were much cheaper than when 'under steam'. Although a premium was paid annually on a regular basis, a new policy was usually issued every five years. Once a policy has been found for a particular person or property it is possible that another policy for the same property will be found five years earlier and five years later. There were many exceptions to this, particularly where the property changed hands, although such changes are recorded in endorsements (if they survive). (See Chapter 3.)

By the beginning of the 19th century many fire insurance companies had established themselves around the country. Their agents may be found in trade directories under 'Fire Offices'. It is helpful to identify the names of the local agents for the period of a search. The *Sun Fire Office* policy registers usually have the agent's name entered in the left hand margin. Rather than read the names of the policy holders at the top of every policy it is quicker to locate the agent's name. It was usual for the agent to return details of policies in 'blocks' of numbers. Thus a number of policies for one agent will be found in the registers entered consecutively.

If a policy holder is known to have died it is likely that his executors will have informed the insurance company. In such a case an endorsement was issued. Searching the endorsement register after the date of death may reveal the policy number. The policy number is always recorded with the endorsement. The policy can then be immediately located in the appropriate policy register as policies are entered in numeric order. It should be noted that in many cases several volumes record policies for one particular date span. Policies are entered consecutively in 'blocks' of numbers with some gaps in the numbering. The numbers missing in one volume will be found in another volume covering the same overall dates and numbers.

Agents' policy registers held in county record offices and other archives (see Appendices 3, 4 and 5) do not usually have name indices, but as each of these is a policy register for one particular agent they usually cover one particular district. They include far fewer policies for a particular period than the company policy registers and are therefore relatively quicker to search.

For those researchers with West Country interests the Devon and Cornwall Record Society published in 1978 *The Devon Cloth Industry in the Eighteenth Century* edited by Stanley D. Chapman. This book has brought together a large number of Sun Fire Office policies relating to all those involved in the weaving trade in the County of Devon. The book has an index of policy holders and another index of all other persons recorded in these policies.

Chapter 7

Policy Registers: Householders, Tradesmen and Inns

London Assurance Corporation

GLDH Ms 21278/1

No. of Policy	1809
Date of Policy	30 Sepr 1723
Assured name and the place of abode	Henry Sproule of Athlone in the County of West Meath, merchant
What is assured and the place where	One hundred pounds on his dwelling house being shingled, & out houses thereto belonging, in sd Town of Athlone, County West Meath, now in his poss^n, fifty pounds on household goods therein & one hundred pounds on goods in trade, except such goods as in the proposals are excepted
	Danl Kennedy
	W by Widd^o Acton
Sum Assured	£250
Continuance of policy seven years	
Annual Premium	8s [*shillings*]

Royal Exchange Assurance

GLDH Ms 725/2

Surveyed and approved	Ed^d Hawkins of Lemon Street, Goodmans Fields, carpenter
Aug ye 6, 1755	On a timber house situate on the Southside of a
Thos Mutter	yard (late a carpenters yard) on the West Side of the Passage leading from the Rosemary Branch of Goodmans Yard in Goodmans Fields aforesaid, now empty

£200

continued on page 98

Warwick CRO 1039/2   *Phoenix Fire Office (Agent's Policy Register)*

Date	Names of persons assured Also their Profession and residence	Sums assured If several different Sums, to be specified	On what property	Where situated
1788 December 25th	Mr Robert Doubleday of Atherstone Warwickshire Gentleman	£200	Insuared for seven years. A dwelling House Brick and Tiled in Tenure of — Redfern, Cordwainer, Situated the Long Street Atherstone	In the Long Street Atherstone
1789 March 25th	Mr John Herbert of Atherstone, Warwickshire Woolcomber	£200	Insuars his now Dwelling House one hundred and Fifty pounds. Household goods therein £30. Stable & Workshop and shed adjoining £20. All brick and Tiled and Situate in +	+ the Long Street, Atherstone
		Memorandum The Interest of this Policy is now become		
March 25th	Mr John Freeman of Atherstone Warwickshire	£100	Insuars a Dwelling House Brick Stone and Tiled in tenure of Mrs Sumerfield Widow Situate in the Long Street, Atherstone aforesaid	In the Long Street Atherstone
June 24th	Mr Richard Harrison Farmer in the Parish of Ansley in the County of Warwick	£400	Insuars a House and out Houses adjoining Brick and Tile, in Tenure of William Minnon victualer £300 also Insuars A House and out Houses Adjoining Brick and tile in Tenure of Joseph Hatherly by Trade A Hatter	In the Long Street, Atherstone
June 24th	Mr Thomas Fielder by Trade A Blacksmith in the Township of Atherstone in the Parish of Mancester in the County of Warwick	£150	Insuars his Household goods and Stock Therein £140 Insuars the Stock of his Shop Adjoining his Dwelling House £5. Insuars the Stock in his yard £5 all Brick and Tile	In the Long Street, Atherstone

Rate of Premium per Cent	Sum received for Premium If any odd Time Over and above 1 year, set forth the No of days	Sum received for Duty	Sum received for Policy and Mark	Total Sum recieved on each Insurance
	£ s d	£ s d	£ s d	£ s d
	One Year 1 4 0	One year 0 18 0	0 8 6	2 10 6
	One Year 0 4 0	One Year 0 3 0	0 8 6	0 15 6

the Property of Wm Herbert of Atherstone, Carpenter.   Entered March 1803   J Owen

	One Year 0 2 0	One Year 0 1 6	0 8 6	0 12 0
	One Year 0 8 0	One Year 0 6 0	0 8 6	1 12 6
	One Year 0 4 6	One Year 0 2 3	0 8 6	0 15 3

31166	On a timber House situate on the West Side of the Passage leading from Rosemary Branch to Goodmans Yard afores^d, now empty	£150
£4-14	Ren'd [*renewed*] from N 13306 29 Aug.1755	£300

Sun Fire Office

GLDH Ms 11936/379

21st Sept 1791

588926	Samuel Swinnerton at *The Rose* in Monkwell Street [London],vintner	
£2-4	On his house only, *The White Hart* situate at	
Mich 1792	Colnbrook, Middx, intended for his own	
£2-4-11	occupation,Brick & tiled	£800
	Stables adjoining each other, separated, brick, timber & tiled	£400
		£1200
		Duty 18/-

Royal Exchange Assurance

GLDH Ms 7253/40

Oct 2nd

177364 Mich Qt^r 1800

Peter Arniraux of the Island of Jersey, gent

1- 1 - 0	On his House and Offices adjoining and	
14 - 0	communicating, all stone built and tiled,	
1-15 - 0	situate in Queen Street in St Helier in the said Island, occupied by Mrs Gardin, Innholder	£700

Sun Fire Office

GLDH Ms11937/73

15th October 1806

794658	Thomas Smith of Maidenhead in Berks, Yeoman.	
	On his Stock & Utensils in all or any of his Barns,	
£2-1-3	Stables, Granaries, other farm Offices, Rick Yards	
Michs 1807	or other parts of his Farm only at Waltham Lawrence	
Ward	in Berks, not exceeding Sixteen hundred & fifty	
Dy £2-1-3	pounds	£1650

N.B. Free from loss on such hay or corn as shall be destroyed or damaged by natural heat.

West of England Fire and Life
Insurance Company

Devon RO Ex 4196B/A1

1021	Lady Day 1809	
	Joseph Hawkins of Radpole in Co. Dorset,	
	brewer & miller	
	On his stock in Trade & utensils as a brewer	
	in his brewhouse, stone & tiled	£600
	On his stock in trade as a miller in	
	his millhouse adjoining, stone & tiled	
	having no kiln therein	160
	On his live & dead stock in stable near, adjg,	
	stone, thatched & yard near	40
	On household goods in his dwg house situate	
	near the above mentioned, stone & thatched	100
	On stock of beer in the cellar adjg the sd dw hse,	
	thatched	100
		£1000

Dorchester, Fisher
premium   £1-14
Duty   £1-5

Sun Fire Office

GLDH Ms 11937/187

26th May 1831

1126060	Messrs Latham & Thomas of the City of Chester,	
8/-	Ironmongers, Brass Founders & Tinmen.	
Midr 1832	On their stock and utensils in their shop and two	
9/-	Rooms over, situate on the North side of Eastgate	
Brooke C.	Street, in said City, a Stove therein well secured for	
13/6	airing the place only. Brick & slated	
Chester	Four Hundred pounds	2/- £400

Sun Fire Office

GLDH Ms 11937/211

30th May 1834

1179819	Joseph Southwood of *The Green Dragon Inn*,	
15/-	Wellington, Somerset, Innholder	
Midr 1835	On his Household Goods, Wearing apparel, printed	
17/2	books & plate in his now Dwelling house & offices,	
Wellington	all adjoining, situate as aforesaid, thatched.	
Dy 9/-	One hundred pounds	5/- 100
	Stock utensils & Goods in trust	
	therein only, two hundred pounds	" 200
		£300

Sun Fire Office

GLDH Ms 11937/224

5th January 1836

1213436	William Wotton Elliott of No. 47 King Street St.		
£2-2	Heliers Jersey, builder		
Xmas 1836	On his now dwelling house only, situate as aforesaid,		
Le Ber	four hundred pounds	1/6	400
Jersey	Household goods, wearing apparel, printed books plate therein only,		
	two hundred pounds	"	200
	Stock of linen, wollen drapery & haberdashery goods therein only,		
	three hundred pounds	"	300
	One years rent on the above,		
	thirty pounds	"	30
	Two houses with outhouses communicating to each, situate in Portland Place, Ann Street, St Heliers aforesaid,		
	three hundred pounds on each	"	600
	One years rent thereon,		
	twenty pounds on each	"	40
	Two houses with outhouses communicating to each situate in Clarendon Place, Clarendon Road, St. Heliers aforesaid,		
	four hundred pounds on each	"	800
	One years rent thereon, thirty pounds on each	"	60
	House called *Argyle Cottage* in Clarendon Road aforesaid, two hundred and fifty pounds	"	250
	One years rent thereon, twenty pounds	"	20
	Shed only in his Yard near, fifty pounds	"	50
	Stock and utensils for building, slated, tiles, scaffolding and other utensils therein not hazardous, fifty pounds		50
	All stone & brick, tiled and slated and in private tenure		£2800

Mem. This Office to be liable for the payment of rent during the time that the premises may be actually untenantable

Norwich Union Fire Insurance Society

NU 30/4/2

215853   September Quarter 1838
                Archibald Clarke of Douglas in the Isle of Man,
                Grocer and Dealer in Wines & Spirits. In Trust
    350   On a Dwelling House only occupied by Davidson
                & others situate in Great Nelson Street, Douglas.
    150   On Household Goods, Apparel, Printed Books and
                Plate therein only
    100   On his Interest as Mortgagee in a Dwelling House
                occupied by William Christian Baker, Situate in
                Sand Street, Douglas. Warranted No Oven therein,
                all Stone & Slate   9

                        [nine shillings; premium]

Sun Fire Office

GLDH Ms 11937/274

             2nd February 1842
1375252   William Todd & Co. of William Street, Limerick,
£9-0-0   hosiers, mercers, linen, woolen and hat merchants.
Xmas 1842 On their now dwelling house, stores, warerooms
Murphy   and dormitory including counters and shop fixtures
Limerick   therein, all communicating, situate as aforesaid,
Irish   stone & slated   750
           Household goods (including china & glass to the
           amount of £10) wearing apparel, printed books
           & plate therein only   250
           Stock & utensils therein only   5000
                            3/-   £6000

           Mem. Similar sums being insured on the within
                mentioned property in the Royal Exchange,
                West of England & the Scottish Union Fire
                Offices is hereby allowed
           Entered in the Office Books 2 Feb. 1842
121/33   125/367

              Endorsement
GLDH Ms 12160/121 page 33
             29th April 1850
1375252   Messrs Todd & Co.
           The af'said have made another addition to their premises con
274   sisting of 3 Apartments over each other the first & second floors
           communicating with the general ware rooms by Door Ways, the
           third Floor is used as a Tailor's work shop, same is hereby
           allowed, one Sum insured on Stock hereby is intended to cover
           same in the above mentioned premises.
Limerick   29th April 1850

continued

Endorsement

GLDH Ms 12160/125 page 367

1375252　　It is hereby allowed & agreed on that the within Insurance shall
　　　　　　extend to cover proportionally the building of the new addition
274　　　　made to the premises as also the stock therein.　　19 Oct 1846

　　　　　　The within assured have added an additional apartment to their
　　　　　　premises with two fire places constructed in the usual manner
　　　　　　which is hereby allowed　　　　　　　　　　13 May '51
Cop^d from L　3 June '51
Limerick　　Murphy

Phoenix Fire Office

Cam Uni PX 990

　　　　　　Agent's Policy Register, Monmouth

5 June 1852　　Mr William Watkins of Monmouth, stonemason.
　　to　　　　On his dwelling house and offices, communicating.
24 June 1853　Occupier, himself. Near the Old Gate called *Dixton Gate* £140
　　　　　　On his brewhouse, store room & mason's workshop,
　　　　　　all under the same roof but not having any internal
No. of Policy　communication.Situated in the back Court or
1036323　　　Garden adjoin^g the above, in equal proportions　　　　15
　　　　　　On a dwelling house & Offices communicating
Dated 10th June　called the *Seven Stars* Public house next to the
　　　　　　above & close adjoin^g *Old Dixton Gate*
　　　　　　Occupier J. Pembridge　　　　　　　　　　　140
　　　　　　On a Shed and brewhouse under the same roof in
　　　　　　the back Court or Skittle Alley belonging,
　　　　　　in equal proportions. Occupier J. Pembridge　　　10
　　　　　　　　　　　　　　　　　　　　　　　　　£405
　　　　　　　　　　　　One Year's Prem　　　　　6s - 0
　　　　　　　　　　　　One Year's Duty　　　　　9s - 8
　　　　　　　　　　　　　　　　　　　　　　　15s - 8
　　　　　　　　　　　　Annual prem　　　　　　5 - 8
　　　　　　　　　　　　do　　　duty　　　　　9 - 2
　　　　　　　　　　　　　　　　　　　　　　　14 -10
　　　　　　Payable annually 24th June

Law Union Fire and Life
Insurance Company

GLDH Ms 21270/1

Policy no. 1099　　Richard Read of　　1. On Agricultural Produce and
29 Sept.1855　　　Freehampton in　　　　Farming Stock, Live and Dead.
　　to　　　　　　the County of　　　　Implements & Utensils of
29 Sept. 1856　　Norfolk, Farmer　　　　Husbandry on his Farm situate
　　　　　　　　　　　　　　　　　　　at Reedham and Linpenhoe,
　　　　　　　　　　　　　　　　　　　adjoining Parishes, and

worked as one Farm.	600
2. On the like on his Farm situate at Freethorp and adjoining parishes	2000
Sum Insured	£2600
Premium	£3-18-0

Sun Fire Office

GLDH Ms 11937/492

29ᵗʰ February 1860

1918624   Richard Lloyd of High Street, Rochester in Kent, Flyman
£3-6   On the following property in his yard, coachhouses,
Xmas 1860   stables, workshops all adjoining or near to each other
Haymen   with the Gas laid on & a stove in the workshop, all well
Rochester   secured, situate in High Street aforesaid, brick, timber
Dᵞ £2-8   & tiled or slated & mostly timber built viz:

On ten horses £20 on each	5/-	200
Barouch [*four wheeled carriage*]	"	130
Clarence [*four wheeled closed carriage*]	"	30
Clarence	"	30
Brougham [*one horse closed carriage*]	"	60
Brougham	"	35
Phaeton [*two horse light four wheeled open carriage*]	"	12
Phaeton	"	30
Chaise Cart [*two wheeled, open travelling cart*]	"	10
Britska [*hooded carriage*]	"	30
Britska	"	20
Dog Cart	"	20
Gig [*one horse, two wheeled carriage*]	"	5
Chariot [*four wheeled carriage with seats at back only*]	"	10
Two Cabs £20 on each [*hackney carriages*]	"	40
Omnibus [*passenger and luggage vehicle*]	"	40
Van [*covered vehicle for carriage of goods*]	"	20
Oat Bruising & Chaff Cutting machine	"	25
Corn	"	26
Fodder	"	4
Set of Plated [*sic*] Pair Horse Harness	"	15
Another set of same Brass mounted	"	10
Two other sets of same £6 on one set & £2 on the other	"	8
Nine sets of Single Harness	"	10
Whips, Rugs & mats therein only	"	10
Stable Utensils	"	5
Household Goods, Wearing Apparel, Printed Books & Plate in his now Dwellinghouse, shop communicating used as a Grocers & Pork Butchers in High Street aforesaid, timber & tiled	3/-	350

continued

Sun Fire Office. Two pages from a Policy Register dated 26 March 1822, showing two of the author's ancestors referred to in the preface

China & Glass therein only	5/-	25
Pictures & Prints therein only	"	10
Fixtures therein only	3/-	50
Stock & Utensils therein only	"	300
		£1600

County Fire Office

GLDH Ms 18816

Agent's Register, Stow-on-the-Wold

Insurance When Commenced	1 June 1861
	No. 408091
Quarter When Annual Premium Due	Midsummer
Name, Residence and Profession	William Hawkins of
of Person to be Insured	Bourton on the Water,
	Gloucestershire, carpenter.

On What Property	{ On his Dwelling House	100
	{ On his Dairy and	
	{ Woodhouse adjoining	20
Occupier, Himself	{ On a Cottage adjoining	30
	{ On his Outhouses all	
	{ adjoining & communicating,	
	{ detached	30
Occupier, Thomas Baylis	On a Cottage	
	(no oven therein)	30
With What Materials Built	Stone Built and Slated	
Situation of Property Insured	Bourton on the Water	

One Years Premium	4s-6d
One Years Duty	6 -0
Renewal Premium	10 -6

Sun Fire Office

GLDH Ms 11937/511

11th September 1861

1967123	John Penn of [blank], engineer. On a Picture by
£1-3-1	Horsely A.R.A. entitled "Lost and Found" in the
14 Feby 1862	rooms of the Liverpool Acadamy in Old Post Office
Bold	Place, Liverpool, lent for exhibition therein, the said
Liverpool	rooms all communicate and are in a pile of brick
Dy 11/7	and slated buildings used as dwelling houses and
6 months	shops and offices, are lighted by gas sun burners
	when artificial light is required and warmcd by
	common fire grates 3/- 770

Prem. 4 : 6
Duty · 1 : 6
   6 : 0

... 1869 · £100 · Christmas

Shadrach Aspinall of Maulden in the Parish of Edlesboro

160

... Mud and Thatch in the occupation of Mrs
... called the Pesthouse in Maulden
... hereby cancelled.

Prem. 1 : 16 : 0
Policy · 12 : 0
   £2 · 8 : 0

No. 647052. Dated 25th Jan'y 1869 - £800 · Christmas.

William Baumbrough of High Street Leighton

Buzzard Grocer.—

450 · On Stock in trade and Fixtures

150 · On Household Furniture plate linen wearing apparel printed
Books China glass earthenware and wines and liquors in
private use therein.

All in his own dwellinghouse and shop adjoining and
communicating Brick and tile

150 · On Stock in trade in warehouse Brick stud and thatch
adjoining and communicating with the above.

50 · On Stock in trade in a room over Kitchen forming part of
Assured's dwellinghouse brick and tile

Warranted no Oil kept on any part of the Premises giving
off an inflammable vapour under the temperature of 110°
Fahrenheit. No. 485939 is hereby cancelled.

   Policy _____ handed over to us

25.1.69 to 25.4.69
Prem. 1 : 15 : 0
Duty · 7 : 6
  £1 : 2 : 6

No. 648499 · Dated 8th Feb'y 1869 · £2000.

Shadrach Tompkins of Leckhampstead Bucks Farmer

2000 · On Wool in a Dwelling-house brick stone and tile situate
as above.

Norwich Union Fire Insurance Society. A page from a Policy Register.
This policy is transcribed on page 108

Sun Fire Office

GLDH Ms 11937/520

2nd Jany 1862

1975835	Michael Hawkins of the *Kings Arms Inn* Wellington		
£1-19-9	in Somerset, Innholder.		
Xmas 1862	On his now dwelling house only called		
£2- 1-5	the *Kings Arms Inn*, Situate as aforesaid	2/6	400
Horsey	Household Goods, wearing Apparel,		
Wellington	printed Books & plate therein only	"	200
Dy £2-5-4	China and Glass therein only	4/6	50
	Stock, Utensils & Goods in trust		
	therein only	2/6	350
	Brewhouse, Stable & Linhays all		
	adjoining, near	"	200
1803777 Canc^d	Stock & Utensils therein only	"	100
1603358 "	Newly Built Carriage Shed only near	"	50
	House & Shop communicating, near,		
	in tenure of James Hall, Cabinet Maker	5/-	100
			£1450

All Brick, Stone & Slated & no Stove therein

London and Lancashire Fire and Life
Insurance Company

GLDH Ms 8747A

Policy No. 225434
Midsummer Quarter 1864
Mr John de Gruchy of No. 33 Charles Street, St. Helier, Jersey, Carpenter

Two Hundred Pounds on the house, shop and offices all
adjoining no.1 St. James Street, St. Helier, aforesaid,
known as *La Motte house* occupied as a Grocers' Shop
(no coffee roasted) and let in lodgings.

	Sum Ass.	Rate/cent
	200	2/6
Five hundred Pounds on the house and		
offices adjoining each other and above in		
Grosvenor Street, occupied by a Shoemaker		
and let in lodgings	500	1/6
	£700	

All Stone and brick built and slated
(Party walls not through roof)
Expired

Premium to Midsm^r/65	13/9	
Annual Prem	12/6	

London Assurance Corporation
Agent's Policy Register

Berks RO D/EX 113/1

Lady Day Quarter 1865

Mr Edwin Moore	On his household furniture, linen, wearing
of No.9 King Street	apparel, printed books, wines & liquors,
Reading	Glass, china, Earthenware, pictures & prints
	(not exceeding Five pounds on any one
Woollen Draper	picture or print) £100

Watches & trinkets, musical Instruments
& music Books in his dwelling house and
offices adjoining thereto, brick & stone
built, slated or tiled, situate & being as
aforesaid.

Prem to Lady 1-10-0
Day 1866

         1- 4-0   No stove
Received   £2-14-0   On his Utensils & Stocks in Trade therein £1400
                                                                 £1500

Premium   1-10-0
Duty   1- 4-0
         £2-12-6   to be paid Annually at Ladyday★

No. 231401
Del^d Policy to Mr Moore *MHD*

★This is presumably the payment made by the agent to head office, being the premium paid by the policy
    holder less the agent's commission of one shilling and sixpence

Norwich Union Fire Insurance Society

NU 38/3/1

     £ s d
Prem 1-16-0 No 647052 Dated 25th January 1869   £800   Christmas
Duty   12-0
     £2 - 8-0 William Baumbrough of High Street, Leighton Bussard, Grocer
      450   On Stock in trade and Fixtures
      150   On household Furniture, plate, linen, wearing apparel,
                  printed Books, China, glass, earthenware, and wines and liquors
                  in private use therein.
                  All in his now dwellinghouse and shop adjoining and
                  communicating Brick and tile.

Cancelled

      150   On Stock in trade in Warehouse, Brick, stud and thatch,
                  adjoining and communicating with the above.
       50   On Stock in trade in a room over Kitchen forming part of
                  Assured's dwellinghouse, brick and tile.
                  Warranted no Oil kept in any part of the Premises giving
                  off an inflamable vapour under the temperature of
                  110° Fahrenheit.
                  N° 485939 is hereby cancelled
                  Policy handed over to Mr B

Note: The original of this document is reproduced on page 106

Law Union Fire and Life
Insurance Company
Agent's Policy Register

Heref RO BB 89/1

114255   The Reverend Rowland Hill of Mancell Lacey, Herefordshire
as mortgagee, and The Ross Royal Hotel Company (Limited),
as mortgagors

	£
On the Buildings of the *Royal Hotel* with passages and offices all communicating situate ar Ross, Herefordshire.	4000
On a range of Stables communicating with Granary over	400
On Stables Coachhouses and sheds all communicating	400
On the *Tap Inn* and brewhouse (no steam Engine therein) both communicating	600
On open carriage sheds in Yard	50
On Billiard Room and Lavatories communicating	100
On one years rent of the said Buildings in relative proportions to be specified on each of the several buildings during such time as the Property may remain untenantable by accident from fire not exceeding twelve calendar months from the time of the breaking out of the said fire	450
	£6000

All the aforesaid buildings adjoin each other are
brick and stone built and slated, and in the occupation
of the Ross Royal Hotel Company (limited)

Policy No. 58096 cancelled hereby returned Premium £2-10-2

October 5/69   September   £6

Law Union Fire and Life
Insurance Company
Agent's Policy Register

Heref RO BB 89/1

114189 William Gadsall of Hereford	£
On his dwelling House, brick, timber and tiled, situate in St. Owens St., Hereford	400
On household furniture, Plate, Linen, Wearing Apparell, Printed Books, Wine and Liquors in private use therein	100
On Kitchen with Two Rooms over near the above, brick and timber built and tiled, occupied by the Insured	100
On a Greenhouse adjoining the last mentioned occupied by the Insured	50
On a Warehouse and Stable adjoining under one Roof near the above, brick, timber & tiled The latter in the occupation of Miss Matthews	

continued

No hazardous goods allowed to be deposited or
hazardous trade carried on therein.   50
On a Barn detached standing upon land called
The Crosses situate in the Parish of Ross stone
and tiled   100
                                                                    ─────
                                                                     £800

October 12/69   September   £1-1-0
Cancelled   See 13144

Law Union Fire and Life
Insurance Company
Agent's Policy Register

Heref RO BB 89/1

114713   Francis Lewis Bodenham of Hereford, Esquire and Thomas
         Clark of Derndale, in the parish of Canon Pyon, in the
         County of Hereford Esq[re]
         On the following buildings situate at Burghill,
         Herefordshire in the occupation of Mr Goatman,
         Farmer. Viz:
         On Gurgill [sic] Lodge, Cider house & Poultry
         house adjoin[g] Greenhouse, Store house & sheds
         in one block, lath and plaster & slated or tiled.   400
         On a gig house and three stall Hackney Stable, with
         lofts over, Dairy, Cider house, & Dove Cot over in
         one Block,brick built & tiled.   150
         On two hop kilnes, Cider house, Farm House
         (unoccupied) Barn & Waggon house with Horse
         trashing [sic] machine attached in one Block, brick
         and Slated and Stone tiled   400
         On Cider Mill house brick slated or tiled.   10
         On Cart, Stable and Cider house with lofts over,
         brick and tiled   140
         On Cider house, Cow houses, Calves Cots,
         Hay Bay with Sheds at back, & Barn adjoining
         in one Block, brick and covered with slates and
         pan tiles, wood and partly thatch & Stone tiled.   400
                                                                    ─────
                                                                    £1500

Nov 9/69   September   £3 - 4 - 0
Cancelled   611385

**Law Union Fire and Life
Insurance Company**
Agent's Policy Register

Heref RO BB 89/1

118779	James Price of Friars Street, Hereford, Fishmonger., On the building of a dwelling house, brick or stone built and slated or tiled, situate and being the *Bush Inn*, Tuder Street, Abergavenny, Monmouthshire, occupied by Thomas Price Innkeeper	£300
	In equal proportions on two private dwelling houses, brick and slated, situate and being N°s 14 & 15 Friars Street, Hereford, occupied by John Walter and Thomas Powell	£200
		£500

March 29/70   March   10/6

Chapter 8

Policy Registers: Land and Property Owners with Named Tenants

Sun Fire Office

GLDH Ms 11936/18

July 30th 1724

32651   Catherine Eston in Flidges Court in Noble Street, in the Parish of St. Olaves, Silver Street, widow, for Sixteen houses (in Trust for Edmund Towse, Watchgilder, and Mrs Mary Shalmer) in Jacob Street, in ye Parish of St Mary Ma^{gn}, Bermondsey as herein after particularly express'd viz.

One House Only in occupation of John Perry Hatter & Ale House keeper, not exceeding Two hundred Pounds	200
One in Possession of Widow Wildes, not exceeding thirty Pounds	30
Six Houses only, not exceeding Sixty Pounds only on Each viz. One inPossession of Jane Man, an Herb Shop. One in Possession of Walter Wyatt, Mariner. One in Possession of Blackwell, Carpenter and Widow Clarke. One in Possession of Thos Gouge and John Gridley. One in Possession of Mary Dudley, Spinster and ye oy^r in Possessⁿ of Mary Gawden, Chandler	360
Three houses only, not exceeding fourty Pounds only on each viz. One in Possⁿ of Stephen Cole, One in Possn of Robt Brack and ye oy^r in Possⁿ of Wm Strechley	120
Three houses only not exceeding fifty Pounds only on Each viz. One empty house lately in Possession of Thos Haddon, Blacksmith. One in Possⁿ of Elizabeth Hall & the other in Possⁿ of Geo. Jones	150

The other two Houses only not exceeding Seventy

	Pounds only on Each. Viz the one in Poss^n of Robt White and ye oy^r in Possn of Mary Besant,	140
6/6	Schoolmistress	
		£1000

July 30th 1724

32652	Catherine Eston in Flidges Court in Noble Street in the Parish of St Olaves, Silver Street, Widow, for Eleven houses (in Trust for Edmund Towse, Watchgilder, and Mrs Mary Shalmer) in Jacobs Street in the Parish of St Mary Magdalen, Bermondsey as hereinafter particularly express'd, viz.	
	Three in the several Possessions of Edward Osbourne, Widow Slaughter and Isaac Nicholls, not exceeding fifty Pounds only on each	150
	Seven in the Several Possession of Edw Sistens, Samuel Peck, Thomas Cook, William Gatlin, James Nightingale, William Cane & Peter Sistens, not exceeding forty five Pounds only on Each	325 [sic]
	And the other in Possession of Elizabeth Gee alias Peak, not exceeding thirty five Pounds	35
3/-		
		[£]500 [sic]

Sun Fire Office

GLDH Ms 11936/306

16th January 1783

470173	On his house at St. Neots, in the County of	
£8-14	Huntingdon, in the Tenure of Francis	
Xmas 1783	Atwood, Shoemaker. Brick, Stud and Tiled not exceeding	
Lawrence	One Hundred Pounds	100
£8-3	House and Brewhouse adjoining in the tenure of	
	Henry Norman, Butcher, Brick, Plaister and Tiled,	
	not exceeding One Hundred Pounds	100
	House only, *The Half Moon*, in the tenure of	
	William Umbley, Victualler, Stud and Tiled, not exceeding	
	One Hundred and Fifty Pounds	150
	Stable and Brewhouse under one roof, separate,	
	Stud and Tiled, not exceeding Fifty Pounds	50
	House, Brewhouse and Offices adjoining	
	in the tenure of Thomas Ladds, draper,	
	Stud and Tiled, not exceeding Two Hundred Pounds	200
	House and Offices adjoining in the tenure	
	of Thomas Gurry, Ironmonger, Stud and Tiled,	
	not exceeding Two Hundred Pounds	200
	House, Brewhouse and Offices adjoining	
	in the tenure of William Emery, Innholder, Brick,	
	Plaister and Tiled	
	The Cross Keys, not exceeding Two Hundred and Fifty P'nds	250

continued

Range of Stables adjoining, Brick, Stud and Tiled,
not exceeding Fifty Pounds   50
House only, *The White Lion*, in the tenure of
Thomas Atkinson, Victualler, Stud and Tiled, not exceeding
One Hundred and Fifty Pounds   150
Brewhouse, Stables and Leantoo adjoining, Stud
and Tiled, not exceeding fifty pounds   50
House only in the tenure of William Joyce, Draper &
William Sommers, Potman, Brick, Stud and Tiled,
not exceeding One Hundred Pounds   100
House only in the tenure of John King, draper,
Brick Stud and Tiled, not exceeding One
Hundred and Fifty pounds   150
Warehouse and Brewhouse in a Range
adjoining, Stud and Tiled, not exceeding Fifty Pounds   50
House only in the Tenure of Widow Smith, Butcher,
Stud and Tiled, not exceeding One Hundred Pounds   100
House only *The Angel* in the tenure of William Wiles,
Victualler, Brick, Stud and Tiled, not exceeding
One Hundred and Fifty Pounds   150
Brewhouse and Stables adjoining, Brick,
Stud and Tiled, not exceeding Fifty pounds   50
House only in the tenure of James Conquest, Glazier,
Stud and Tiled, not exceeding One Hundred Pounds   100
House only in the tenure of Thomas Hunt,
Glazier, Stud and Tiled, not exceeding
One Hundred and Fifty Pounds   150
House and Brewhouse adjoining in the tenure of
Thomas Abbott, Glover, Stud and Tiled,
not exceeding One Hundred Pounds   100
House only in the tenure of William Fairy,
Glazier, part thatched, not exceeding One Hundred Pounds 100
House only in the tenure of Ann & John Smith,
Butchers, Stud and Tiled, not exceeding
One Hundred Pounds   100
House only in the tenure of John Bridges, Butcher,
Stud and Tiled, not exceeding
One Hundred and Fifty Pounds   150
Brewhouse, Stable and Granary adjoining,
stud and Tiled, not exceeding fifty Pounds   50
House only in the tenure of Widow Lewis,
Stud and Tiled, not exceeding One Hundred Pounds   100
House only *The Golden Ball* in the Tenure
of Thomas Palmer, Victualler, Stud and Tiled,
not exceeding One Hundred and Fifty Pounds   150
Butchers Shop, Brewhouse and Stable
adjoining, Stud and Tiled, not exceeding Fifty Pounds   50
House only in the tenure of Richard Wiles, Farmer,
Stud, Tiled and Thatched,
not exceeding One Hundred and Thirty Pounds   130

Wheat Barn and Barley Barn only separate,	
Thatched not exceeding Forty Pounds on each	80
Barns and Stables in a Range, separate,	
Thatched, not exceeding Forty Pounds	40
The aforesaid at St. Neots in the County of Huntingdon.	
House only at Wintringham in the Parish	
aforesaid in the Tenure of Robert Achurch, Farmer,	
stud and Tiled, not exceeding One Hundred Pounds	100
Barn only, separate, Thatched, not exceeding Forty Pounds	40
Barns and Stables in a Range, separate, Thatched,	
not exceeding Sixty Pounds	60
House only at Eynesbury in the County aforesaid in	
the tenure of Widow Gale & William Dixey, Fisherman,	
Stud and Tiled, not exceeding Fifty Pounds	50
House only at Eynesbury aforesaid in the	
tenure of Jane Briggs, Victualler, Brick, Stud and	
Tiled, not exceeding Fifty Pounds	50
Brewhouse and Stable adjoining, Brick, Stud and Tiled	
not exceeding Fifty Pounds	50
House only at Eynesbury aforesaid in the tenure	
of Andrew Simons, Butcher, Stud and Tiled,	
not exceeding Fifty Pounds	50
House, Brewhouse & Offices adjoining at Eynesbury	
aforesaid in the tenure of George Careless, Farmer,	
Stud and Thatched, not exceeding One Hundred	
and Fifty Pounds	150
Stable & Barn adjoining, Thatched,	
not exceeding Sixty Pounds	60
Barn only, separate, Thatched, not exceeding Forty Pounds	40
House only at Eynesbury aforesaid in the	
tenure of Simon Staughton, Farmer, Brick	
and Tiled, not exceeding One Hundred Pounds	100
Stables & Barn in a Range, separate, thatched,	
not exceeding Sixty Pounds	60
Barn only, separate, not exceeding Forty Pounds	40
House in the Parish of St. Neots aforesaid with	
Water Corn Mill adjoining, Brick, Stud, Timber	
and Tiled in the tenure of Henry Dobson, Miller,	
not exceeding Two Hundred Pounds	200
House & Brewhouse adjoining at Brampton in	
said County in the tenure of John Hull, Farmer,	
Stud & Tiled, not exceeding Two Hundred Pounds	200
Barns & Stables in a Range, separate, thatched,	
not exceeding Sixty Pounds	60
Barn only separate, Thatched, not exceeding Forty Pounds	40
House & Brewhouse adjoining at Little Stukeley	
in said County late in the tenure of	
William Banks, Stud and Tiled,	
not exceeding One Hundred and Twenty Pounds	120

continued

Barn & Stables in a Range, separate, Thatched, not exceeding Fifty Pounds	50
Barn only, separate, Thatched, not exceeding Thirty Pounds	30
House & Brewhouse adjoining at Little Stukely aforesaid in the tenure of John Hull, Farmer, Brick and Tiled, not exceeding Fifty Pounds	50
Stable only adjoining, Stud and Tiled, not exceeding Ten Pounds	10
Barn only separate, Thatched, not exceeding Thirty Pounds	30
Wind Corn Mill only in the Parish of Little Stukely in the tenure of Thomas Howe, Miller, Timber, not exceeding Sixty Pounds	60

£4900

Duty   £3-13-6

Royal Exchange Assurance

GLDH Ms 7253/40

Michaelmas Qr 1800
Oct 8th Stephen Round
         of New Windsor
         in The County
         of Berks, Gent

177488

1450	2/-	1 - 9
5000	3/-	7-10
100	5/-	5
		9 - 4
		6-11
		£15-15

Ren[d] f[m] 166479
              172350

On his Dw House and Offices adjoining
sit. In Pescod Street in New Windsor in
the County of Berks af[d] Tim[r] and tiled   500   3/-
Furniture   200   3/-
Plate   50   3/-
P Books   } in the same   50   3/-
Apparel   50   3/-
On a Building called the Office near
in his own Occupation, Timber and tiled   150   3/-
Fur[r]   } in the same   25   3/-
P Books   50   3/-
On a Dw House near, Tenant
Thomas Greener, Whitesmith Timber b[k]   50   3/-
tiled
On two Dw Houses near and adj[g],
Tenants Caroline Barlett Widow & Eliz[th]
Bailey Widow, Timber and tiled, not
exceeding £200 on each   400   3/-
On two Washhouses and Chambers
over, belonging, Timber built and tiled   50   3/-
On three Cottages adjoining in Clewer
Lane near the bottom of Pescod St[t] af[d].
Tenants Henry Winter, Shoemaker, and
W[m] Jorden, Gardener, and one
unoccupied. Timber built and tiled   150   3/-
On a Stable and Lofts over, near, in his
own Occupation, Timber and tiled   100   3/-
On a House Situate in Pescod Street af[d]

Ret^d [returned] £3-0-6d Pc^y
and £2-6 duty for 6 mos
unexpired time on 166479
for £4600

Ret^d 5s Pc^y and 5s duty
for 6mos unexpired time
on 172350 for £500

Windsor

Tenant Mrs Richardson, Tim^r & tiled	400	3/-
On a Farm House sit. at Spittle Hills in the parish of New Windsor af^d, Bk & tiled	50	2/-
On a Barn, Stable, Cowhouse and Buildings adjoining, Timber built and tiled, near	200	3/-
Utensils and Stock therein	150	3/-
On a Granary belonging, Timber built and tiled	25	3/-
Utensils and Stock therein	50	3/-
On stock in the Rick Yard and Close adj^g and belonging	100	3/-
On a House, Timber built and tiled, situate in Deans Yards in New Windsor af^d Tenant Robert Muiller Gent	200	3 /-
On a Cottage situate at Dedworth Green near Clewer in the C^o of Berks, Tenants Peter Appleton and Henry Sumber, Laborers, Bk B^t and tiled	100	2/-
On a Cottage, Timber built and tiled called *Birch Piddle Cottage* near Sunninghill Bog, in the County aforesaid, Tenant a laborer	50	3/-
On a House and Gardener's Cottages adjoining, Timber built and tiled, situate at Kings Beach Hill in the parish of Old Windsor in the County of Berks in his own Occupation	300	3/-
On a dwelling House called *Shrubs Hill House* near Cowarth in Old Windsor af^d, late in the Occupation of the Earl of Chatham, but now unoccupied. Brick & slated	500	2/-
On a Coach house, Stable, Lofts and Landry [*sic*] belonging and adjoining Bk and tiled	200	2/-
On a New Stable, Timber and tiled, belonging	50	3/-
On a Dwelling House and Offices adjoining, Timber built and tiled, situate at Old Windsor Green in the parish of Old Windsor aforesaid. Tenant Robert Brooker, Farmer	150	3/-
On two Cottages in the parish of Egham in the County of Surry, opposite *Shrubs Hill House* aforesaid. Tenants Laborers. Timber built and tiled.	25	3/-
On a New built Barn near and belonging. Timber built and tiled.	100	3/-

continued

On Stables, Coach houses and Buildings adjoining at Laleham in the C° of Middx, Tenant John Coggan Esq. Timber built and tiled.	100	3/-
On a Public House called the *Rose and Crown* at Thorpe Green in the county of Surrey, Tenant Mrs Edge, vict^r, Bk built and tiled.	200	2/-
On a Barn belonging. Timber built and thatched.	25	3/-
On a Farm House and Offices adjoining situate at Clewer Green, Tenant Wm Gotolee, Farmer, Brick built and tiled	200	2/-
On the Great Barn, thatched, near	50	3/-
On the Little Barn, stable and Outhouses adjoining, thatched, near	50	3/-
On a Cottage situate at Buckets Hill, in the parish of Winkfield in the County of Berks aforesaid, tenant John Steer laborer	25	5/-
On a newly built Cottage, Brick built and tiled situate at Buckets Hill aforesaid. Tenant [*blank*] Blackmore, shoemaker	50	2/-
On two Houses adjoining, situate in Nonsuch Lane in Wokingham in the County of Berks, tenants John Lawrence, carpenter and [*blank*] Laborers. Brick built and tiled not exceeding £25 on each	50	2/-
On two Houses adjoining, near, Tenants [*blank*] labourers. Brick built and tiled not exceeding £25 on each	50	2/-
On a Dw^g House situate at Iver Heath in the parish of Iver, in the County of Bucks, Tenant Thos Randall, Farmer, Brick built and tiled	50	2/-
On a Barn, thatched, near	50	3/-
On a Farm House sit^e at Lovegreen in the parish of Iver af^d in his own Occupation. Timber & Tiled.	200	3/-
Furn. therein	25	3/-
On two Barns, Henhouse and offices adj^g, thatched, belonging	100	3/-
Utensils and stock therein	100	3/-
On a Carthouse, Stables, Cowhouse adj^g, thatched, belonging	100	3/-
Utensils and Stock therein	100	3/-
Do Do in the brick yard and Closes adj^g & belonging	250	3/-
On a Public House at Sheading Green in Iver af^d Tim^r & thatched called the *Red Lion*, Ten^t Wm Hunt	50	5/-

On a Barn and Stable belonging,
Tim^r and thatched   25   3/-
On a House, Timb. built and tiled situate
at White Leaf in the parich of Monks
Risborough in the County of Bucks,
Tenant John Rogers, Shoemaker   25   3/-
On a House and Barn adjoining, Timber
built and tiled, situate in Copper
Beech Lane in the parish of Wokingham
in the County of Wilts [sic], tenant John
Leman, Nurseryman   100   3/-
On a newly built Farm House, Brick
built and tiled at Easthampstead in the
County of Berks, Tenant James Stroek,
Farmer   50   2/-
On a Barn and outhouses adj^g and,
thatched   25   3/-
On a Cottage, thatched, situate at
Dunsden in the parish of Sunning [sic]
in the County of Oxford Tent [blank] a
Laborer   25   5/-
Free as usual   £6550

Sun Fire Office

GLDH Ms 11937/187

26th May 1831

1126062	Henry Deacon & Thomas Rose of Portsmouth in		
£17-11-0	Hants Receivers & Managers of the Estate of William		
Lday 1832	Deacon Esq.		
Poulden			
D £25-4-0			
Hants			
Tenants Names	The following Property in Portsmouth in Hants Viz:		
	House & Offices all adjoining in Penny Street,		
	one thousand pounds	1/6	1000
W. Deacon Esq	Brewery & Plant in said Street with Coopers'		
	& Carpenters' shops, Beer & Spirit Stores,		
	all adjoining, no kiln nor steam engine		
	& no pitch nor tar heated, nor stove therein,		
	two thousand three hundred pounds	3/-	2300
	Stock & utensils including Casks & Vats in		
	said Brewery in the brewery yard, &		
	in all other before mentioned premises,		
	two thousand four hundred pounds	"	2400
	Counting House & Stables, all adjoining in		
	said brewery yard, four hundred & fifty pounds	2/6	450
	Furniture in said Countinghouse only		
	forty pounds	"	40
	Stock & utensils in said stables only		

continued

	fifty pounds	"	50
	All the above are brick & tiled except the		
	Louvert Boards & a very small part Timber		
	Tenement only in Keppel Row.		
Gammons	Seventy five pounds	1/6	75
Bytheway	Tenement only adjoining. Seventy five pounds	"	75
Frost	Tenement only adjoining. Seventy five pounds	"	75
Churcher & { Whitehouse	House only in two tenements in Smith Court, Keppel Row aforesaid, one hundred & fifty pounds	"	150
Spratt	House only in Keppel Row aforesaid, two hundred pounds	"	200
Caston	House only in Keppel Row aforesaid adjoining the last above mentioned, one hundred & fifty pounds	"	150
Way	House & Offices, *The Portsmouth Arms*, all adjoining in Penny Street, three hundred pounds	"	300
Dubber & Salter	House in two tenements & offices all adjoining & to the last above mentioned, Two hundred pounds	"	200
Way & Brunt	House Offices & Stables all adjoining in High Street, one hundred & thirty five pounds	"	135
Taylor	House & Offices, *The Three Tuns*, all adjoining in High Street, Four hundred pounds	"	400
Wyld	House & offices all adjoining, *The Antelope* on the Grand Parade, brick, timber & tiled, three hundred & fifty pounds	2/6	350
Brunt	House & offices all adjoining, *The Royal Mail* in St Thomas's Street, three hundred & fifty pounds	1/6	350
Hatch, Way & Brunt	Store, Stables & Washhouse, all adjoining & to the last above, mentioned, three hundred pounds	"	300
Gloge	Bonding Stores with vaults under adjoining *The Royal Mail*, aforesaid no hazardous goods therein. Four hundred pounds	"	400
Coopers	House & Offices with rooms all adjoining *The London Tavern* in Warblington Street, brick timber & tiled. Two hundred pounds	2/6	200
Haywood	House & Offices *The Blacksmiths Arms* all adjoining in Prospeck Row, one hundred & fifty pounds	1/6	150
Haywood	Stable & tenement adjoining & to the last above mentioned but not communicating therewith, a brick wall between, brick timber & tiled, thirty pounds	2/6	30
Wickendon	House & Offices all adjoining *The Jolly Brewers* in Armbury Lane, two hundred & seventy pounds	1/6	270
Wickendon	Kitchen only near, twenty pounds	"	20
Wickendon	Stable only in Armbury Lane, thirty pounds	"	30

Daniel	House & Offices *The Naked Boy* all adjoining in Crown Street, Two hundred pounds	"	200
Daniel	Outbuilding only, near, Timber & tiled, thirty pounds	2/6	30
Colenutt	House, offices & tenement all adjoining *The Phoenix* in King Street, three hundred pounds	1/6	300
Thornton	Tenement Stable & Wheeler's Shop,all adjoining in King Street aforesaid, brick, timber & tiled, one hundred pounds	5/-	100
Thornton	Blacksmiths shop only near brick timber & tiled, Forty pounds	3/-	40
Harvey	House & Offices all adjoining *The King of Prussia* in Broad Street, two hundred pounds	1/6	200
Harvey	Store only, behind, near, brick, timber & tiled, two hundred pounds	2/6	200
Witteridge	House & offices, all adjoining, in Broad Street adjoining the last above mentioned but not communicating therewith, a brick wall between two hundred pounds	1/6	200
Lyons	House & offices, all adjoining & to the last above mentioned, two hundred pounds	1/6	200
Fogwill	House & Offices, all adjoining & to the last above mentioned, two hundred pounds	"	200
Grinder	House & offices, all adjoining, *The Bengal Tavern* in Broad Street aforesaid. Three hundred pounds	"	300
Haynes	House & offices, all adjoining, *The Neptune & Mars* in Broad Street aforesaid, two hundred & fifty pounds	"	250
Gregory	House & offices, all adjoining, *The Lord Hood & General Elliott*, in Broad Street, two hundred pounds	"	200
Rogers	House & offices, all adjoining, *The Nelsons Arms* in East Street, one hundred & fifty pounds	"	150
Perry	House & offices, all adjoining, *The Packhorse* in West Street. Two hundred pounds	"	200
Perry	Outbuildings all adjoining & to the last above mentioned but not communicating therewith, a brick wall between, brick, timber & tiled, thirty pounds	2/6	30
Parrott	House & offices, all adjoining, *The Jolly Waterman* in West Street, brick, timber & tiled, one hundred& fifty pounds	"	150
Duckett	House & offices, all adjoining, *The Old Plough* in Tower Street, near brick & tiled except a small part timber, one hundred pounds	2/-	100
Matthews	House & Offices, all adjoining, *The Plymouth Arms* in Tower Street aforesaid,		

continued

	one hundred pounds	1/6	100
Matthews	Tenement only, adjoining the last above mentioned but not communicating therewith, a brick wall between, brick, timber & tiled, thirty pounds	2/6	30
	All above in Portsmouth in Hants		
	The following in Portsea		
Mills	House & Offices, all adjoining, *The Golden Fleece* on the Common Hard or Ordnance Row, three hundred pounds.	1/6	300
Mills	Tenement only behind, near, one hundred pounds	"	100
Martin	House & offices, all adjoining, *The Sheer Hulk* on the Hard aforesaid, brick, timber & tiled, three hundred pounds	2/6	300
Martin	Kitchen only, behind, near, forty pounds	1/6	40
Huxford	House, offices & Skittle Alley all adjoining, *The Royal Marine* in Queen Street, Four hundred & twenty pounds	1/6	420
Yardley	House & offices, all adjoining, *The Admiralty Arms* in Spring Street. Three hundred pounds	"	300
Baker	House & offices, all adjoining, *The Lord Wellington* at Hyde Park corner, two hundred pounds	"	200
Fletcher	House & Offices, all adjoining, *The Nelsons Arms* on the London Road. Four hundred pounds	"	400
Fletcher	Stable only, behind, near, fifty pounds	"	50
Stevens	House, offices, stable & Outbuildings, all adjoining, *The Blue Anchor* at Kingston. Five hundred pounds	"	500
Dovey	House & offices, all adjoining, *The Old George* at Buckland, a very small part timber, three hundred & forty pounds	2/-	340
Dovey	Stables, all adjoining, near, brick, timber & tiled, twenty pounds	2/6	20
Dovey	Skittle Alley & Room over, near, brick, plaster timber & tiled, one hundred pounds	"	100
Smith	House & offices, all adjoining, *The Travellers Joy* at Milton, two hundred & fifty pounds	1/6	250
Smith	Tea rooms, Skittle alley & offices, all adjoining, near, Brick, timber & tiled two hundred pounds	2/6	200
			£1680

All brick or stone & tiled except as aforesaid, no
hazardous goods nor trade therein unless mentioned
& where expressed as being a small part timber it is

warranted that the timber is less than one eighth of
the whole building, and said Public houses in tenure
of Victuallers

Sun Fire Office

GLDH MS 11937/354

11th July 1848

1577857
£15-11
Midsr 1849
Surridge
Romford
Duty £14-15-2
Chester

Samuel Richard Green Francis of Cranham Place in
Essex Esqr & Henry Hawkins of The Inner Temple,
London, Esqr.

On the Following Buildings situate in the Parish of
Wistaston in the County of Chester

Tenants Names	Description of Buildings		Amount Insured
Samuel Basford	Farmhouse only, Brick, Timber & Slated	2/6	200
	Stable, Cowhouse & Barn all		
	under one Roof, near, Brick & Tiled	3/-	120
Jno Brotherton	Cottage only near	4/6	100
	Shed only near		10
Johnson Cappur	Two Cottages adjoining near	"	100
Thos Allmans Thos Cappur Wm Cappur	Cottage only near		50
	Cottage & Cowhouse adjoining, near, Brick & Tiled	1/6	100
Thos Cooper	Cottage only near	4/6	70
Saml Mottrum	Public house and Brewery called *The Rising Sun* adjoining near	"	150
	Cowhouse & stable adjoining near, brick & slated	1/6	50
Thos Dodd	Cottage only, near	4/6	70
Josh Downing	Cottage only near, Brick & Tiled	1/6	100
	Shed only, near	4/6	10
Jno Fisher	Public House called the *Rockwood* & Stable under the same Roof, near.	"	120
	Shed & Cowhouse adjoining, near Brick & Slated	1/6	20
Josh Gibson	House & Blacksmith's Forge under one Roof, near, Brick & Slated	2/-	100
	Shed only, near, Brick & Tiled	1/6	20
Thos Hector	House only, near, Brick & Tiled	"	100
	Cowhouse only near	4/6	10
Sarah Hopley	Cottage only near	4/6	70
Sparkes	Cottage (*Newlodge*) near, Brick & Slated	1/6	50
Jno Leigh	House & Wheelwright's Shop, Brick & Tiled & Cowhouse & Workshop.		

continued

	Thatched, all communicating, near	7/6	150
Martha Perrin	House only near, Brick & Tiled	1/6	120
	Cowhouse only near, Brick & Tiled	"	10
Ja^s Morris	Farmhouse only near, Timber & Tiled	2/6	250
	Cowhouse & Barn adjoining, near, Brick & Tiled	3/-	150
	Stable & Bay adjoining, near, Brick & Tiled	"	100
Wm Mottram	Farmhouse only near	5/-	150
	Cowhouse, Stable & Barn under one roof, near, Brick & Tiled	3/-	120
Elizth Mullock Thos Timmis	Two Cottages near, £50 on each	4/6	100
Ja^s Pace	Cottage only near	"	70
Ja^s Pennell	Farmhouse only, Brick, Timber & Tiled	2/6	200
	Stable & Cowhouse adjoining, near, Brick, Timber & Tiled	3/-	70
	Cowhouse & Barn under one Roof, near, Brick & Tiled	"	150
	Carthouse only near, Brick & Tiled	"	20
Robt Pennell	Farmhouse only near, Brick & Slated	1/6	300
	Barn & Cowhouse all adjoining near, Brick & Slated	3/-	200
	Shed & Stable under one Roof near, Brick & Slated	"	100
Elliza Melling	House only near, Brick & Slated	1/6	200
Wm Perrin	House only near, Brick & Tiled	"	250
	Stable only near, Brick & Slated	3/-	20
	Pigsties & Stable adjoining near, Brick & Slated	"	80
	Barn, Cowhouse, Granary & Cartshed all adjoining near, Brick & Tiled	"	200
Wm Powell	Cottage only, near	4/6	70
Jno Roberts	Cottage only at Rogess Hill, near, Brick & Slated	1/6	50
Ja^s Smit Saml Whithingham	Two Cottages adjoining, near, Thatched	4/6	100
Jos^h Smith	Cottage only, near	"	70
	Cowhouse & Pigstye adjoining near, Brick & Tiled	1/6	10
Thos Smith	Cottage & Cowhouse adjoining near, tiled & Thatched	4/6	70
Thos Wade	Cottage & Shed adjoining, near	"	80
Sarah Wilkinson	Farmhouse only, near	5/-	200
	Cowhouse, Stable & Cartshed, all adjoining, near, Brick & Slated	3/-	100
	Barn only, near	"	150
Jno Johnson	Dwellinghouse only, near, Brick & Slated	1/6	200
	Cowhouses & Barn, thatched,		

Penelope Hammond	Carthouse & Stable, Brick & Tiled all adjoining, near	3/-	300
	Mansion House only, near, Brick & Tiled	1/6	700
	Stables, Coachhouses & Cowhouse all adjoining, near, Brick & Tiled	3/-	300
Richd Pedley	The following in the Township of Haslington in the said County Dwelling house only situate at Hall on Heath, Brick, Timber & Tiled	2/6	250
	Cowhouses, Barn, Stable & Cartshed, all adjoining, near, Brick & Tiled	3/-	250
Thos Rowley	The following in the Parish of Nantwich in the said County Dwellinghouse, Stable, Barn & Granary & Cowhouse & Cartshed all communicating, Brick & Tiled & Slated	3/-	400
Jn° Mason Wm Mason Jos^h Hockenhull Geo Peers Ralph Breaford	Beam Street. Five Cottages with sheds communicating with each, Brick & Tiled £60 on each	1/6	300
Jn° Bebbington Sarah Church Wm Church Mary Rigby	Church Lane. Four Cottages with Sheds adjoining to each. £60 on each	4/6	240
Jn° Bebbington Thos Jarvis Thos Moulton Jn° Till	Hospital Street. Four Cottages with Sheds adjoining to each. £60 on each	"	240
Jn° Robinson Jon° Palmer	Hospital Street. House, Carpenters Shop & Granary all communicating, brick, tiled & slated. Shed & Stable adjoining, near,		
		5/-	120
	no pitch or tar heated nor stove therein, nor in the building last above described	4/6	50
	Wall Lane		
Thos Downes	Shed only used by a Tanner	4/6	20
	Another Shed only, near, also used by a Tanner, Timber & Slated	"	20
	Snow Hill		
Wm Robinson P. Bailey M. Moulton	Ten Cottages Thatched & Slated Thatched Thatched		

continued

Tho⁵ Robinson	Thatched		
Wᵐ Bafford	Thatched		
Jaˢ Chefters	Thatched		
Edwᵈ Bulge	Brick, Timber & Slated		
Peter Bellington	Thatched		
Jnᵒ Bellington	Thatched		
Jnᵒ Smith	Thatched £40 on each	4/6	400
Jnᵒ Bostock	Stable only near	"	20
Cauley	House. Smith's Shop & stable all		
	adjoining, near	7/6	70
Jaˢ Sherrett	Cottage only, near, Brick & Slated	1/6	70
Samˡ Bellington	Thatched		
Wmˡ Brainnell	Thatched		
Tho⁵ Bostock	Thatched		
Jaˢ Wade	Thatched		
Wᵐ Harding	Thatched		
Robᵗ Farmer	Thatched		
Tho⁵ Reade	Thatched		
Tho⁵ Nixon	Thatched		
Tho⁵ Gilbert	Thatched		
Chaˢ Robinson	Thatched		
Wᵐ Robinson	Thatched		
	being Eleven Cottages £40on each	4/6	440
Edwᵈ Tomkinson	Cottage only near, Brick & Tiled	1/6	70
			£9840
Farm House	All Thatched & no hazardous trade		
Farm Bgs	therein except otherwise described		
Carpenters			

Sun Fire Office

GLDH MS 11937/490

14ᵗʰ July 1859

1897603	The Executors of the late Abraham Totman		
	of Finchingfield in Essex, Farmer.		
£5-3-6	On household goods, wearing apparel, printed		
Midr 1860	books & plate in the dwelling house &		
Portway	offices all communicating, called *Howe Hall,*		
Braintree	Finchingfield aforesaid, in tenure of Mr		
Dʸ £4-4	Totman, plaster & tiled	2/6	300
	China & glass therein only	4/6	20
	Farmhouse called *Swallows Farm,*		
	Finchingfield aforesaid, in tenure		
	of Chapman	5/-	70
	Wheat barn, Horse shed & henhouse all		
	adjoining, near	3/-	400
1832513 Cᵈ	Stable & strawhouse adjoining, near, thatched	"	65
	Barley barn only near	"	260
	Small henhouse only near	"	5
	Seven cottages all adjoining at Finchingfield		

	called *Sharps* in tenure of Townsend & others	4/6	200
	Three cottages at Little London, near, in tenure of Sullen & others. £100 in equal proportion	"	100
Essex	Six cottages in tenure of Turpen & others £200 in equal proportion	"	200
	Two cottages near in tenure of R. & J. Stock, & John Lewsey. £50 on each	"	100
	Cottages in three tenements, near, in tenure of Whitehead & others	"	50
	Cottage only, near, in tenure of Digley	"	20
	Six cottages near in tenure of Chapman, Danes & others. £250 in equal proportion	"	250
	Two cottages, near, in tenure of Thomas & George Turpin, £50 on each	"	100
	Cottage in four tenements at Finchingfield aforesaid in tenure of Frost & others, plaster & tiled	2/6	200
	Double tenement only, near, in tenure of Ridgwick plaster & tiled	"	100
	Four tenements near, in tenure of French & others. £50 on each	4/6	200
	Tenement only called *Clapgates*, Finchingfield aforesaid	"	50
	Double tenement only at Little London aforesaid in tenure of Turpin & another	"	100
	Bake office & stable adjoining, near, plaster & tiled	"	10
			£2800

All thatched except as aforesaid &
in no hazardous tenure

Sun Fire Office

GLDH Ms 11937/526

	10th July 1862

10th July 1862

1992687	Ambrose Goddard Lethbridge, Charles Agustus Thurlow & Hugh
£15-5-5	Fitz Roy, Trustees under the Will of
Mids^r 1863	the late Sir T. B. Lethbridge, Bart
Easton	On the following property forming the
Taunton	Luxborough Estates, Somerset.The
	following on *Gupworth Farm* in Withiel
Dy £12-18-1	Florey, Tenant John Vicary

Farm house & Offices all communicating stone & slated	1/6	140
Stable, stone & slated	3/-	40
Pigsties and Granary, all adjoining, near, slated	"	20
Barn & linhays all adjoining, stone and slated	"	50

continued

Linhay by the Carthouse, slated	"	20
The following on *Ford Farm* in Withiel Florey, tenant Mark Coles		
Farm house & Offices, all adjoining, stone & thatched	5/-	100
Barn, stable, Cowsheds & stalls all adjoining, near, stone & thatched	5/-	50
The following on Part of *Goosemoon* [sic] *Farm* in Withiel Florey, Tenant John Greenslade		
Dwelling house & Cowshed adjoining, stone & thatched	"	100
The following on Castle Hill in Withiel Florey, Tenant William Tarr		
Farm house & Offices adjoining, thatched	"	250
Home Barn, near, Stone & slated	3/-	20
Stable & Upper Linhays all adjoining, near the above, stone & slated	"	30
New Waggon house, near, stone & slated	"	20
Edgerton Barn & Linhays all adjoining, thatched but laying off at a distance from the above	5/-	50
The following on *Withiel Farm* in Withiel Florey, Tenant John Cornish		
Barton or Linhays all adjoining, south of the Home Garden, stone & thatched	"	20
Farm house & offices all communicating, stone and slated	1/6	180
Stable, stone, Cob & Slated	3/-	30
New Barn, stone & slated	"	30
Blagdon Barn & Linhays, all adjoining, stone & thatched (standing alone).	"	30
Davis Barn & Linhays all adjoining, stone & thatched (standing alone)	5/-	30
The following at Higher Eastcott in Withiel Florey, Tenant Wm Langdon		
Farm house & Offices all adjoining, thatched,	"	150
Upper barn near, slated	3/-	20
Linhay near the Barn, thatched	5/-	10
Stable, Linhays, Pigsties & Calves houses all adjoining, detached thatched	"	20
Linhay in the Green, thatched	"	10
The following on *Holworthy Farm* in Kingsbrompton, Tenant John Warren		
Farm house & Offices all communicating, stone & slated	1/6	250
Barn, stable & Linhay, all adjoining, near, thatched	5/-	80
Upper barn, near, thatched	"	20
Upper linhay, slated (standing alone)	3/-	50

Waggon house, stone & slated, near	"	20
The following at Cophole & Stoford in		
Kingsbrompton, Tenant Thomas Cornish		
Farm house & Offices all communicating,		
stone built & slated	1/6	200
Home Linhays & stable, all adjoining, near,		
thatched	5/-	50
Home Barn, stone & slated	3/-	20
Stoford Barn & Linhay adjoining, near,		
standing alone & thatched	5/-	40
New Waggon house on Cophole, stone		
and slated	3/-	20
The following on *Leigh Farm* in		
Kingsbrompton, Tenant John Lucas		
Farm house & offices, all adjoining, thatched	5/-	250
Barns, Stable & Linhays, all adjoining, near,		
thatched	"	100
New Linhays & Stalls, all adjoining in the		
Green, thatched (standing alone)	"	20
Linhay, stone & slated, in the Green near	3/-	10
Waggon house, thatched	5/-	10
Small Moor new Barn & Linhays, all		
adjoining, near Stone & Slated	3/-	30
Small Moor two Cottages, standing alone		
under one Roof, slated	"	30
The following on *Hurscombe Farm* in		
Kingsbrompton, Tenant William Baker		
Farm house & Offices, all adjoining, thatched	5/-	200
Stable adjoining the Farm house, thatched	"	40
Linhay in the Court, thatched	"	10
Barn & Linhay adjoining, stone & slated,		
standing alone	3/-	30
Waggon House, thatched, standing alone	5/-	10
The following at *Higher Goosemoor* [*sic*] in		
Kingsbrompton, Tenant, Abel Scott		
Dwelling house, barn & linhay, all adjoining,		
thatched	"	100
Two dwellings under one roof standing		
alone in Kingsbrompton William Blackmore,		
Tenant, Thatched £20 on each	10/6	40
The following on *Woolcott Far*m in		
Kingsbrompton, Tenant William Corner		
Dwelling house, thatched	5/-	70
Waggon house, thatched	"	25
Another Linhay, thatched	"	10
Barn & Linhays all adjoining, thatched	"	50
House occupied by John Quarterly, thatched,		
standing alone	"	50
Linhay near, slated	3/-	20

continued

The Following on *Goosemoor* [sic] *Farm* in
Exton, Tenant Joseph Davey

Barn & Linhays, all adjoining, stone and thatched	5/-	70
Cottage at a distance from the other buildings & alone, stone & thatched	7/6	100

The following on *Armoor Farm* in Exton,
Tenant William Ridler

Farm house & offices all adjoining, thatched	5/-	200
Barn, Stable & Linhays all adjoining, near, thatched & slated	"	60
Crosses house, near, thatched	"	20
Weekfields Farm house, thatched	"	50
Barn & Linhays adjoining each other & the above, thatched	"	30
Small Moorehouse & Linhay adjoining, in Kingsbrompton, thatched	5/-	30
Barn & Linhay adjoining, near, thatched	"	20

The following on *Langham Farm* in
Luxborough, Tenant Edward W. Rocket

Farm house & Offices all, communicating stone & slated	1/6	150
Stable & Linhay adjoining, near, stone & slated	3/-	30
Home Barn & Linhays, all adjoining, near, thatched	5/-	30
Blindwell Barn & Barton, all adjoining, slated & thatched, standing alone	"	30

The following on *Poole Farm* in Luxborough,
Tenant Thomas Webber

Farm house & Offices adjoining, thatched	"	200
Cottage & Barn adjoining, near, thatched	"	40
Higher Barn, near, newly built, stone & slated	3/-	20
New Stable, near the above, stone & slated	"	30
Pound house, thatched	5/-	10
Linhay near the Pound house, thatched	"	10
Slowley Barn & Barton, all adjoining, stone & slated, standing alone	3/-	20
Linhay at West Slowley, thatched	5/-	20

The following at Newcombe in Luxborough,
Tenant William Lucas

Farm house Offices & stable, all communicating, stone & slated	1/6	180
Western Barn & Linhay adjoining, near, stone & slated	3/-	20
Eastern Barn & linhay, adjoining, near, thatched	5/-	20
Kernisham Farm house & stable, adjoining, thatched, standing alone	"	50

Barn & Linhays, adjoining, thatched	"	30
Colly hill house & offices all adjoining, thatched, standing alone	"	60
Barn & Linhays, all adjoining, near, thatched	"	30
The following on *Wescott Farm* in Luxborough, Tenant Thomas Dallyn		
Westcott [*sic*] *Farm* house & ,Offices all communicating, stone & slated	1/6	200
Home barns all adjoining, near, thatched	5/-	50
Stable & linhay, adjoining, near ,thatched	"	30
Granary & Cellar or Offices under, slated	3/-	30
Home Linhays all adjoining, near, thatched	5/-	30
Newly built Wood & poultry house adjoining, stone & slated	"	10
Ditch linhay, stone & tiled & *Ditch Cot* house adjoining , thatched, standing alone	5/-	20
Ditch Barn & linhays adjoining, near, thatched	"	30
Woodlands House Barn & Linhays all adjoining, thatched, standing alone	"	30
Throat house & Linhays all adjoining, tiled, standing alone	3/-	20
The following at Lype & Hole Stowey & Cutcombe, Tenant John Joyce		
Lype house Barn & Linhays all adjoining, thatched	5/-	40
Barn with Linhay under, near, stone & slated	3/-	40
Hole Stowey Farm house cellars & Offices, all under one roof, thatched standing alone	5/-	200
Barn, stable & shed, all adjoining, near, thatched	"	20
Barn, thatched	"	20
Linhays all adjoining near thatched	5/-	10
The following at Nurcott & Will in Luxborough, Tenant Robert G. Norman		
Farm house & Offices all communicating, stone & slated	1/6	200
Linhays & Pound house adjoining, thatched	5/-	40
Stable, detached, thatched	"	20
Two Barns & Linhays all adjoining, near, thatched	"	40
Will house now two Cottages standing alone, slated	3/-	30
New Barn & linhay adjoining on the Hill (part of *Bearsham*) stone & tiled	"	50
The following on *Kersham Farm* in Cutcombe, Tenant Richard Barton		
Farm house, offices & sheds, all adjoining, thatched & slated	5/-	200

continued

Upper Barn, Stable & Linhays, all adjoining, near, thatched	"	60
Hill barn & Linhay adjoining,thatched, standing alone	"	30
The following at Hazery in Treborough, Tenant Thomas Webber		
Farm house & Offices, all adjoining, thatched	5/-	100
Barn, Stable & Linhays, all adjoining, near, thatched	"	50
The following at New Mill & part of *Washers* in Luxborough, Tenant James Bryant		
Dwelling house & Water Grist Mill adjoining & communicating, stone & tiled, said Mill not working more than two pair of stones, no kiln therein and no oats shelled nor ground therein	7/6	100
Cowshed, near, thatched	5/-	10
New shed adjoining the Road, stone & thatched	"	20
Washers Barn, sheds & stable, all under one roof, stone & thatched, standing alone	"	40
Waggon house & Granary over. Stone & slated	3/-	30
The following at *Old Hall* in Luxborough, Tenant Robert James & others		
Dwelling house & cottages all adjoining called *Old Hall*, stone & thatched, standing alone	5/-	80
The following at *Charcote Lodge* & Premises in hand in Luxborough		
Dwelling house & Offices, all communicating, brick stone & tiled, no stove therein	1/6	1250
Household goods (china & glass excepted), wearing apparel, printed books & plate therein	"	400
Stables, coachhouse & shed, all adjoining, near, stone & tiled	3/-	100
Cattle sheds all adjoining, near, tiled	"	30
Bailiffs house called *Washers*, stone & thatched, standing alone	5/-	40
The following on *Coomberow Farm* in Old Cleve, Tenant Mrs Jewell		
Dwelling house, stone & slated	1/6	40
Barn, stable & Pigsties under one roof, near, thatched	5/-	20
New Linhay near, Stone & Slated	3/-	10
		£8605

Sun Fire Office

GLDH Ms 11937/526

1997001   10th September 1862
£8-19-9 Sir Frederick Ulrick Graham Bart of Netherby Hall near
2nd February   Carlisle in Cumberland
1863
Baty
Longtown
Dy £9-4-6
Annual
Cumbd
192001 Canc*d*

	Sum Insd	Totals	Rates	Premium	Duty
On farm buildings at Longton in Cumberland called *Longton Farm* occupied by Robert Hendrie farmer viz:					
On dwelling house	80		1/6		
Potato house stables & gighouse all adjoining	100		3/-		
Barn & Byre adjoining	50		"		
Pothouse & piggeries all adjoining	20	250	"	6 5	7/6
Hallburn Farm occupied by Richard Coulthard					
On dwelling house	50		1/6		
Loose box, pothouse piggeries, cattle sheds & calfhouse all adjoining	70		3/-		
Byre Barn & stable all adjoining	50		"		
Thrashing mill house	30	200	"	5 3	6/-
Stoneygate occupied by Robt Wilson Innkeeper					
On dwelling house	25		1/6		
Barn & Byre adjoining	25	50	3/-	1 2	1/6
Dykeshead Farm occupied by Mrs Ellen Armstrong					
Dwelling house	50		1/6		
Byres, calfhouse & pothouse all adjoining	30		3/-		
Cattle sheds, Piggeries & barn, all adjoining	100		"		
Loose box, stable & cartshed all adjoining"	70	250	"	6 9	7/6
Cottage at Roadend occupied by William Blaylock					
Cottage	25		1/6		
Barn & Byre adjoining	25	50	3/-	1 2	1/6
Sunneyrigg Farm occupied by William Johnston					
On dwelling house	50		1/6		
Stable & loose Box adjoining	40		3/-		
Byre, Barn & Cartshed all adjoining	40		3/-		
Pothouse & piggeries all adjoining	20	150	"	3 9	4/6
Cottage at Cleugh Head occupied by William Baty	50	50	1/6	9	1/6
Buildings of Easton occupied by John Carruthers					
On cottage	30		1/6		
Blacksmith's shop	20	50	3/-	1 1	1/6
Buildings at Easton occupied by					

continued

	Sum Insd	Totals	Rates	Premium	Duty
Thomas Fairburn					
House Joiners shop & byre all communicating	50	50	5/-	2 6	1/6
Building at Heatherhead occupied by					
Francis Blaylock					
On dwelling house	50		1/6		
Barn stable & Byre all adjoining	50	100	3/-	2 3	3/-
Buildings called *Browhead* occupied by					
William Sirey					
Cottage thatched	50		5/-		
Stable Barn & Byre adjoining near	50	100	3/-	4 -	3/-
Buildings at Hemplands occupied by					
Robert Johnson					
On cottage & Blacksmith's shop communicating	50	50	2/-	1 -	1/6
Farm Buildings called *Longtown Moor* occupied by John Baty					
On house & Barn communicating	50		1/6		
Stable & Byre adjoining near	25		3/-		
Piggeries & Pothouse all adjoining near	25	100	"	2 3	3/-
Farm Buildings called *Robriedsboy* occupied by David Coulthard					
On dwelling house	50		1/6		
Stable Barn Byre & Piggery all adjoining to said house	50	100	3/-	2 3	3/-
Farm Buildings called *High Planes* occupied by M. Lawson					
On dwelling house stable & cartshed all communicating	100		1/6		
Byres, Turnip house calfhouse & cattle sheds all adjoining near	80		3/-		
Piggeries all adjoining near	20	200	3/-	4 6	6/-
Buildings at Sandysyke occupied by Joseph Tweddle					
Double cottage	70		1/6		
Stable only adjoining	30	100	3/-	2 -	3/-
Buildings called *Cleughead* occupied by Adam Riddley					
Cottage & Joiners shop communicating	50		5/-		
Barn, stable & Byre all adjoining to the last above named but not communicating therewith a stone wall between slated & thatched	50	100	3/-	4 -	3/-
Farm buildings called *Redcleugh* occupied by Rob[t] Sander					
Dwelling house thatched	40		5/-		
Stable Loosebox & cartshed all adjoining to the last above named thatched	30		"		
Barn only near thatched	30	100	3/-	4 5	3/-

	Sum Insd	Totals	Rates	Premium	Duty
Farm buildings called *Slealandburn* occupied by John Armstrong					
On dwelling house	40		1/6		
Barn stable byre & piggeries all adjoining to said house	60	100	3/-	2 6	3/-
Farm buildings called *South Slealand* occupied by Wm Johnstone					
On dwelling house	50		1/6		
Stable Barn & Cartshed all adjoining to said house	100		3/-		
Byres, Piggeries & Pothouse all adjoining to last named	25		3/-		
Byre & cattle sheds all adjoining near	25	200	"	5 3	6/-
Farm buildings called *Bruntfould* occupied by James Armstrong					
On dwelling house, stable & barn all communicating, thatched	50		5/-		
Byre only near	10		3/-		
Piggeries & cattle sheds all adjoining near	40	100	"	4 -	3/-
Farm Buildings called *Hill Top* occupied by Jane Forrest					
On dwelling house	40		1/6		
Stable only adjoining	30		3/-		
Byre, pothouse & piggeries all adjoining	40		"		
Barn only adjoining	40	150	3/-	4 -	4/6
Farm buildings called *Hallburn* occupied by Jno Forster					
On house	40		1/6		
Stable & Byre adjoining	30		3/-		
Barn only near	30	100	"	2 6	3/-
Farm buildings called *Beyond Wood* occupied by Andrew Holston					
On dwelling house	50		1/6		
Stable & Byre adjoining	50		3/-		
Barn only near	50	150	"	3 9	4/-
Farm buildings called *Glendenning Rigg Crofts* occupied by Archibald Armstrong					
On dwelling house	30		1/6		
Cattle sheds & piggeries all adjoining	40		3/-		
Stable & Byre adjoining	30	100	"	2 8	3/-
Buildings called *Scotchdyke* occupied by Ja^s Armstrong, carrier					
On dwelling house	50		1/6		
Stable & Warehouse adjoining near	50	100	3/-	2 3	3/-
Farm buildings called *Lyne Moor* occupied by George Ferguson					
On dwelling house & byre adjoining slated & thatched	50		5/-		

continued

	Sum Insd	Totals	Rates	Premium	Duty
Barn & stable adjoining near clay & slated	50	100	3/-	4 -	3/-
Farm buildings called *Station* occupied by W Gibson					
On dwelling house	40		1/6		
Potato house, Turnip house & byre all adjoining	40		3/-		
Barn & stable adjoining near	40		"		
Piggeries, pothouse & sheds all adjoining	30	150	"	4 -	4/6
Farm Buildings called *Fineview* occupied by Thomas Ferguson					
On dwelling house	40		1/6		
Stable & Barn adjoining near	40		3/-		
Byre & potato house	20	100	"	2 6	3/-
Buildings called *Edwardstown* occupied by George Graham					
On cottage, blacksmith's shop, barn & byre all adjoining thatched	100	100	7/6	7 6	3/-
Farm buildings called *Nookfoot* occupied by Richard Forrester					
On dwelling house	50		1/6		
Stable, Barn & cartshed all adjoining near	100		3/-		
Calfhouse, byre & turnip house all adjoining	50		"		
Cattle shed, Piggeries & pothouse all adjoining	50		"		
Threshing machine (driven by water) in said Barn	50	300	"	8 3	9/-
Farm buildings called *Hobbies Farm* occupied by Thomas Vast					
On cottage	40		1/6		
Barn, Byre & stable all adjoining	60	100	3/-	2 6	3/-
Farm buildings called *Longtown Moor* occupied by Wm Little					
On dwelling house & byre adjoining thatched	40		5/-		
Barn only near thatched	20		3/-		
Stable only near	20		"		
Sheds all adjoining near	20	100	"	3 10	3/-
Farm buildings called *Ninevah* occupied by Simon Johnston					
On dwelling house & barn adjoining thatched	40		5/-		
Stable & Byre adjoining thatched	30		"		
Cattle sheds & piggeries adjoining thatched	30	100	"	5 -	3/-
Farm buildings called *Frankstown* occupied by Thomas Graham					
On dwelling house stone & slated	100		1/6		
Barn, Potatoe house, stable, Byre & pothouse all adjoining near thatched	100		3/-		
Room without fire place, shed, byres and piggeries all adjoining near thatched	100	300	"	7 6	9/-

	Sum Insd	Totals	Rates	Premium	Duty
Farm buildings called *White Close Rigg* occupied by W. Irving					
On house & stable adjoining & communicating	80		1/6		
Carshed [sic] barn & stable & byre all adjoining near	100		3/-		
Cattle sheds & piggeries all adjoining near	20	200	3/-	4 10	6/-
Farm buildings called *Millees* occupied by Joseph M. Edgar					
On pothouse, piggeries & cattle sheds all adjoining	30		3/-		
Byre, Barn & cartshed all adjoining near	60		"		
Gighouse & Granary with loft over all adjoining near	60	150	"	4 6	4/6
Farm buildings called *Hobbies Barn* occupied by Rob* Fenton					
On cottage, stable & Byre all adjoining, thatched	50	50	5/-	2 6	1/6
Farm buildings called *Punkins* occupied by Ja* Armstrong					
House & Barn communicating	60		2/-		
Byre & stable adjoining to the above slated	40	100	3/-	2 6	3/-
Farm buildings called *Glendinnings Croft* occupied by Jared Dixon					
On dwelling house	40		1/6		
Barn adjoining	20		3/-		
Stable & Byre adjoining	40	100	"	2 6	3/-
Farm buildings called *Dashwell Green* occupied by Jn° Palmer					
Stable, Barn, Cartshed & Byre all adjoining	100	100	3/-	3	3/-
Farm buildings called *Chapletown* occupied by Miss Twining					
On house	50		1/6		
Stable & Byre adjoining to the house but not communicating therewith a stone wall through the roof between thatched	30		5/-		
Byre Barn loose Box byre & piggeries all adjoining near thatched	20	100	3/-	3	3/-
Farm buildings called *Reburnside* occupied by W. Baty					
On house, stable & cartshed all adjoining thatched	50		5/-		
Barn & Byre adjoining near thatched	50	100	3/-	4	3/-
Farm buildings called *Pladdo* occupied by Mrs Jane Baxter					
On dwelling house	40		1/6		
Stable & Barn adjoining	40		3/-		
Byre & piggeries all adjoining	20	100	3/-	2 6	3/-

continued

	Sum Insd	Totals	Rates	Premium	Duty
Farm building called *Toddle Riggs* occupied by Robert Johnston					
On dwelling house & stable communicating	50		1/6		
Barn & Byre adjoining	50	100	3/-	2 3	3/-
Buildings called *Road End Croft* occupied by Thomas Bonch					
On cottage	50		1/6		
Joiner's shop & byre adjoining to the above but not communicating therewith					
a stone wall between	50	100	5/-	3 3	3/-
Farm buildings called *Liddle Strength* occupied by Peter Morton					
On dwelling house & pot house communicating	50		1/6		
Cottage & stable adjoining near thatched	25		5/-		
Barn & Brye with loft over adjoining near thatched	25	100	3/-	2 9	3/-
Farm buildings called *Barn* occupied by Andrew Hill					
On dwelling house & stable communicating	40		1/6		
Piggeries & Byre, adjoining	20		3/-		
Barn, Cartshed & cattle shed all adjoining	40	100	"	2 6	3/-
Farm buildings called *Lamb Hill* occupied by Ja⁵ Graham					
On dwelling house	30		1/6		
Stable, Barn, cartshed, byre and piggeries all adjoining	70	100	3/-	2 8	3/-
Farm buildings called *Longtown Moor*, occupied by Wᵐ Murrey					
On dwelling house	40		1/6		
Stable & Barn adjoining near	60	100	3/-	2 6	3/-
Farm buildings called *Sanders Bush* occupied by John Johnston					
On dwelling house & pothouse adjoining clay & thatched	50		5/-		
Piggeries all adjoining to said house but not communicating therewith clay & thatched	20		"		
Barn and gin shed adjoining to the above clay and thatched	50		5/-		
Stable and Byre adjoining near clay and thatched	30	150	3/-	7	4/6
	£6,150		£8	19 9	£9-4-6

Farm
Outbuildings
Carpenters

All stone & slated except as aforesaid & no pitch nor tar heated nor stove therein

N.B. The aforesaid buildings are all situate in the County of Cumberland and a plan of the same deposited in this office

Note: The plan referred to in this policy does not survive.

Chapter 9

Policy Registers: Official and Commercial Buildings

The Chapel of St. George, Windsor

Sun Fire Office

GLDH Ms 11936/300

8th March 1782

457035	The Rev[d] Dean & Canons of the Kings Free Chapel of St George, within his Castle of Windsor, in the County of Berks.	
£10-10	On the Buildings as particularly expressed	
L'day 1783	on the back of this Policy viz:	
£10-18	On a Brick & Timber House & Offices	
Tildesley	adjoining called the *Deanery* in the tenure of the Hon[ble] & Rev[d] John Harley DD, not exceeding nine hundred & seventy five pounds.	975
	On the *Deans' Cloister* adjoining. Stone, not exceeding two hundred & seventy five pounds.	275
	On the Southside of the *Canons' Cloister* containing part of the house of the Revd Dr Bray's house. House of the Hon[ble] & Rev[d] D[r] Shute Barrington, the Lecturers House for the time being & Shift Gate house all adjoining. Brick & timber not exceeding six hundred pounds.	600
	On the Eastside of the said Canons' Cloisters containing the other part of the Rev[d] Dr Bray's house & the Rev[d] Mr Hattam's house all adjoining. Brick & timber, not exceeding five hundred pounds	500
	On the North of the said *Canons' Cloisters* containing the Houses of the late Revd D[r] Barnard, Rev[d] D[r] Duval & the Rev[d]	

continued

Dr Shepherd, all adjoining. Brick & timber,
not exceeding nine hundred pounds.   900
On a brick house on the *King's Wall* in the
tenure of the Revd Dr Bostock, not exceeding
four hundred & seventy five pounds.   475
On the Westside of the said *Canons' Cloister*
containing the house & offices adjoining of the
late Revd Dr North. Brick, not exceeding
three hundred & seventy five pounds   375
On a Brick & timber house adjoining North
of the said Revd Dr North's house & South of
the Chapter house in the tenure of the Rev^d
Mr Buller, not exceeding four hundred & fifty pounds.   450
On the Chapter house with the Tower adjoining.
Brick & Stone not exceeding one hundred
& twenty five pounds.   125
On a Brick & stone house with offices adjoining
in the tenure of the Revd Dr Majendie, not
exceeding three hundred & twenty five pounds.   325
On a Brick house adjoining, South of the said
Revd Dr Majendie's house in the tenure of the
Revd Dr Hurdes, not exceeding five hundred pounds.   500
On a brick & timber house adjoining East of the
said Revd Dr Hurde's house, with offices adjoining,
in the tenure of the Revd Dr Lockman, not
exceeding three hundred & twenty five pounds.   325
On a Brick & timber house on the *Kings Wall* in
the tenure of the Revd Mr Clark, not exceeding
fifty pounds.   50
On a Brick & timber house in the tenure of the
Verger for the time being, not exceeding
one hundred & seventy five pounds.   175
On a Range of Brick & timber Buildings with
cloisters & sheds adjoining containing three
dwelling houses in the tenure of the Rev^d
Mr Vanderman, Revd Mr Champnes &
Mr Hartley, with a Singing School, all adjoining,
not exceeding three hundred & fifty pounds.   350
On a Brick & stone Building with offices under
(called the *Library*), not exceeding
two hundred & fifty pounds.   250
On a Range of Brick & timber Buildings
containing fourteen houses with Cloysters
& sheds, all adjoining (called the *Horshoe
Cloisters*) in the tenure of the Minor Canons,
Singing Men and Organist, not exceeding
seven hundred & fifty pounds.   750

                                                                    £7400

All tiled, slated or leaded & situate as aforesaid

Photograph of Battersea Bridge from Chelsea Church Tower, c.1875

Battersea Bridge

Sun Fire Office

GLDH Ms 11936/387

	14th June 1792
601413	The Proprietors for the time being of Battersea Bridge. On the said Bridge, not exceeding two thousand pounds. £2000

£4

Midr 1793

£4-3-4

Mem[dum] Three Thousand Pounds being insured on the within mentioned Bridge viz. Two thousand pounds in the Phoenix Fire Office & one thousand pounds in the Royal Exchange Assurance Office is hereby allowed & agreed

Ent[d] 13 June 1792

Arms, Accoutrements and Cloathing of the First Regiment of Essex Local Militia

Royal Exchange Assurance

GLDH Ms 7253/63

9th July 1810

254030   Joshua Pattison, quarter Master of the First Regt
of Essex Local Militia
On the Arms, Accoutrements & soldiers' cloathing
belonging to the said regiment deposited in the
storerooms & Chamber over, being part of a
building Brick, Timber & tiled, situate in the
Back Lane in the Parish of Saint Rumwald in
Colchester, Co. of Essex, next to the Melting [*sic*]

Colchester   Office belonging to Messs Jones & Chennery
but having no communication therewith   [£]2500
            Warrd that no Ammunition nor gunpowder
                   be deposited in the premises.
            Memo   £3000 being afsd on the above mentioned
                   property in the Essex Equitable Fire Office
                   the same is hereby allowed

            £6-5-0
5/- dy   3-2-6
            £9-7-6

            Sketch of the Premises in agents letter dated
            July 13th, 1810

Arms of the First Regiment of Warwickshire Local Militia

Sun Fire Office

GLDH Ms 11937/95

12th December 1810

851946   Capt. Hawkings of Coventry
            On the Arms only belonging to the First regiment of
£18-18   Warwickshire Local Militia, deposited in a room in St
Xmas 1811 Mary's Hall, Coventry part of which is used as a Theatre,
£20-1-8   stone & leaded, not exceeding eighteen hundred pounds   £1800
Carter   To be relinquished when entered
P.G.   Refused
Dy £2-7-9

Synagogue in Queen Street, Golden Square

Globe Insurance Company
GLDH Ms 11679

21ˢᵗ November 1823

83779	The Treasurer & trustees for the Time being of the Synagogue in Queen Street, Golden Square.	
AP to Mich	Their Desks, Seats, Altar Clock & other fixtˢ in	
24	their Synagogue & Vestry Room adj. &	
£2-5-0	com[*municating*] sit[*uate*] in Cordwell Yard,	
W.O.J.B.	Queen Street. afd. Bk[*brick*] & Tl [*tiled*].	195
26/522	Chandeliers, Candlesticks & other Brass Work the 7	70
	Manuscript Copies of the Law written on Parchment	
	viz Nos 1,2,3,4,5,6,&7 th [*therein*] in EP	200
	Decorations and drapery used in the service th [*therein*]	
	Plate th [*therein*]	145
	Hᵒhold Goods & Furnᵉ in said Vestry Room	40
	DH [*dwelling house*] of the Sexton sit [*situated*] in the	
	Burying Ground in Globe Lane, Mile End. Bk[*brick*].	500
		£1200

N to Mr Hyams
£1-16-0

Gloucester Union Workhouse

Sun Fire Office
GLDH Ms 11679

20ᵗʰ April 1835

1274752	The Guardians of the Poor of the Gloucester Union in the parish of St Catherine in the City of Gloucester,	
£1-15	for the time being.	
L'day 1839	On the front or Entrance building comprising	
Carter	the Board Room, Chapel, Clerk's Room, Porter's	
Gloster	Lodges, Receiving and Probationary Rooms &	
Dy £2-2	Booths, all being on the Ground Floor &	
	communicating, one hundred pounds.	100
	On the centre or main building, this comprises	
	in the centre thereof an Octangular Building	
	containing the Governor & Matron's rooms &	
	other rooms and at the back, the kitchen for	
	cooking for the establishment, & the other parts	
	or wings of this building consist of workshop,	
	school, Day rooms & sleeping rooms for the	
	several classes of Paupers in the House, all	
	communicating, near, One thousand pounds	£1000

On the Back building, the centre part of which is
one story high & consists of rooms for the Medical
Officers, Nurses & for the sick, being the Infirmary
of the establishment, the wings to such building
being on the ground floor and consisting of the
bakehouse, washhouse, laundry, workrooms, dead
rooms & refractory cells, all communicating near,
three hundred pounds   300
                                          2/6 £1400

All brick & slated & unfinished &
situate as aforesaid

Isle of Man Library

Sun Fire Office
GLDH MS 11937/252

                        1st May 1839
1303175   The Trustees of the Isle of Man Library in the
           Isle of Man, Gentn
10/-   On their stock of printed books Charts and
L'day 1840 Utensils in their library only, situate at the north
Moore   Quay, Douglas aforesaid, the shop & cellar
Douglas   under in tenure of Thos. Kelly a Spirit Dealer.   2/6   £400
           Stone & slated

Methodist Chapel, Peel, Isle of Man

Sun Fire Office
GLDH Ms 11927/271

                      5th February 1841
1346720   The Trustees of the Wesleyan Methodist Chapel
           of Peel in the Isle of Man, for the time being.
12/-   On their Chapel with vestry communicating
Xmas 1841 including Pulpit, Pews, Desks and Furniture
Moore   belonging, situate at Peel aforesaid   1/6   £800
Douglas   All stone and slated

Property of St Mary Magdalene College, Cambridge

Sun Fire Office

GLDH Ms 11937/271

19th May 1841

1356739   The Master & Fellows of St. Mary Magdalene
College, Cambridge for the time being. On House

£1-2-6   & offices (in three tenements) all under one roof

L'day 1842   called the *Half Moon Inn* situate near The Iron

Nickolds   Bridge, in the Town of Cambridge in tenure of

Saffron   Francis Eaden & others, brick, plaster & tiled   4/6   £500

Walden

Dʸ 13/-

Cambridge

Hertford Jail and House of Correction

Sun Fire Office

GLDH Ms 11937/282

13th June 1842

1387041	The Justices of Peace, for the County of Hertford for the time being. On the County Jail & House of Correction	
£7-10-0	& other Buildings as per plan deposited in this office	
Mids 1843	situate in the Town of Hertford viz. On the Buildings	
£8-11-10	Marked *No.1* on said plan	600
Sworder	On the Building marked *No.2* on said plan	3000
Hertford	On the Buildings marked *No.3* on said plan including	
Dʸ £17-3-9	the Pulpit, Pews, Desks & furniture in the Chapel therein	3000
	On the Buildings marked *No.4* on said plan	1000
	On the Buildings marked *No.5* on said plan	500
Herts	And on the Buildings marked *No.6* on said plan	1700
	Bedding in said Buildings	100
	Clothing therein	100
		£10,000

All brick & tiled or slated and two Arnott Stoves
well secured allowed in said Buildings viz. one
in the Chapel & one in the store room

Note: The plan referred to in this policy does not survive.

The Galway Union Workhouse, Ireland

Sun Fire Office

GLDH Ms 11937/274

2nd Feb. 1842

1375265   The Guardians of the Galway Union Workhouse,
for the time being

£3-15-0   On the entrance building of said Workhouse in
the New castle road in the Parish of Rahoon in

Xmas 1842   the County of the town of Galway   250

On household Furniture, Bedding & wearing

Wilde   apparel therein only   100

On the Main Building   1750

Galway   On household furniture, bedding & wearing

Irish   apparel therein only   650

Hall, Kitchen, Laundry & offices all
communicating & with the aforesaid
(fixtures therein included)   750

On Household Furniture, Bedding & Wearing
apparel therein only   200

Hospital & Lunatic Wards, all communicating   750

On household goods, Bedding & wearing
apparel therein only   50

On year's rent on the aforesaid Buildings in
Proportion to the Sums Specified thereon   500

All Stone, Brick & Slated   1/6   £5000

Mem: This Office to be liable for the Payment
of rent during the time only that the Premises
may be actually untenantable

Paisley, Greenoch, Port Glasgow, Pollocks Laws and Renfrew Prisons

Sun Fire Office

GLDH Ms 11937/402

11th January 1853

1696073   The Renfrewshire Prison Board for the time being

On the Building of Paisley Prison (consisting of

£1-16-0   two wings connected) in which are a Chapel, Cells,

Xmas 1853 Bath & Class room, matron's & warders'

Dunn   apartments, cooking house, washing house,

Paisley   drying room, airing yards on the roof of the

Dy £3-12-0 south wing & cellars under both wings all
communicating. In the cellars of the south
wing are two boilers one for hot water for
heating the Prison which is conveyed thro'

the building in Iron pipes, the other for Steam
for Cooking. In the cellar of the North wing are
two furnaces for hot air for heating the Prison
which passes thro' flues in the Walls.   1000
Building in front of said Prison consisting of
the Governor's House with Governor's & Clerks'
Offices.   200
Building of Keeper's house, Cooking house &
cellars in the court in front of said Prison to the
north, forming part of, & attachment to, the County
Offices, Court house & Police Offices but not
communicating therewith.   200
Building of the Prison of Greenoch, consisting of
three stories, with keeper's house & cooking houses
in the centre of the Building & with the room used
as a Chapel a pipe stove well secured.   450
Building of the Prison of Port Glasgow, consisting
of keeper's house & Prisoners' Cells, public &
private Offices & shops.   200
Building of the Prison of Pollocks Laws, consisting
of Prisoners' Cells, keeper's house, washing house
& bath room, a boiler with a common furnace
being in the Washing house.   200
Building of the Prison of Renfrew, consisting of
two stories & communicating with county Hall
Council Room & other apartments which
are all in the same building.   150
                                                                            £2400
All stone & slated & situate in the County of
Renfrew   1/6

Liverpool Commercial Banking Company

Sun Fire Office

GLDH Ms 11937/496

6th June 1860

1926671 The Trustees for the time being of The Liverpool
         Commercial Banking Company.

£63   On the building *No.1* on the plan annexed hereto,
Midsʳ 1861 the ground floor used as a bank & bullion office there
£72-3-9 being in the cellar a secure furnace for smelting
Bold   gold, the rooms occupied as offices by other parties. 3600
L'pool   Building *No.2* on the said plan in tenure of The
Dy £72-3-9 Electric Telegraph Company, a secure stove
         allowed for warming a room therein.   3600
         Building *No.3* on the said plan used as the bank
         of the assured & club rooms.   9000

continued

1619691 C^d	Fixtures, furniture & stationery therein.	1000
	Building marked *No.4* on said plan.	3420
	Arched Vaults under, all communicating.	180
	Building marked *No.5* on said plan.	1842
	Arched Vaults underneath, all communicating.	198
	Building marked *No.6* on said plan communicating with the building No.5 aforesaid, the cellars underneath being used as a brewers store.	3000
	Building marked *No.7* on said plan.	3600
	Building of that portion of the arched vaults underneath *No.7* having a communication with the cellars under *No.6* aforesaid, also occupied by the same parties as a Brewers store.	300
	On the other portion of the said Arched vaults used as the dwellinghouse of the bank porter.	300
	Building of *No.8* on the said plan.	1716
	Arched vaults underneath, all communicating, in tenure of Jno Dawson, wine and spirit merchant.	204
	Building marked *No.9* on said plan.	2070
	Arched vaults underneath all communicating.	210
	Building *No.10* on the said plan.	1800

Twelve months rent viz:

Of the building *No.1*	504
Of the building No.2	360
Of the building *No.3*, viz of the Bank portion.	604
And of the club rooms portion.	400
Of the building *No.4*	1128
Of the arched vaults underneath.	72
Of the Building *No.5*	438
Of the arched vaults underneath.	42
Of the building *No.6*	816
Of the building *No.7*	552
Of the two portions of the Arched vaults underneath, £24 each.	48
Of the building *No.8*	348
Of the arched vaults underneath.	54
Of the building *No.9*	378
Of the arched vaults underneath.	36
and of the building *No.10*	180
	£42,000

The aforesaid are all situate in Liverpool &
are brick & stone & slated or covered with metal
or flags & *No.3,4,5,6,7,8,9 & 10* are occupied by
various persons as commercial offices & the
arched vaults except as above stated as wine
& spirit stores, packing & bottling allowed therein.

N.B. This Office to be liable for payment of
rent during the time only that the premises
may be rented.

Note: The following illustration refers to the policy above. It is a rare example of a plan drawn in a policy
register.

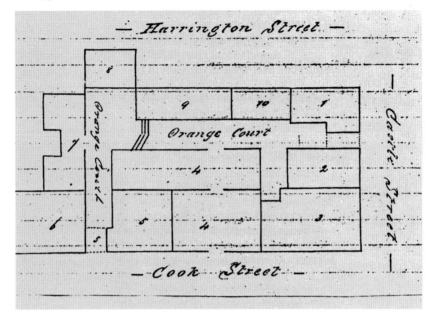

The Globe Iron Works, Pendleton, Lancashire

Sun Fire Office

GLDH Ms 11937/493

12th September 1860

1931961	The Globe Iron Works Company for the time being, of Brindle Heath, Pendleton, County of		
£3-8-2	Lancaster, Machine Makers & Iron & brass founders		
L'day 1861	On mechanics shop marked *No.3*	7/6	100
Holton	Steam engine therein	"	50
Manch^r	Shafting, gearing & all fixed utensils therein	"	50
Dy £2-5	Lathes, tools, stock & all moveable utensils therein	"	200
	Patterns, their own & in trust therein	"	30
	Iron foundry or castings shop adjoining the above marked *No.2*	"	80
	Crane, fan & all fixed utensils therein	"	80
	Stock & all moveable utensils therein	"	100
	Building of countinghouse (fixtures therein included) marked *No.1*	1/6	130
	Stock, their own or in trust therein	"	120
1851879 C^d	Brass foundry & joiners' shop adjoining but not communicating with last aforesaid, a brick wall between marked *No.4*	5/-	20
Lanc^r	Stock & all moveable utensils therein	"	30
	Patterns, their own and in trust therein	"	20
	Live & dead stock & all moveable utensils in stable & pattern rooms over marked *No.5*, no joiners work done therein	2/-	30
	Patterns, their own & in trust therein	"	120
	Smithy & shed adjoining near marked *No.6 & 7*	2/6	20
	Stock, fixed & all moveable utensils therein	"	10
	Dwellinghouse (late in tenure of Jones & Co.) including pattern rooms & stable, all communicating, near, marked *No.8*, no joiners work done therein	2/-	125
	Cottage adjoining	1/6	30
	Three cottages all communicating & adjoining last named	"	50
	Dwellinghouse adjoining	"	80
	Cottage only adjoining	"	25
	All brick & slated situate at Brindle Heath, Pendleton aforesaid & said numbers refer to a plan deposited in this office		__£1500__
	158/51		

Note: The plan referred to in this policy does not survive.

GLDH Ms 12160/158 page 51

Endorsement
29th Oct. 1860

1931961 Mem. Joiners' work being now done in the Buildings
Globe Iron Insured by the 14th, 15th & 18th Items of this Policy (but no
Works Co. stove therein) the Annual Premium is increased to £3-1-6
  and the sum of 4/2 having been received for the extra
493 Premium from this date to the 25th March 1861 the same is
  allowed.

Police Stations at Spalding, Holbeach and Long Sutton, Lincolnshire

Sun Fire Office

GLDH Ms 11937/500

2nd October 1860

1935624 Her Majesty's Justices of the Peace for the parts
  of Holland in the County of Lincoln, for the
13/3 time being.
Michs 1861 On a building used as a Police Station situate at
Maples Spalding in said Parts and County, comprising
Spalding dwelling house occupied by the Superintendent
D^y £1-4-3 of constabulary, Offices, Guard room, Lock ups

or Cells & other buildings all communicating.	1/6	150
Furniture, fittings & fixtures therein only	"	20
House only, adjoining & under the same roof		
as the above, occupied by a Police Constable	"	100
Stable & Carthouse with granary over & Out		
Lincoln Offices & Yard Walls all adjoining, near	2/6	40
Stock & Utensils in the last mentioned buildings	"	10
Building used as a Police Station situate at		
Holbeache also in said Parts & County		
comprising Dwelling House occupied by an		
Inspector of Constabulary, Office, Guard Room,		
Lock ups & Cells & other Offices, all adjoining	1/6	150
Fixtures, Furniture, Utensils, fittings therein only	"	20
Dwelling House only adjoining & under the same		
roof as the last mentioned, occupied by a Police		
Constable	1/6	100
Stable & Carthouse with Granary over & Out		
Offices & Yard Walls. All adjoining, near	2/6	40
Stock & Utensils therein only	"	10
Building used as a Police Station at Long Sutton		
also in the said Parts & county, comprising		
Dwelling House occupied by a Sergeant of		
Constabulary, Office, Guard room, Lock ups		
or Cells & Offices, all communicating	1/6	150

continued

Furniture, Utensils, fixtures & fittings therein
only   "   20
                                                                     £880*
Building of Courthouse only adjoining with   70
last named fur, fix. & fittings therein only

*This figure was originally £810 and altered after the last item (70) was added later.

Bristol Lunatic Asylum

Sun Fire Office

GLDH Ms 11937/505

1ˢᵗ Febʸ 1861

1949102	The Corporation of The Governor, Deputy Governor, assistants and Guardians of the Poor of the City of	
£5-12-6	Bristol, for the time being	
Xmas 1861	On the building on the East Side of the yard	
Barrow	consisting partly of the Lunatic Asylum for Males,	
Bristol	with Brewhouse under *A*	650
Dʸ £6-15-0	The building *B* situate on the West side of the yard con-	
Average	sisting partly of the Lunatic Asylum for Females, in occupation of Visitors of the said Asylum & partly of the the Workhouse Laundry & drying room & Cooking	
Cancelled	Kitchen stores & offices, occupied by the said Corporation	1000
1345800	On building *D* (being partly under the same roof) & partly occupied by the said visitors as an Asylum for female Lunatics & partly by the said corporation as a Workhouse & offices, stone timber & tiled	1500
	Workhouse building *C* consisting of Male Receiving Ward, Medical and Surgical Wards, Old mens' Ward and Offices occupied by the said Corporation	350
	The following property in all or any of the aforesaid buildings subject to the aforesaid conditions of average viz. Stock of Oakham, Timber & Leather	25
	Household fixtures, household Goods, including Iron & tin cans, Brewing Utensils, wearing apparel, Woollen and Linen Drapery	900
	China, Glass & Earthenware	50
	Dispensary Fixtures	25
		£4500

Memo   Said Letters refer to a plan deposited
              in this office [*The plan does not survive*]
              All brick, stone & tiled except as aforesaid
              & situate in Peter Street, Bristol & Known
              as St Peters Hospital.
                There is a stove in the Tailor's Shop, a
              stove in the Hall & a Gas stove in the
              Matron's store room in Building *D*, also a
              stove in the Medical Ward No16 in

Building *C*, the same being used for
warmth only, well secured & allowed.

NB   The aforesaid conditions of average apply
            to the 5th, 6th, 7th & 8th Items separately

Mem°   Similar sums being insured on the aforesaid
            property in the Imperial Fire Office and
            £600 on the property described by the 6th
            Item of this Policy in the London Assurance
            Company, the same is hereby allowed

Entered in the Office Books this
1st of February 1861
H. P. Kingston

173/145★

★ This endorsement volume is missing.

Bristol and Clifton Zoo

Sun Fire Office

GLDH Ms 11937/513
965144

	16th August 1861	
	The Treasurer for the time being of the Bristol &	
12/6	Clifton Zoological Society .	
22 Oct.1861	On a Building situate in their Gardens near Bristol,	
Barrow	built of timber & covered with glass and no fire heat	
Bristol	allowed therein.	80
D[y] 3/9	An American Aloe★ now being exhibited in the	
	above	420
	2/6	£500

★ A tall tropical plant that blooms once every ten to thirty years.

Chapter 10

Policy Registers: Railways

The Grand Junction Railway and The Liverpool and Manchester

Sun Fire Office

GLDH Ms 11937/513

11ᵗʰ October 1838

1285393 The Grand Junction Railway Cᵒʸ for the time being
         On Goods, their own in trust or on commission in all
£25   or any of the Carriages & Waggons on the Grand
L'day 1839 Junction Railway, or on the Liverpool & Manchester
Bold   Railway between Birmingham, Manchester and
L'pool   Liverpool   Ten thousand pounds   5/- [£]10000
Dʸ £15

Memᵈᵘᵐ Warranted that passengers' baggage is not
       included in this Insurance nor is any thing which
       may be conveyed upon or by the passenger trains to
       be brought into the average after mentioned.

Memᵈᵘᵐ It is hereby declared & agreed that in case
       the property aforesaid shall at the breaking out of
       any fire or fires be collectively of greater value than
       the sum insured, then this Company shall pay &
       make good to the assured such a proportion of the
       loss or damage as the sum insured shall bear to the
       whole value of the Goods in the Carriages &
       Waggons & all the goods carried, or in transit, on all
87/245 the trains on that day when the fire happens.

GLDH Ms 12160/87 page 245

Endorsement
14th Dec 1838

250   Be it remembered that Goods as well of the within named
Company as of all persons if carried by the said Company
and whether under the care of the said Company or of such
other persons and whether carried at the risk of
the said Company or of such other persons are
comprised in the insurance by the within written policy.

The Shropshire Union Railway and Canal Company

Sun Fire Office

GLDH Ms 11936/435

18th April 1855

1766208   The Shropshire Union Railway and Canal
Company for the time being.

£1-17-9   On Offices, Warehouses & shed all communicating
on the North side of the Yard at the Crane in said

L'day 1856 City of Chester, in tenure of Joseph Williams,
Oil Merchant & Grease Manufacturer, no tar

Bowers   nor tallow melted nor oil boiled therein,

Chester   but opposite to a building about 9 feet distant

D^y 10/9   in which Grease is made and there
are windows and a door in the wall facing the same,
brick & slated   10/6   [£]360

    Mem° In the above Oil, Tallow & Grease is stored,
          & in the upper story sails are made & in the
          shed firstly described, ship Carpenters'
          Work is allowed to be done & a stove with
          about 3 feet of pipe well secured and used

151/7   for warmth only, allowed therein

GLDH Ms12160/151 page 7

Endorsement

435   1858, Oct 2nd It is hereby allowed and agreed that
the manufacturer of Zinc is now only carried on
in the premises insured within.

The North Union Railway – Preston Station

Sun Fire Office

GLDH Ms 11937/446

7th May 1856

1796985	Emmeline Lambert of Preston in the County of Lancaster, bookseller.	
7/6	On her bookcases and fixtures on the platform	
L'day 1857	at the East side of the North Union Railway	
Jennings	Station at Preston aforesaid.	7
Preston	Stock and printed books & Newspapers therein only	43
Dy 4/6	Her bookcases & fixtures on the platform at the	
	West side of said Station	7
	Stock of printed books & newspapers therein only	43
1699567 Cd	Stock, utensils & fixtures, viz:–	
	In her storeroom on the West side of said Station	20
	And in her newspaper folding room near	30
		£150

The Bristol and Exeter Railway
Taunton, Tiverton and Exeter Stations

Sun Fire Office

GLDH Ms 11937/491

25th November 1859

1908757	The Directors for the time being of the Bristol & Exeter Railway Company at Bristol		
£10-0-9	On the following at their Taunton Station, Taunton		
Mich. 1860	in Somerset,		
Barrow	Two buildings (used as Booking Offices		
Bristol	& waiting rooms) detached from each other		
Dy £7-10	& marked A on plan. £566-10 in equal proportion	2/6	566-10
	Furniture therein only £24-10 in equal proportion	"	24-10
	Stores & utensils (not machinery) therein £24-10 in equal proportion	"	24-10
	Two carriage sheds adjoining to the above but not		
Somerset	communicating therewith, a brick wall between		
	marked B on the said plan, timber & tiled. £123		
	in equal proportion	5/-	123
	Goods shed & offices communicating & cranes		
	belonging thereto marked C on said plan	"	200
	Two platforms extending through the buildings		
	aforesaid not adjoining each other, with the		
	water cranes therein £61-10 in equal proportion	2/6	61-10
	The following at their Tiverton Station, Tiverton		
	in Devon.		

Building used as a booking office & waiting rooms with sheds adjoining & described on said plan, stone, timber & tiled & marked *A* on said plan	4/6	301-10
Furniture & stores (not machinery) therein only	"	32
Goods shed with cranes belonging thereto timber & tiled & marked *B* on said plan	5/-	119
Two platforms & water cranes belonging to the first above named, stone, timber & tiled & marked *A* on said plan £47-10 in equal proportions	4/6	47-10
The following at their Exeter Station, Exeter in Devon.		
Two buildings used as Booking Offices & waiting rooms marked *A* on plan. £750 on each	2/6	1500
Furniture in each of said buildings. £175 in equal proportion	"	175
Shed marked *B* on said plan, large engine shed with fitting shop adjoining, stone, timber & tiled	7/6	250
Coke therein only	"	200
Three buildings marked *C* on said plan, timber & tiled £200 on each	5/-	600
Shed marked *D* on said plan being engine shed, timber & tiled	7/6	75
Building marked *E* on said plan used as a goods shed, stone, timber & tiled	5/-	625
Two platforms belonging to the passengers station marked *F* on said plan £75 in equal proportion	2/6	75
		£5000

All brick, stone & tiled, except as named

N.B.	No workshop allowed within said buildings or communicating therewith or so near thereto as to endanger them in the event of a fire
Mem.	Similar sums being insured in the aforesaid property in the West of England Fire Office the same is hereby allowed.

Entered 24 Nov. 1859
Jos. Richardson

Note: The plan referred in this policy does not survive.

The Bristol and Exeter Railway – Bristol Station

Sun Fire Office

GLDH Ms 11937/489

16th March 1860

1920501	The Directors for the time being of the Bristol and Exeter Railway Company.		
£12-4-6	On the building of their Bristol Station		
Xmas 1860	comprising Booking Offices, Waiting Rooms,		
Barrow	Storerooms, Sheds and Platforms all under one		
Bristol	roof or communicating, situate at Temple Gate,		
Dy £5-8	Bristol, built of stone or wood and covered with slate and marked *No.1* on the plan deposited in this Office	7/6	1500
	Stock, fixtures, utensils and stores in their Storehouse & Steam Engine House all under one roof, brick or stone & tiled or slated & marked *No.4* on said plan	10/6	1500
1887403	Building of a Carpenters' shop under the		
Can[d]	same roof with the last above named, no pitch nor tar heated nor stove therein.	"	150
	New Goods shed, & Excursion Platform near marked *No.5* on said plan	5/-	800
	Cranes & other lifting machinery & utensils therein only	"	200
	Furniture in the Company's new Offices all communicating near, stone & slated & marked *No.3* on said plan	1/6	250
	Coke shed near built of wood & marked *No.6* on said plan	5/-	200
			£4600

N.B.	No workshop allowed within said buildings or communicating except otherwise described.
Mem	In the Buildings described by the 2nd item aforesaid there is a Steam Engine, seven carpenters' benches & seven workers in wood.
Mem[d]	Like sums in like manner being Insured on the within mentioned property in the West of England Fire Office the same is hereby allowed.

Entered 16th March 1860

W Dickens

Note: The plan referred to in this policy does not survive.

The West Somerset Railway

Sun Fire Office

GLDH Ms 11937/518

7th May 1862

1988681	The Managers for the time being of the West Somerset Railway Company		
£1-7-0	On Four houses adjoining at Watchet in Somerset,		
L'day 1863	in tenure of J. Strickland & others, of no hazardous		
Easton	trade stone & slated		
Taunton	£450 on each	1/6	[£]1800
D'£2-14			
Som'			

The Llanelly Railway and Dock Company
Stations at Llandovery, Lampeter, Llangadock and Glanrhyd

Sun Fire Office

GLDH Ms 11937/526

1st May 1863

2016865	The Llanelly Railway and Dock Company		
	On the following buildings & contents belonging		
£3-12-9	to the said Llanelly Railway and Dock Company.		
L'day 1864	On the building of the Station & House under		
Griffiths	one roof at Llandovery, Wales. Stone & slated	2/-	451 -19 - 7
Swansea	Warehouse only near stone & slated	4/6	301 - 6 - 4
D' £3	Stock and utensils therein only	"	150 -13 - 2
	Coke shed only near, timber built	4/6	30 - 2 - 8
	Carriage shed only, near, timber & iron roof	"	135 -11 -10
	Guards box near, timber built	"	18 16 - 8
301152	Two Weighbridge houses near, stone & slated		
L'pool &	£37-13-4 in equal proportion	2/-	37 -13 - 4
London F.O.	Warehouse only Lampeter Road Station, in the		
	parish of [*blank*] stone & slated	4/6	188 - 6 - 6
	Stock and utensils therein	"	7 - 6 - 7
	Passengers station including fittings therein, near, timber & zinc roof	3/-	112 -19 -10
	Weighbridge house only, near, timber built	4/6	15 - 1 - 4
	Warehouse only at Llangadock Station, stone & slated	4/6	188 - 6 - 6
	Stock & utensils therein only	"	75 - 6 - 7
	Passengers station including fittings therein, near, timber & zinc roof	3/-	112 -19 -10
	Weighbridge house only, near, timber built	4/6	15 - 1 - 4
	Station only at Glanrhyd, stone & slated	2/-	90 - 7 -11
			£2000 - 0 - 0

160

Sun Fire Office Policy dated 3 June 1812
Messrs Hawker and Sons of Plymouth

Chapter 11

Policy Registers: Ships

Royal Exchange Assurance

GLDH Ms 7252/2

2nd August 1755

31101 Capt. John Grant of North Shields in the Co. of
       Northumberland, owner
       On a ship called the *John & Elizabeth* burthen
       about 180 tons the said John Grant Commr now
       lying at Pelican Stairs in the River of Thames or
       any part of the said River as low as Gravesend
       with Liberty to Dock   £600

£1 - 4 - 0
——7 - 6
£1-11 -6   The Policy to Mr James Mangles, Wapping
            New Stairs

Royal Exchange Assurance

GLDH Ms 7253/66

16th December 1811

264430 Benjamin Gowland of Whitby Co. York
        On his Brigantine called *Lady Mineli*
        [blank] Commander burthen about [blank] tonnes
        while lying in Whitby Harbour, Co. afsd or in
14/6   any Port or Harbour in Great Britain with
Whitby liberty to Dock.   £400

Sun Fire Office

GLDH Ms 11937/99

3rd June 1812

870979 Mess Hawker and Sons of Plymouth in Devon,
Merchants and Agents for the Captors. On the
cargo of the American Ship *General Gates* master*
1812 detained by his Majesties ships *Belle, Poule, Dryad,*
Pridham & *Abercrombie*, now on board the said ship lying
D^y £6-11-3 at the Rock Tier [*sic*] in the Harbour of Catwater,
within the Port of Plymouth, or in all or any of the
Warehouses in the said Port, five thousand pounds   £5000

Memorandum £15000 being Insured on the
within mentioned property viz. £10,000 in the
Phoenix Fire Office is hereby &c.

Entered in the Office Books
3 June 1812
T J Sterry

* It is not clear if the ship is called 'General' or 'General Gates' or whether the master is called Gates.

Royal Exchange Assurance

GLDH Ms 7353/81

24th September 1821   On forty three Fishing Vessels,
327297   their names whose property
Thomas Harris of Fisher Street, they are and Tonnage of the same
Barking, Co. of Essex as Treasurer more particularly described on the to
the Fishing Society held   back hereof, not exceeding £50 on
at the Sign of the *George*   the Hull of each Vessell and £50 on in
Barking afs^d   the stores , tackle, Cabin Furniture
3/-   6 - 9 - 0   and Wearing Apparel on Board each
dy   6 - 9 - 0   of the same, while the said Vessels are
       £12-18 - 0   lying in the Creek at Creeks
                              Mouth in Barking afs^d or in any Port
                              or Harbour in Great Britain with
                              liberty to dock   £4300

	Owners Names	Vessels Names	Tonnage
Rend [renewed] from No 321200	Jonathan Ling	*Sea Adventurer*	50
	John Brown	*Reliance*	50
	do	*Fortitude*	50
	do	*Traverse*	50
	John Harris	*Mary Ann*	50
	do	*Blossom*	50
	James Laby	*Laby*	47
	do	*Ditchburn*	50

Henry Shellitoe	*Ceres*	50
do	*Flora*	48
Edward Smith	*Ann*	50
do	*Hercules*	54
Scrymgcour Hewitt	*Flemming*	50
do	*Fyfeshire*	54
do	*Liberty*	38
Thomas Whennell	*Brothers*	53
Charles Baxter	*Rising Sun*	55
William Gardner	*Hebe*	50
do	*Olive Branch*	50
Benjamin Hagar	*Good Heart*	48
J Knowles	*William &* *Thomas*	47
Joseph Reed	*Maria*	49
James Harris	*Dove*	40
do	*Ebenezer*	47
Thomas Harris	*Pacific*	50
do	*Providence*	47
Sarah Bowers	*Fortune*	50
J. Chalk	*Minerva*	46
H. Thredder	*Tabez*	48
Robert Mullet	*Ranger*	50
James Morgan	*Sociable*	50
Daniel Burchell	*Fanny*	36
James Davis	*Dependence*	50
J. Topsom	*Lora Kenyon*	48
James Orsborn	*Experimental*	50
William Shellitoe	*Laurel*	50
Thomas Harris	*Hope*	50
William Reed	*Friends*	53
S. Hewitt	*Matchless*	54
Thomas Whennell	*Active*	54
Thomas Plows	*Choice*	54
William Gardner Jun[r]	*Alert*	54
Barking	Jacob Spashetti	*Prosperous*	56

Sun Fire Office

GLDH Ms 11937/157

12th December 1826

1052857	The Owners of the Steam Boat *St. George* for the time being on the said Steam Boat burden about
£3-15	310 tons with stores, tackle & furniture belonging
14th May 1827	on board now lying in the Port of Liverpool three thousand pounds

2/6   £3000

continued

Pole
D^y £2-5   N.B. The steam engine & boilers are not
6 mos [*months*]   included in this insurance. The boilers
                   are allowed to be heated once a month
                   only for the purpose of cleaning the
                   cylinders & engine but not for any other
                   purpose.

                   Mem^{dum} This office is not to be answerable
                        for any loss or damage that may
                        happen by explosion or in
                        consequence thereof

Sun Fire Office

GLDH Ms 11937/162
                          15th August 1827
1064525   John Featherstone of Hull, shipowner
Bolton   On his ship *John Bainbridge* Irving master,
£1-5   Burthen about 365 tons with stores tackle &
6 Aug 1828   furniture belonging either on board or on
D^y £1-10   shore or in any Port, Harbour or Dock in
                   Gt Britain or Ireland   2/6   £1000

Sun Fire Office

GLDH Ms 11937/167
                          14th May 1828
1077384   Charles Pole of Liverpool, Esq.
                   On the Steam Packet *Restauraden Lusitatno*
15/-   burden about 173 tons Lourenco Germack
30 July 1828   Passodo commander, with stores tackle &
Pole   furniture belonging (including the steam
D^y 2/3   engine and boilers) now lying in the Port of
3 mo^s Liverpool, three hundred pounds   [£]300

                   N.B Leave to be given to repair the vessel &
                        steam engine & to put on board new boilers
                        which are included in this insurance & also
                        to heat the new boilers to dry them & the
                        steam engine after repairing it but not
                        more than twice.

                   Mem^{dum} This Office is not to be answereable
                        for any loss or damage that may happen by
                        explosion or in consequence thereof.

Sun Fire Office

GLDH Ms 11937/271

	9th February 1841		
1346771	The Directors of the Great Western		
	Steam Ship Company for the time being		
£17-10	On the *Great Western* Steam Ship including		
15 March 1841	the stores, tackle, furniture, Engines and		
Barrow	Boilers on board belonging now lying in the		
Bristol	Port of Bristol	3/6	£10,000

D^y £1-17   Mem. £10,000 being insured on the within
mentioned property in the Bristol
Union Fire Office, the same is
hereby allowed.

Ent^d 8 Feb 1841

Sun Fire Office

GLDH Ms 11937/519

	11th November 1862		
2002000	Horatio Nelson Ley & Captain Sherard		
	Osborne CB as Agent for the Emperor of		
£25	China & John White of Medina Docks,		
5 May 1863	West Cowes, Hants, Ship Builder		
Dear	On a steam ship of about 1000 tons		
Cowes	(with materials for finishing the same)		
6 months	either on board or in the yard undermen-		
SHIP	tioned now building on the Slip nearest		
	the Steam Saw Mills in Medina Yard, West		
	Cowes aforesaid.	5/-	£10,000

Memo: Said steam Ship when launched
is allowed to dock & undock, get
up steam occasionally & run her
trial trip, also if it is required to
facilitate the work the gas is allowed
to be lead into her.

Chapter 12

Policy Registers: Policies Linking two or more Places in Great Britain, the Channel Islands and Ireland

Liverpool, Newry, Belfast, Dundalk and Dublin

Royal Exchange Assurance

GLDH Ms 7152/4

Aug 19th 1756

32275   Dan¹ McNeal of Liverpool, Hen. Courtney
of Newry, Revᵈ Jaˢ Hamilton Clewlow of
Belfast, Rev. Jnᵒ Skelton & Nich. Ekson of
Dundalk, Edwᵈ Noy, Wᵐ Richardson &
Percival & Jnᵒ Hunt of Dublin
On their new Sugar House & warehouses
adjoining, warranted to be brick built &
tyled or slated and likewise warranted to
have arch'd Stoves & Iron Doors, situated

Return £17.7.6   at Dundalk in the Kingdom of Ireland
for 11 months   £1400
1 week 6 days
expired Time on   Renewed from 32249
No. 32249   To Mr Champion in St Martins Lane

Storgursey, Somersetshire and Andover, Hampshire

Sun Fire Office

GLDH Ms 11936/326

12th March 1785

502322   William Poole of *Shurton Court*, in the
Parish of Stogursey, in the County of Somerset.

£1-1-0   On his Household Goods in the dwelling house
L'day 1786   only of the *White Hart* , situated in the Town
£1-1-10   of Andover in Hants in the tenure of
Jones W   George Score, Innholder. Stone & tiled,
                  not exceeding six hundred and forty pounds   640
                  On his Plate therein only, not exceeding
                  sixty pounds   60
                                                                   £700
                                                                   Duty
                                                                   10/6

London, and Milverton, Somersetshire

Sun Fire Office

GLDH Ms 11936/365
                        21ˢᵗ October 1789
562193   Edith Norrish of the City of London, widow.
                  On a House called the *New Inn*, Brewhouse,
10/-   Stable and Linneys all adjoining in the tenure
Mich. 1790   of William Webber, Innholder, not exceeding
Jones   one hundred pounds.   100
                  Two houses adjoining in the tenure of
                  Rᵈ Roberts & others, not exceeding one
                  hundred pounds   100
                  All Tiled & Thatched & situate at Milverton   [£]200
                  in the County of Somerset.   Duty
                                                                    3/-

Padstow, Cornwall and Southwark, Surrey

Sun Fire Office

GLDH Ms 11936/364
                        11ᵗʰ November 1789
563067   William Sheppard of Padstow in Cornwall,
                  sergemaker
18s   On his utensils, stock & goods in trust, or
Xmas 1790   on Commission in warehouses in one
£1-0-3   Building at Toppings Wharf, Tooley Street,
                  in the Borough of Southwark. Brick &
                  Timber, not exceeding six hundred
                  pounds   [£]600
                                                                    Duty
                                                                    9s
                                                                    10/1

Bath and Taunton, Somersetshire; Thatcham, Berkshire and Hungerford, Wiltshire

Royal Exchange Assurance

GLDH Ms 7253/53

		30th Aug. 1805	

30th Aug. 1805

217581 Geo. Hare of Taunton, Som^t, coachmaster
On Ut^s & Trade in a Stable & corn loft sit. in
15-0 Milk Street, Bath £300
1-6 On Ut^s & Trade in a stable sit. at the *Crown*
16-6 *Inn*, Thatcham in Berks £100
duty 13-9 On Ut^s & Trade in a stable sit. at the *John of*
£1-10-3 *Gaunt Inn* at Hungerford, Wilts £100
£500

Taunton   All brick or Stone & Tiled

Stogumber, Taunton and Wilton, Somersetshire and Exeter, Devonshire

Sun Fire Office

GLDH Ms 11937/137

22nd January 1822

988433 The Revd John White of Stogumber in Somerset
and Samuel White Esqr of Exeter, Exors in trust.

£10-12-6	On cellar and chambers over behind the dwelling			
Xmas 1822	house of Wm Turle at Taunton Somerset, grocer,			
Jones W.	four hundred pounds	2/-	400	
Dy £10-13	Stock & utensils not hazardous therein only,			
	two hundred pounds	"	200	
	Malthouse only adjoining but not communicating,			
	a brick wall between, not used as such,			
	five hundred pounds	"	500	
	Brewhouse & cellars not used as such all			
	adjoining near, eight hundred pounds	"	800	
	Stock & utensils not hazardous therein only,			
	one hundred pounds	"	100	
	House, *The George Inn*, and offices all			
	adjoining near in tenure of Wm Wood,			
	Innholder, twelve hundred pounds	3/-	1200	
	Stables & rooms over all adjoining in a Court			
	behind, two hundred pounds	"	200	
	House and Bakehouse (oven included) adjoining			
	near now or late in tenure of Priscilla Body, baker,			
	five hundred pounds	"	500	
	House, Brewhouse, Cellars & Stable all adjoining			

behind near, *The Spread Eagle Inn*, in North street near, now or late in tenure of James Barker, Innholder. Timber, Plaster & tiled, six hundred pounds	5/-	600
Two cellars behind near in equal proportion, one hundred pounds	2/-	100
House & Shop adjoining & to *The Spread Eagle Inn* but not communicating, a brick wall between, in tenure of Rew, plaster & tiled, three hundred and fifty pounds	3/-	350
Three Cottages behind near in tenure of John Wake and others, private, plaster & tiled, fifty pounds on each	"	150
House, Brewhouse, Cellars, stable, Ciderhouse, Lofts over and Slaughter House, all adjoining at Wilton in Somerset, now or late in tenure of Wm Knight, butcher. Stone, Cob & tiled, four hundred pounds	2/-	400
Twelve Cottages near called *Turkey Court* in tenure of Saml Bidgood & others, thatched, in equal proportion, eight hundred pounds	5/-	800
House and Offices all adjoining in High Street, Taunton in Somerset in tenure of Jno Hawkins, private, two hundred & fifty pounds	2/-	250
House, Cellars & Offices *The New Angel Inn*, all adjoining the corner of High Street near, now or late in tenure of Wm Clarke, Innholder, four hundred pounds	3/-	400
Brewhouse and Stable adjoining near, fifty pounds	3/-	50
House only at Shuttern near, now or late in tenure of Thos Burrough, private, one hundred pounds	2/-	100
All brick & Slated as aforesaid and no hazardous trade unless mentioned.		£7100

NB This policy is hereby declared void in
   case the aforesaid Malthouse &
   Brewhouse be used as such.

Henley-on-Thames, Oxfordshire and Liverpool

Sun Fire Office

GLDH Ms 11937/157

12ᵗʰ December 1826

1052856	The Revᵈ John Owen Parr of Ravenham near Henley on Thames in Oxon
£2-8	On his warehouse only on the east side of
Michs 1827	John Street, Liverpool, in tenure of Willis &
Pole	Vaughan in plurality of tenure, hazardous goods
Dʸ £1-14	but not hazardous trade therein, brick & slated,
	eight hundred pounds 6/- [£]800

St Helier, Jersey and Plymouth, Devonshire

Royal Exchange Assurance

GLDH Ms 7253/95

7ᵗʰ February 1828

372179	Benjamin Hooper of St. Helier in the Island of Jersey, gent Plymouth	On a House & Offices adjg No.2, Stone & Slated in Regent Place in Plymouth in the County of Devon in the occupation of Mrs Gordon
	1/6 6s	
	dy 12s	
	——— 18s	
		1/6 [£]400

London , and Hemyock, Devonshire

Sun Fire Office

GLDH Ms 11937/193

20ᵗʰ June 1832

1142275	Edward Manfield Junʳ of St. Mary Woolnoth, London, gent	
5/-	On two cottages adjoining at Hemyock in	
Mids 1833	Devon in tenure of Edᵈ Manfield Senʳ and	
Wellington	Jas. Goff, private, thatched, eighty pounds	£80
Dʸ 3/-	Blacksmith's shop only, opposite near, thatched	
	Twenty pounds	£20
		——— £100

Langley Park, Buckinghamshire and Crowcombe, Somersetshire

Royal Exchange Assurance

GLDH Ms 7253/97

7th May 1833

412075

200 2/6	5-0	Robert Harvey of Langley Park, Co.			
500 4/6	1-2-6	Buckingham, Esq.			
	1-7-6	On a Farmhouse, Brewhouse, cellars,			
		Pumphouse and Stable, all adjᵍ	200	4/6	
duty	1-1-0	On a large Barn, grannary, two waggon			
	£2-8-6	houses and Linhays all adjᵍ about 20			
Taunton		yards from the above	80	2/6	

200 2/6   5-0   Robert Harvey of Langley Park, Co.
500 4/6   1-2-6   Buckingham, Esq.
             1-7-6   On a Farmhouse, Brewhouse, cellars,
                      Pumphouse and Stable, all adjᵍ   200   4/6
duty   1-1-0   On a large Barn, grannary, two waggon
            £2-8-6   houses and Linhays all adjᵍ about 20
Taunton   yards from the above   80   2/6
                      On the lower ox Linhays and Pigsties
                      adjᵍ each other and the Brook near.   20   "
                      The above are occupied by Chas.
                      Newton and called *Lawford Farm*.
                      On a Newbuilt House with the Old
                      Farm House, Cellars, Milkhouse,
                      Brewhouse and Washouse all adjᵍ
                      & communicating called *Truscombe
                      Farm*, occupied by Moses Squibbs.   300   4/6
                      On the Barn, Ciderhouse & Long
                      Linhay all adjoining, detached,
                      belonging.   80   2/6
                      On a Stable & Linhay adjoining,
                      detached, near. All Stone & Cob and
                      Thatched except otherwise described.   20   "
                      All sitᵈ in the parish of Crowcombe,   £700
                      in County of Somerset.

Staines, Middlesex and Hockworthy, Devonshire

Sun Fire Office

GLDH Ms 11937/219

17th July 1835

1201780   The Rev. Robert Govett of Staines in Middlesex
           On house, malthouse (not used as such) & stable
Mich. 1836 all adjoining called *Bences*, situated at Hockworthy
Tiverton   in Devon in tenure of Elizabeth Gamlen, one
Dʸ 6/-   hundred pounds   100
           Barn & out buildings all adjoining, new,
           one hundred pounds   100
           All thatched   £200

           N.B. This policy is hereby declared void if
                  said malthouse is used as such

Old Brentford, Middlesex and Strowbrook [Shobrooke?] Devonshire

Sun Fire Office

GLDH Ms 11937/233

23rd February 1837

1246632	Thomas Berry Rowe and Laurence Rowe of Old Brentford in Middlesex, soap and alkali Manufacturers.		
£42-1-9	On their now dwelling house only situate as		
Xmas 1837	aforesaid marked *A* on a Plan deposited in this		
Cridland	Office, brick & tiled, twelve hundred pounds	1/6	1200
Brentford	Household goods, wearing apparel, printed books		
D^y £24-9	& plate therein only, twelve hundred pounds	"	1200
	China & glass therein only, one hundred pounds	4/6	100

Soaphouse, counting house, warehouse & chaisehouse all communicating near, marked *B* on said plan, brick timber & tiled, two thousand five hundred pounds — 5/- — 2500

Stock & utensils therein only, five thousand five hundred pounds — " — 5500

Alkali Manufactory all under one roof, near, marked *H* brick, timber & tiled, two thousand pounds — 10/6 — 2000

Steam engine therein only, two hundred pounds — " — 200

Mem: There are four furnaces, four coke ovens, two crystallizing coppers & steam boiler for boiling Palm Oil by steam only in said Alkali Manufactory, but they are not included in this Insurance.

Melting house only *C* adjoining *H* aforesaid, but not communicating therewith, a brick wall between, brick & tiled, one hundred pounds — 7/6 — 100

Stock & utensils therein only, one hundred pounds — " — 100

Laboratory & warehouse *I* and *K* communicating near, brick, timber & tiled, one hundred pounds — 10/6 — 3100

Stock & Utensils therein only, three hundred pounds — " — 300

Carthouse & Stable in one building *D* including the loft over, brick, timber & tiled, one hundred & fifty pounds — 3/- — 150

Stock & Utensils, live stock included therein only, two hundred pounds — 5/- — 200

Nagstable *E* with Granary over, near, brick, timber & tiled, one hundred pounds — 3/- — 100

Stock & Utensils, live stock included therein only, two hundred & fifty pounds — 5/- — 250

Warehouses & Carpenters Shop in one building

near, marked *G*, no pitch nor tar heated nor stove therein, brick, timber & tiled, four hundred pounds	6/-	400
Stock & Utensils therein only, two hundred pounds	6/-	200
House, cellar, loft & offices all adjoining at Strowbrook [*sic*] in Devon, called *Rew Farm*, in tenure of [*blank*] thatched, five hundred & fifty pounds	4/6	550
Two Stables, Gateway, Sheep pen, Loft & Barn all adjoining near, thatched, one hundred & twenty pounds	3/-	120
Poundhouse (pound engine & mill therein included) Cellar & lofts over, all adjoining, near, thatched, one hundred pounds	"	100
Linhey & Shippen & lofts over, all adjoining, near, thatched, thirty pounds	"	30
Barn only in the Court, near, thatched, fifty pounds	"	50
Linhey with loft over, near, thirty pounds	"	30
Cellar with loft over in the Orchard, near, thatched, twenty pounds	"	20
Four Cottages at Brentford in Middlesex in private tenure, brick & tiled, fifty pounds on each	1/6	200
Five cottages near, brick & tiled, three hundred pounds in equal proportions	"	300
Stationhouse only, near, in tenure of the Police, brick & tiled, three hundred pounds	"	300
		£16300

120/365

GLDH Ms 12160/120 page 365

Endorsement
May 27ᵗʰ 1850

policy number
1246632
Thomas Berry
Rowe, Esq

Mem. A Brick & tiled room having been added to the Building marked B on the plan deposited in the office the same is allowed to be included in the amount covered by the 4ᵗʰ Specification hereof. The said Room is heated by Two Stoves on the outside with 60 feet of pipe well secured & is used for drying soap. In consequence of the above addition to a risk already under rated 1/- p cent beyond the present charge is required on the amount covered by the 4ᵗʰ & 5ᵗʰ Specifications of the Policy thereby making the future Annual premium £46.1.9 & the receipt of 5/- is hereby acknowledged as the proportion of the additional premium for the unexpired currency of the Policy. The above is a copy of an Endorsement directed to be made by John Richards Esqʳ Secretary to the Sun Fire Office by his letter dated 5ᵗʰ December 1849 & the receipt of £2-10-0 this day in addition to 15/- and £1-10-0 paid before is hereby acknowledged

Wᵐ Henry Sanders, agent
Brentford

Note: The plan referred to in this policy does not survive.

London and Bristol

Sun Fire Office

GLDH Ms 11937/279

12th April 1842

1380177	Capt. David Chambers of London. RN.	
6/-	On a house & shop communicating at Stokes	
L'day 1843	Croft, Bristol in tenure of Biggs, a baker, no	
Barrow	oven therein, brick, stone and tiled	£400
Bristol		
D[y] 12/-		
Somerset		

Overne Hill, Gloucestershire; and Wimborne and Haselbury Bryan, Dorsetshire

Sun Fire Office

GLDH Ms 11937/286

17th October 1842

1396421	Sophia Cox & others of Overne Hill in the County of Gloster.		
9/-	On a farmhouse only situate on *Beare Barn*		
Mich. 1843	*Farm* near Wimbourne in the county of		
Roe	Dorset in tenure of Edward Elliott, brick & tiled.	1/6	100
Blandford	Barn only adjoining but not communicating,		
D[y] 9/-	brick & tiled	2/-	50
	Farm house only at Hazlebury Briant, near, in tenure of Widow Upshall, thatched, standing alone.	5/-	100
	Barn, stable & Cowhouse all adjoining near thatched	3/-	50
			£300

Lynn, Norfolk, Oathill, Sussex and Wyke Regis, Dorsetshire

Sun Fire Office

GLDH Ms 11937/491

31st August 1860

1931739	Harriett Hawkins of Lynn in Norfolk, and Emily Jane Bent of Oathill in Sussex, gent[wm]		
8/3	On four cottages at Wyke Regis near Weymouth		
Mich. 1861	in Dorset, private, brick & slated £50 on each	1/6	200
9/7	Cottage only adjoining but not communicating		
Hancock	therewith, a brick wall carried thro' the roof		
Weymouth	between, thatched but not in a row with other		
D[y] 8/8	thatched buildings	10/6	50
Dorset			£250

St Columb, Cornwall and Outwell, Norfolk

Sun Fire Office

GLDH Ms 11937/515

5th February 1862

1979741	Elizabeth Schultz of St Columb, Cornwall, spinster. On a dwelling house only at Outwell in Norfolk,		
£1-1-6	brick and tiled, in tenure of Andrews, private.	1/6	200
Xmas 1862	Three tenements all adjoining near thatched,	5/-	300
Goward	private.		
Wisbech	Blacksmith's Shop adjoining but not		
D[y] 18/9	communicating, a brick wall carried through the Roof between, brick & tiled	5/-	30
	Two tenements adjoining near brick & tiled, private, £75 in equal proportion	1/6	75
	Stable & Outhouse adjoining near brick & tiled	3/-	20
			£625

Manchester and Wellington, Somersetshire

Sun Fire Office

GLDH Ms 11937/516

30th October 1862

2001623	Joseph John Pyne of No. 63 Piccadilly, Manchester, Chemist		
15/6	On a Farmhouse and offices all communicating		
Mich 1863	called *Cades Farm* Wellington, Somerset, in		
Horsey	tenure of William Pring	1/6	300
Wellington	Barn poundhouse and Waggon House all		
D^y 18/-	adjoining, near	3/-	100
Somerset	Long linhay with lofts over all adjoining, near	"	75
Farm	Stable and linhay adjoining, near	"	25
Outbgs	Linhay with loft over, near, thatched	5/-	100
			£600

All brick stone and tiled except as named

Chapter 13

Policy Registers: Policies Linking Places in Great Britain and Ireland with Places Abroad

Southampton and Calcutta

Sun Fire Office

GLDH Ms 11936/356

25th September 1788

548470	Thomas Calvert of Calcutta in Bengal, Esq.
	On his House only situate above Bar in the
£2-7-6	parish of All Saints, in the Town County of
Mich[s] 1789	Southampton, in the tenure of Sir Yelverton
Dated 29th	Peyton, Bart. Brick & tiled not exceeding
Guillaume	Fifteen Hundred Pounds

Fifteen Hundred Pounds   1500
Household Goods therein, only, not exceeding
Five hundred pounds   500
                                                          £2000
                                                          Duty
                                                          £1-10-0

Exeter, Devonshire and Philadelphia, America

Sun Fire Office

GLDH Ms 11937/20

11th October 1797

671330	John Carpenter of Philadelphia in America, currier
	On his house only in two tenements in Guinea,
4/6	Street in the City of Exeter, in the tenure of Anstis,
Mich. 1798	whitesmith & Williams, hair dresser. Brick, plaister
Webber	& slated, not exceeding one hundred & fifty pounds [£]150

                                                          D[y] 3/-

Stoke Fleming, Devonshire and Oporto, Porgugal

Sun Fire Office

GLDH Ms 11937/20

20th October 1797

671567   Dixon Nicholas Land of Oporto in Portugal, merchant.
            On his House & Offices adjoining at Stoke Fleming
6/-   in Devon late in tenure of J. Teague, stone & slated,
Mich. 1798 not exceeding two hundred and fifty pounds   250
Oxenham   Stable adjoining, stone and slated, not exceeding
            fifty pounds   50
                                                                          £300
                                                                        Dy 6/-

Edinburgh and Jamaica

Sun Fire Office

GLDH Ms 11937/107

7th June 1814

896169   William James of Jamaica, Esq.
            On his household goods, wearing apparel,
7/6   printed books & plate in a house only, head
Mich. 1815 of Pleasance [*sic*] opposite crosscauseway, Edinburgh,
Dy 8/9   private, two hundred & fifty pounds   250
Allen E.   China & glass therein, fifty pounds   50
                                                                          £300

            All stone & slated

Culmstock, Devonshire and Jamaica

Sun Fire Office

GLDH Ms 11937/284

5th August 1842

1390862   James H Wood of the Island of Jamaica,
            Dissenting Minister.
            On House and Offices all adjoining at
£1-2-6   Nicholson, in the parish of Culmstock in Devon,
Mich.1843   in private tenure, thatched & standing alone   7/6   220
£1-7   Stable, Gighouse and Hogstye all adjoining,
Horsey   near, thatched   40
Wellington Cottage only adjoining in private tenure,
Dy 10/10   thatched   40
Devon   £300

Wellington, Somersetshire and Rathcormac, County Cork, Ireland

Sun Fire Office

GLDH Ms 11937/485

6th October 1859

1903796	Sarah Land of Rachcormac in the county of Cork, Ireland, widow. On five cottages called	
£1-2-6	*Colburns*, Wellington, Somerset, in private	
Mich. 1860	tenure, thatched and not adjoining other	
Horsey	thatched buildings, £150 in equal proportion	£150
Wellington		
D^y 4/6		

Limerick, Ireland and Rome, Italy

Sun Fire Office

GLDH Ms 11937/520

11th November 1862

2003091	Isabella Sherlock at present residing at Rome, widow. On two houses adjoining, situate at Brunswick Street,		
£1-18-0	city of Limerick, one partly occupied as a spirit shop		
Xmas 1863	& the other let in tenements. £100 on each	3/-	200
£2-6-7	Corn store only adjoining the ground floor, used by		
Murphy	O'Neill as storage for his coach factory	3/-	100
Limerick	Two dwelling houses adjoining to the last		
Irish	named fronting Brunswick Street aforesaid,		
	the under part or ground floor used as other rooms		
	by said O'Neill. £150 on each.	3/-	300
	Stores, workshop & other offices, all adjoining,		
	behind the above, occupied by said O'Neill as a		
	Coach Factory or his undertenants (no artificial		
	heat used therein). £400	5/-	400
			£1000

Chapter 14

Policy Registers: Some well known Companies and Famous People

Sir Christopher Wren, Architect

Sun Fire Office

GLDH Ms 11936/12

6th Decembr 1720

20324   Sr Christopher Wren in St James's Street Knt for his House only
at Hampton Court in the Co. Middx, in his own Tenure

£60

Memdum Sr Christophen Wren Knt above mentioned
being deceased the sole Interest of this Policy is now to

7/-   Christopher Wren Esqr his son, now resident in the said
house above mentioned.
Enterd 19th April 1723

See Ind No 6 Page 251

20325   Sir Christopher Wren as before for his goods in his above said
7/-   Dwelling House only, not Elsewhere.
£60

Memdum Sr Christopher Wren Knt above mentioned being
deceased, the sole Interest of this Policy is now to
Christopher Wren Esqr his son, now resident in the said
house above mentioned.
Enterd 19th April 1723

See Ind. No 6 Page 251

GLDH Ms 12160/6 page 251

Endorsement
23rd August 1748

20324   Chrisr Wren, Middx, now Stephen Wren Esqr, of the
20325   same place, Son & heir of the said Christopher Wren Esqr,
12*345   deceased   7 Apl CZ

David Garrick, Actor Manager

Sun Fire Office

GLDH Ms 11936/89

26th Feby 1749

120177	David Garrick on the East Side of Southampton Street in the Parish of St. Paul Covent Gardens Esqr	
£1-2	On his Household Goods & Furniture in his now	
L'Day 1751	dwelling House only, Brick, situate as aforesaid,	
£1-3-10	not exceeding	600
	Six Hundred Pounds	
Quineo	On his Wearing apparel therein only,	
	not exceeding Two Hundred Pounds	200
		£800

Thomas Chippendale, Cabinet Maker

Sun Fire Office

GLDH Ms 11936/111

10th May 1755

146588	Thomas Chippendale of St Martins Lane in the Parish of St Martins in the Fields & James Rennie of [*blank*] Cabinet makers & upholsterers.	
£10-2-0	On the now dwelling house of the said	
Midsr 1756	Thomas Chippendale with a Warehouse	
£11-7	behind adjoining and communicating on the Right Hand side of the yard, situate aforesaid, not exceeding Nine Hundred Pounds	900
	Household Goods, Utensils, Stock & Goods in Trust therein, and under the said Warehouse & on the roof thereof, not exceeding Two Thousand five Hundred Pounds	2500
	Glass therein only, not Exceeding Two Hundred & Seventy pounds	270
	Wearing apparel in the dwelling house the Property of the said Thomas Chippendale, not exceeding Sixty pounds	60
	On their shop only on the Left hand Side of the said yard & separate from the aforesaid, not exceeding Two Hundred & Eighty pounds	280
	Utensils Stock & Goods in Trust therein only, not Exceeding Two Hundred and ninety Pounds	290

continued

Utensils Stock & Goods in trust in a House
on the Left hand Side of the Said yard &
Communicating with the above mentioned
Dwelling house, not exceeding

Three Hundred pounds	300
The buildings brick & timber	£4600

The Right Honourable William Pitt

Sun Fire Office

GLDH Ms 11936/113

Octr 1st 1755

148806

£2-10-0
Mich 1756
Allen

The Right Honble William Pitt of Whitehall Esqr.
On his new built House only Stone and Tiled, not
yet occupied, Situate in the Circus near Queens
Square in the Parish of Walcott within the Liberty
of the City of Bath, in the County of Somerset, not
exceeding Two Thousand pounds £2000

The Leiutenant Governor of North Carolina

Sun Fire Office

GLDH Ms 11936/154

27th June 1764

210087
£1
Mich^s 1771
£6-4

His Excellency Colonel William Tryon Leiutenant
Governor of North Carolina. On his Dwelling
House Stables & Coach house only, adjoining &
Communicating, situate in Upper Grosvenor Street,
brick built not exceeding One Thousand Pounds £1000

Josiah Wedgwood, Manufacturer of Earthenware

Sun Fire Office

GLDH Ms 11936/331

13th August 1785

508865

£7-10
Mich. 1786
£8-11-10

Josiah Wedgwood of Portland House in Greek
Street, Soho, manufacturer of earthenware.
On his utensils and stock in his now dwelling
house and warehouse communicating, situated
as aforesaid, brick, not exceeding three thousand
pounds £3000

Mem^{dum} Fifteen hundred pounds being insured
on the within mentioned utensils and   Duty
stock in the Royal Exchange Assurance   £2 - 5 - 0
Office is hereby allowed & agreed to.   £2 - 11 - 6

Ent^d 13 Aug. 1785 B.P.

47/330

48/372 & 388

GLDH Ms 12160/47 page 330

Endorsement
7th October 1795

508865   Josiah Wedgwood of Greek St, now Josiah Wedgwood
          The Son & Thos Byerty he being admitted into partnership
331

GLDH Ms 12160/48 page 372

Endorsement
12th January 1797

508865   Josiah Wedgwood, Greek Street, Soho. Removed
331   six hundred pounds on utensils & stock to a House
          Chapel in York Street, St James's Square. Brick
          where the same &c
JR

GLDH Ms 12160/48 page 388

Endorsement
15th February 1797

508865   Josiah Wedgwood & Co, Greek Street. Remov'd
          Fourteen hundred pounds, Utensils & Stock to a House &
331   Chapel communicating in York Street, St James's Square.
          Brick where the same continue &c   *JE*

Benjamin D'Israeli, grandfather of
Queen Victoria's Prime Minister

Sun Fire Office

GLDH Ms 11936/347

11th December 1787

528185   Benjamin D'Israeli of Little Winchester Street, merchant
£3-15   On his utensils, stock & goods in Trust or on Commission
Xmas 1788 (not hazardous) in Hands Warehouses in one building in
£2-18-1   Wormwood Street: brick   £3000
                                                             Duty
                                                             £2-5
                                                             £2-6-10

Richard Tattersall, Horse Dealer

Sun Fire Office

GLDH Ms 11936/349

8th January 1788

538984	Richard Tattersall of Grosvenor Place, Dealer in Horses.	
	On a brick and tiled House and Brewhouse adjoining at	
£5-7	Great New Barns near Ely in Cambridgeshire, in his own	
Xmas 1788	occupation: not exceeding two thousand pounds	2000
Griffin	Household Goods therein only, not exceeding one	
	thousand pounds	1000
	Barn and two stables near, thatched not exceeding	
	three hundred pounds	300
	Bullock House and Stables near, thatched,	
	not exceeding two hundred pounds	200
	Brick & tiled House at Little New Barns in his	
	own occupation, not exceeding six hundred pounds	600
		£4100
		Duty
		£3-1-6

John Debrett, Bookseller

Sun Fire Office

GLDH Ms 11936/349

23rd April 1788

543604	John Debrett, Opposite Burlington House, Piccadilly,	
	bookseller.	
£5-18-6	On his household Goods in his now Dwelling House	
L'day 1789	only. Brick. Situate as aforesaid, not exceeding two	
Griffin	hundred pounds	200
	Utensils & stock therein only not exceeding	
	two thousand five hundred pounds	2500
	Wearing apparel therein only, not exceeding	
	two hundred pounds	200
	Plate therein only, not exceeding	
	one hundred pounds	100
	Utensils and stock in a Shop behind Cooper's	
	a printer in Bow Street, Covent Garden.	
	Brick, not exceeding Fifteen hundred pounds	1500
	Utensils and stock in the Dwelling House.	
	Brick, of Nicholls a milkman in Printers	
	Court, Duke Street, St. James's. Brick,	
	not exceeding three hundred pounds	300
	41/343 [*This endorsement volume is missing*]	£4800
	47/66	Duty
		£3-12

GLDH Ms 12160/47 page 66

Endorsement
7th April 1794

543604	John Debrett , Piccadilly, rem^d [*removed*] his Utensils & Stock from Princes Court, Duke St to a private House
349	Brick n.50 Picadilly

Samuel Whitbread, Brewer

Royal Exchange Assurance

GLDH Ms 7252/4

32735	Samuel Whitbread of Chiswell Street, Brewer	
	On Household Furniture in his dwelling House,	
1757 Jany 12	brick built, situate next Door but one to White	
	Cross Street in Chiswell Street aforesaid	£800
	Wearing apparel	100
	Plate	100
	Surveyed X f21	£1000
	Ren^d from 26300	

Samuel Whitbread, Brewer

Sun Fire Office

GLDH Ms 11936/366

13th April 1790

568077	Samuel Whitbread of Chiswell Street, brewer	
	On his utenstils & stock viz:	
£23-2-6	In Maylings granary at Bankside, Southwark. Brick,	
L'day 1791	not exceeding six thousand pounds	6000
	In Winksworth Warehouses only, communicating in two stacks of Building, situate at Broken Wharf, Upper Thames Street. Brick, not exceeding two thousand five hundred pounds	2500
	In Tegons Warehouses only, in one Building at Pauls Wharf in said Street. Brick, not exceeding one thousand pounds	1000
	In Wilsons Warehouses only, at Dowgate Dock in said Street. Brick & Timber, not exceeding three thousand pounds	3000
	In Winksworths Warehouse in one Building in Gardners Lane, Upper Thames Street. Brick, not exceeding two thousand pounds	2000
		£14500
44/350		Duty
46/460		£10-17-6
48/442		

GLDH Ms 12160/44 page 350

Endorsement
23rd April 1793

568077   Samuel Whitbread, Bankside, Removed Six Thousand
            Pounds Utensils & Stock from Maylin's Granary to Hammand's,
366   Brick Granary at Bankside aforesaid where the same Continue &c

H

GLDH Ms 12160/46 page 460

Endorsement
13th May 1795

568077   Samuel Whitbread, Bankside. Removed the Six Thousand
            pounds, Utensils & Stock back again from Hammond's Granary to
            Maylin's Granary, Bankside where the same &c
366

JC

GLDH Ms 12160/48 page 442

Endorsement
12th April 1797

643911*	Saml Whitbread	Chiswell St	
402	do	White Lion St	
594589*	do	Chiswell St	now Saml Whitbread Esq.
384	do	Up^r Tha^s St	
585950*	do	Bankside	
378			
555063*			
359			
568077*			
366	Son of Saml Whitbread, Deceased		

* These are other policies for Samuel Whitbread not reproduced here.

Josiah Spode, Potter

Sun Fire Office

GLDH Ms 11936/365

15th Oct 1789

561856   Josiah Spode at N° 45 in Fore Street, Cripplegate.
            Dealer in China, Glass & Earthenware. On his
£6-17-6   household Goods in his now dwelling house, only,
Mich. 1790 situate as aforesaid. Brick, not exceeding

Two Hundred Pds	200
Utensils therein only, not exceeding	
Two hundred Pounds	200
Wearing Apparel therein, only, not exceeding,	
One hundred Pound	100
Stock therein, only, not exceeding Two Thousand	
Five Hundred Pounds	2500
	£3000
	Duty £2-5

William Grimaldi, Miniature Painter

Sun Fire Office

GLDH Ms 11936/373

	16th Feby 1791	
580046	W[m] Grimaldi at No 7 in King Street, St James's, Enamiel & Miniature Painter.	
17/6	On his household Goods in his dwelling House.	
L'day 1792	Brick, situate as aforesaid. Not exceeding	
19/4	three hundred & Eighty pounds	380
	Printed Books therein, only, not exceeding thirty pounds	30
	Pictures therein, Miniatures excepted, only	
Griffin	not exceeding one hundred & Eighty pds	180
	Utensils & Stock of Colours therein only, not exceeding Twenty Pounds	20
	Wearing Apparel therein, only, not exceeding One Hundred pounds	100
	Plate therein, only, not exceeding Forty pounds	40
	China & Glass therein, only, not exceeding Fifty pounds	50
		£800
47/280		Duty 12/-
		13/6

GLDH Ms 12160/47 page 280

Endorsement

580046	W[m] Grimaldi, King Street, St James's. R[d] [*returned*] to his dwelling
373	House Brick, N° 2 Albemarle St.

His Majesty King George the Third

Sun Fire Office

GLDH Ms11937/45

	20th Feb[y] 1802	
729528	The Right Hon[ble] The Lord Chief Baron and Barons	
£8-10-	of the Court of Exchequer of Scotland for the time	
L'day 1803	being for behoof of His Majesty King George the Third	
£9-7-8	On the Place of Holyrood House as p. Plan	
Allan E	lodged in this office viz.	
	On Ranges *No. 1 & 3* not exceeding sixteen Hundred fifty Pounds on each	3300
	And on Range *No. 2* not exceeding seventeen Hundred Pounds	1700
	Household Goods in Ranges *No. 2 & 3* not exceeding One Thousand Pounds	1000
	All stone & slated & leaded	£6000

Mem^{dm} £13,550 being Insured on the within mentioned   D^y £6
property in the following Manner Viz. £2000 on each   £6-12-0
Range *No. 1, 2 & 3* & £1550 on the Household Goods
in the Ranges *No 2 & 3* in the Royal Exchange Assurance
Office £1650 on each Range No. 1 & 3 & £1700 on
Range *No. 2* & £1000 on Household Goods in Ranges
No. 2 & 3 in the Edinburgh Friendly Fire Office &c

Enter'd 20th Feby 1802
TJS

Note: The plan referred to in this policy does not survive.

The Wife of Admiral Bligh

Sun Fire Office

GLDH Ms 11937/68

2nd May 1806

789604	The Trustees of Mrs Mary Bligh wife of Admiral Bligh and Margaret Golightly of [*blank*]	
£1-0	On a house & Offices only, adjoining, facing the	
Mids 1807	*Two Brewers* at Clapham in Surrey in tenure of	
£1-4-11	Mrs Marsden private. Brick & Tiled, not exceeding	900
P.G.	nine hundred pounds	
	Coachhouse & stable adjoining, near, timber &	
	tiled, not exceeding one hundred pounds	100
		£1000
	D^y	1-5
		1-9-8

Sarah Siddons, Actress

Sun Fire Office

GLDH Ms 11937/101

13th May 1813

882747	Sarah Siddons of Westborne Green, Paddington, gentlewoman.	
£4	On a house & Offices adjoining in above Bar	
L'day 1814	Street in the Town of Southampton, untenanted,	
D^y £5	brick & tiled.	
	Four thousand pounds	£4000

The Duke of Wellington

Sun Fire Office

GLDH Ms 11937/130

8th August 1820

969714   The Most Noble Arthur Duke of Wellington
            of Stratfield Saye in Hants.

£30-10-0   On his now dwelling house and offices all
Mich. 1820 adjoining situate as aforesaid. Three thousand
£34-18-11   pounds   2/-   3000
Dy £49-16-10 Household goods, wearing apparel, printed
            books and plate therein only, twenty three
            thousand pounds   2/-   23000
            China and Glass therein only, two thousand
            pounds   5/-   2000
            Stables, Coach House and Offices all adjoining,
            near, two thousand pounds   2/-   2000
                                                                      £30000

            All brick and tiled

Arthur Guinness & Sons & Co., Brewers

Sun Fire Office

GLDH Ms 11937/176

29th Apl 1829

1091456   Arthur Guinness & Sons & Co. of St James Gate,
            Dublin, Porter Brewers

£18-5-0   On their new dwelling house & Counting house (a
Lday 1830   stove therein for warming the place only) with malt
Pegg   store over, situate as aforesaid five hundred pounds   500
Irish   Household goods, wearing apparel, printed
            books, plate & office fixtures therein, only
            seventy five pounds   75
            Brewhouses, 2nd malt store, steam engine, house
            coolers, Tun Rooms, Old & new Vat houses with
            hop store over, porter store, cellars & vaults all
            communicating & adjoining the first mentioned
            buildings but not communicating therewith,
            except by a metal shoot from said malt store,
            fifteen hundred pounds   1500
            Steam engine & machinery thereto belonging
            therein only, two hundred pounds   200
            Fixed machinery, horse mill & fixed utensils
            therein only, seventeen hundred & fifty pounds   1750
                                                                  continued

Stock & moveable utensils therein only three thousand pounds		3000
Cooperage Offices, Cooperage & Carpenters sheds & workshop (no pitch nor tar heated therein) Coachhouses, workshops, outloft & Dormitory over stables, sawpit, all communicating on the opposite side of the yard near, one hundred & twenty five pounds		125
Stock & utensils including furniture of said Dormitory therein only, one hundred & twenty five pounds	5/-	125
		£7275

All brick stone & slated & no kiln nor corn mill nor
gasometer

Her Royal Highness the Princess Augusta

Sun Fire Office

GLDH Ms 11937/208

23rd Jany 1834

1171553	Her Royal Highness the Princess Augusta On a Dwelling house and Building adjoining		
£3-12-0	on *Shaws Farm* in Berks. Six hundred pounds	2/6	600
Xmas 1834	Cart Horse Stable and coach Horse stable		
Windsor	adjoining, near, Two hundred and fifty pounds	3/-	250
£3-15-0	Cow and Ox Houses and Sheds all adjoining the Garden Wall near, Three hundred pounds	"	300
	Barley Barn and Leantoos all adjoining, Four hundred pounds	"	400
Berks	Sheds all adjoining in Rick Yard, near. Fifty pounds	"	50
	Wheat Barn, Nag Stable and Sheds all adjoining, near. Four Hundred pounds	"	400
	Stable Mill House, Coachhouse and Cartsheds all adjoining, near. Three hundred and fifty pounds	"	350
94/319	Granary only, near. One hundred and fifty pounds	"	150
	All brick timber, tiled and slated		£2500

GLDH Ms 12160/94 page 319

Endorsement

18th Jany 1842

1171553 208	The interest in this Policy is now become the property of Mr Robert Watkins of *Shaw Farm*, Windsor, Berks

William Davenport, China, Glass and Earthenware Manufacturer

Sun Fire Office

GLDH Ms 11937/245

14th Nov. 1837

126097	William Davenport & Co. of Longport in the County of Stafford, China Glass & Earthenware Manufacturers		
£49-9-3	On the following buildings in their own tenure,		
Mid[r] 1839	stone & slated and brick & tiled , situate as		
£81-8	aforesaid and marked by numbers & letters on a		
Hyde	plan deposited in this Office, viz House, Offices &		
Newcastle	Workshops, all communicating, *A*, six hundred		
Dy £66-14-6	pounds	2/6	600
Yr & half	Wine in the cellar of the last mentioned building.		
& 7w	Three hundred pounds	"	300
	Wharf Warehouse only, *C*. Two hundred pounds	1/6	200
	Office & Workshops over, *E* adjoining to, but not communicating with *No.12*, a brick wall between. Twenty five pounds	2/6	25
	New Counting house & Warehouse over, *G*. Eight hundred pounds	1/6	800
	Blacksmiths Shop only, *I*, fifty pounds	2/6	50
	Porters Lodge & Dwelling House communicating, *K*, fifty pounds	1/6	50
Stafford	Three houses, *L*, one hundred pounds in equal proportion	"	100
	Joiners Shop & Storerooms all communicating, *M*, no pitch nor tar heated nor stove therein, forty pounds	2/6	40
	Coopers Shop & Storeroom communicating, *N*. Twenty five pounds	2/6	25
	Workshops & Mold Chambers all communicating, *O*, one hundred & fifty pounds	"	150
	Sagger House only, *S*. Ten pounds	"	10
	Stable only, *F*, fifty pounds	"	50
	Glass Cutting Shop & Engine House communicating, *P*, near *No.7*, heated by Steam from the Engine house. Six hundred pounds	"	600
	New Wharf Warehouse adjoining buildings marked *O* on the line of the Dock. Three hundred pounds	"	300
	Workshop & Warehouse over, *Q*. One hundred pounds	"	100
	Workshops & mold Chambers all communicating, *R*. Two hundred & fifty pounds	"	250

New Mill & Engine communicating (all fire
proof except the roof) *I*. One hundred pounds   "   100
Workshop only *No.O*. Twenty five pounds   "   25
Glass Shew room, Packing room, Weighing room
& Glass warehouse all communicating *No.6*
adjoining to, but not communicating with
No.12, a brick wall between.
Fifteen hundred pounds   "   1500
Workshop only *No.4*.
One hundred & fifty pounds   "   150
Glass Shrower [*sic*] & Glass warehouse over
No.7, forty pds   "   40
Glass Lodge & Mixing rooms & Storerooms
over, all communicating *No.8*.
Seventy five pounds   "   75
Enamelling Kilns with workshops over, all
communicating *No.9*. Fifty pounds   "   50
Glass Pot rooms all communicating *No.10 & 11*,
one hundred pounds   "   100
Ranges of workshops & Warehouses over, all
communicating *No.12* adjoining to *E* but
separated therefrom as aforesaid.
Three thousand three hundred pounds   "   3300
South West range of Workshops all adjoining
being *No.13,* Eight hundred pounds   "   800
Workshop only *No.14* ~~Twenty pounds~~ *   2/6 300   (20)
Workshops all communicating *No.15*
~~One hundred pounds~~*   "   300 (100)
Workshops all communicating *No.16*,
fifty pounds   "   50
Workshops *Nos.18 & 19* all communicating.
Two hundred pounds   "   200
Workshop only *No.20*, fifty pounds   "   50
Workshop only *No. 21*. One hundred pounds   "   100
The following buildings are not on the Plan, Viz
House only near the Road leading to Newcastle,
private Eighty pounds   1/6   80
Seven houses all adjoining, near, private,
forty pounds on each   "   280
On Stock & Utensils in the aforesaid Buildings
on the Plan Viz. In *C*. Two hundred & Fifty pds   4/6 250
In *E* including engraved copper plates,
five thousand pds   "   5000
In *G*, five hundred & fifty pounds   "   550
In *I*. Twenty pounds   "   20
In *M*. Twenty pounds   "   20
In *N*. Ten pounds   "   10
In *O*. Two hundred pounds   "   200
In *P*. Two hundred pounds   "   200
In the said New Wharf Warehouses adjoining

the building marked *O*. Five hundred pounds	"	500
In *Q*, fifty pounds	"	50
In *R*. Two hundred pounds	"	200
In *T*, fifty pounds	"	50
In building Number *O*. Twenty five pounds	"	25
In *No.4*. One hundred & fifty pounds	"	150
In *No.6*. Fifteen hundred pounds	"	1500
In *No.7*. Two hundred pounds	"	200
In *No.8*. Ninety pounds	"	90
In *No.9*. Fifty five pounds	"	55
In *No's 10 & 11*. One hundred & fifty pounds	"	150
In *No.12*. Six thousand four hundred & Seventy five pounds	"	6475
In *No.13*. Three hundred & forty five pounds	"	345
In *No.14*. Twenty pounds	"	20
In *No.15*. Sixty pounds	"	60
In *No.16*. Twenty pounds	"	20
In *No's 18 & 19*. One hundred & fifty pounds	"	150
In *No. 20*. Twenty pounds	"	20
And in *No. 21*, fifty pounds	"	50
		£27030

Mem^{dum} It is warranted that there is no
communication between the buildings
marked C G K & L & the workshops
aforesaid.

** These have been crossed through and the figures in the right hand column each changed to 300.
The original figures are shown in brackets underneath. The total sum does not include these changes.*

Note: The plans referred to in this policy do not survive.

Tussaud Wax Work Exhibition

Sun Fire Office

GLDH Ms 11936/589

	9th June 1843
1412231	Joseph & Francis Tussaud of Baker St , Portman Square, Proprietors of the Wax Work Exhibition
£15-15	On wax & other Figures, Dresses, Ornaments,
11th May 1844	Pictures, Prints, Looking Glasses, Busts,
Duty	Devices & Decorations, fixed & moveable,
£2-5	Musical Instruments & other property composing their exhibition in their Room at the Bazaar & dwelling House adjoining & Communicating Baker St., Portman Square, as per catalogue deposited in the Office
Baker S^t CC	(with liberty to alter the numbers therein & in which case the identity of the figures shall be established under the description thereof in the said Catalogue)

21/-   £1500

continued

Mem^m A portion of the said Bazaar as well as
the yard belonging thereto is allowed to be
used for Prize Cattle Shows & the remaining
portions for Saddlery, Ironmongery, Furniture
& other purposes.

Watney Brewers

Hand in Hand Fire and Life Insurance Society

GLDH Ms 8764/150

25th March 1850

119675		
Prem 4-16	Messrs Elliott Watney & Co^y of Pimlico,	2/-
Duty 7-4	Brewers.	800
	£800 on a House situate on North side of	
House cellar *21 }840	Willow Walk, St Georges Row, Pimlico,	Renewed
& 3 stories *40	known as the "*Monster*" Public House &	10 Oct1857
Out Houses*19 }152	in occupⁿ of Geo. Turner	for £800
Sto *8		for seven
		years

N.B. Commencing 2 Sept. 1850

*Sizes of rooms in feet, with areas in square feet.

Horatio Nelson

Sun Fire Office

GLDH Ms 11937/409

7th Decr 1853

1725098	The Rt Honble Horatio Earl Nelson of Trafalgar Park in Wilts		
15/-	One a House in Two Tenements at Whiteparish		
Xmas 1854	in Wilts in tenure of Chas Stone.		
16/10	Brick & Slated & not hazardous	1/6	125
Salisbury	Stable & Piggery adjoining, near. Brick &		
Cooper	Slated	3/-	75
D^y 18/2	Barn, Strawhouse & Cowpens, all adjoining near, thatched.	"	200
6 mo.	Brick house only, near	"	100
	Stable only, near. Brick & tiled	"	25
	Cart Shed only, near. Thatched	"	15
			£540

Farm Houses and Bgs.

Sir Robert Peel

Sun Fire Office

GLDH Ms 11937/444

7th March 1855

1781397	Sir Robert Peel of Drayton Manor near		
15/-	Tamworth in the County of Stafford, Bart.		
Mich[s] 1856	On his farm only situate at Fisherwick in		
Hill	the parish of Whittington in said county,		
Tamworth	and called *Fisherwick Park Farm*	3/-	£500

Isambard Kingdom Brunel

Sun Fire Office

GLDH Ms 11936/711

6th January 1859

1877741	Isambard Kingdom Brunel of no. 17 & 18		
	Duke Street, Westminster, Engineer		
£4	On House and Offices all communicating,		
Xmas 1859	being no.18 Duke Street, aforesaid. Brick.	2/-	£1000
£4-3-4			
Duty	Memo. A Stove on the hearth in the front		
£18-12-3	office and a stove with perpendicular		
1496104 Can[d]	pipe in the back office on the Ground		
	Floor allowed		
	The above house communicates with		
	no.17 in same street in the occupation		
	of the assured but not included in this		
	insurance		
	152/292★ and 375★		

6th January 1859

1877742	Isambard Kingdom Brunel of No. 17 &		
	18 Duke Street, Westminster, Engineer.		
£19-18-6	On Fixtures & Office fittings in his now all		
Xmas 1859	dwelling house being two houses and offices		
£20-15-2	communicating, situate as aforesaid,Brick.	2/-	500
Duty	Household goods, Bed & Table linen,		
£18-12-3	wearing apparel, watches, trinkets,		
1496104 Can[d]	Printed books, wine & liquors in private		
	use therein only	"	3670
	Plate therein only	"	1500
	Musical Instruments therein only	"	650
	Pictures, Prints & Drawings as per		
	catalogues deposited in this Office	5/-	4829
	China & Glass therein only	"	500
			£11900

152/292★ and 375★

★ These endorsements are missing.

continued

Memo. A stove on the hearth in the front
office and a stove with perpendicular
pipe in the back office on the ground
floor allowed.

Bass Brewers

Sun Fire Office

GLDH Ms 11937/480

2nd March 1859

1886832   Michael Thomas Bass, Samuel Ratcliff,
John Gretton, Charles Walter Lyon and
£11-1   Joseph Spender Clay, trading under the
L'day 1860   Firm of Bass, Ratcliff & Gretton of
£12-13-2   Burton-on-Trent in the county of Stafford,
Spooner   Brewers, Maltsters & Coopers.
Burton-on-   On their stock of Malt Barley & other Grain
Trent   Utensils, fixtures, sacks, screens, casks wet
Dy £10-8-1   & dry & malt liquors in their Malthouse
known as *Grettons Malthouse* marked *S1*
on plan *No.3* lodged in this Office situate
on the North West side of Guild Street,
Burton-on-Trent, aforesaid.   3/-   2000
The like in their Malthouse adjoining
communicating known as *Sanders* &
marked *S2* on plan *No.4* lodged with
1861905 Cd.   this Office situate on the South West side
of Anderstaff Lane, Burton-on-Trent,
aforesaid.   "   1000
The like in their Malthouse adjoining
& communicating known as *Sanders*
& marked *S3* on plan *No.4* aforesaid.   "   1000
The like in their Malthouse adjoining
& communicating known as *Musgroves*
& marked *S4* on said plan *No.4* situate
on the North side of Bridge street,
Burton aforesaid   "   100
The like in their Malthouse known as
Hodsons & marked on plan *No.1*
lodged with this Office situate in the
West side of High Street, Burton aforesaid.   "   25
The like in their Malthouse known as
Ratcliff & marked *S6* on plan *No. 2* lodged
with this Office situate in the West side
of High Street aforesaid.   "   37-10
The like in their Malthouse known as
Paynes & marked *S7* on said plan *No.2*
in the West side of High Street aforesaid.   "   25

The like in their Malthouse known as *Dyches 30 Quarter Malthouse* & marked *S8* on said plan *No.4* situate on the south side of Hornington Street, Burton aforesaid.	"	90
The like in their Malthouse known as *Dyches 25 Quarter Malthouse* & marked S9 on said plan *No.4* adjoining last mentioned.	"	75
The like in their Malthouse known as *Evans 25 Quarter Malthouse* & marked *S10* on said plan *No.4* adjoining last mentioned.	"	75
The like in their Malthouse known as *Evans 15 Quarter Malthouse* & marked *S11* on said plan *No.4* adjoining last mentioned.	"	37-10
The like in their Malthouse known as the *Plough Inn Malthouse* & marked *S12* on said plan *No.4* situate on the North side of Hornington Street aforesaid.	"	900
Steam Pumps, Boilers & machinery therein	"	100
Stock of Malt Barley & other Grain, Utensils, fittings, sacks, screens, casks, wet and dry & Malt Liquors in their Malthouse known as *Roes S13* on a plan *No.5* lodged with this Office situate at Bond End, Burton aforesaid, high dried malt made therein.	5/-	87-10
Stock of staves, timber & truss hoops (subject to the conditions of average subjoined) in the timber yard adjoining Messrs Bass & Smiths Sawmills at Hornington, Burton-on-Trent aforesaid & marked *K* on plan *No.6* lodged with this Office.	10/6	500
		£6052-10

All brick & slated or tiled.

N.B. The within mentioned conditions of
average apply to the last Item only.

N.B. Well constructed kilns allowed &
warranted that Pale Malt only is made
in the before named Malthouses except
151/361   otherwise stated.

Note: The plans referred to in this policy do not survive

continued

GLDH Ms 12160/151 page 361

Endorsement

2 Mar. 1859

1886831	Bass	Mem Like Sums being insured on the within
1886832	Bass	Mentioned property in the County, Royal
480		Exchange & Royal Liverpool Insurance Offices
Burton		the same is hereby allowed

Queen Victoria

Sun Fire Office

GLDH Ms 11936/711

23rd March 1859

1888726	Her Majesty the Queen	
	On the following Farm Building on High	
15/-	Lodge Farm, Whichwood, Oxfordshire	250
19 June 1859	Barn	150
D^y 7/6	Cattle Shed near,Cart Shed stable,	
3 mos	Implements, house & covered yard	600
	All adjoining near	£1000
Farm Buildings	All stone & slated	

Michael Faraday

Sun Fire Office

GLDH Ms 11936/711

7th April 1859

1888755	Michael Faraday of the Royal Institution,		
	Arbermarle Street, Esq		
9/9	On his household goods, wearing apparel,		
L'day 1860	printed books & plate in house situate on		
D^y 13/6	Hampton Court Green Private.		
	Brick & tiled & slated	1/6	343
	Musical instruments therein	"	22
	Pictures & Prints therein	4/6	52
	China & glass therein	"	33
			[£]450

Sir Moses Montefiore and
Lionel Nathan de Rothschild

Sun Fire Office

GLDH Ms 11936/705

1ˢᵗ November 1859

1904682	Sir Moses Montefiore Bart & Lionel Nathan de Rothschild Esq., M.P. as mortgagees & Messrs J & R White of		
£33-8-6	West Cowes as mortgagors		
Michs. 1860	On a dwelling house & outbuildings all		
£37-7-9	adjoining. Brick & timber built marked *A*	3/-	125
Duty	On the Model Room. Brick & timber built *B*	"	65
£7-3-3	On the Office. Timber built *C*	5/-	100
3 wks	In equal proportions on fourteen dwelling houses called Thetis Terrace. Brick built *D*	1/6	700
	On the Joiners' & Boatbuilders' Shops, Painters' & Copper Stores all communicating. Brick built having Dumpy stove with fourteen feet of horizontal pipe and four feet of vertical therein *E*	25/-	750
	On the Blacksmiths' Shops all communicating. Brick built having ten forges, a boiler & steam engine therein *F*	"	475
	On the said boiler & steam engine	"	150
	On the Iron Store Shed. Timber built *G*	10/6	20
	On the Brass Shop, Chaisehouse & Gatekeeper's Office all communicating. Timber built *H*	5/-	25
	On the Saw pit sheds. Timber built *I*	25/-	65
	On the Shed & Drawing Office adjoining the last mentioned, Timber	25/-	15
	On the Engine House & Sawing Mills with Coal Store under, all communicating with each other having two boilers, steam engine, pump & machinery therein. Brick built *K*	25/-	500
	On the said boilers, steam engine pumps & machinery	"	350
	On the Steam Tanks adjoining the Blacksmiths' shops. Timber built *I*	5/-	10
Annual	On the Dry Dock *M*	7/6	500
Average	On five timber Cranes subject to the within		
last 2 items	mentioned conditions of average	3/-	150
	On the Tramways, Staging Wharf Walls, Slip & Slipway subject to similar but separate conditions of average	5/-	500
			£4500

The said buildings form the Premises known
as the *Medina Ship Building Yard* are situate
at West Cowes & are in the occupation of the
said Mess[rs] J & R White. The letters refer to a
plan deposited in the Alliance Fire Office

Note: The plan referred to in this policy does not survive.

Stead and Simpson, Boot and Shoe Manufacturers

Sun Fire Office

GLDH Ms 11937/496

27th December 1859

1912419	Messrs Stead & Simpson of Belgrave Gate, Town of Leicester, Boot & Shoe Manufacturers		
£4-10 Xmas 1860	On stock & utensils viz. In their warehouse & workshops all communicating situate as		
£5-1-3	above	3/-	2950
Stone	In their warehouse in yard, near	3/-	25
Leicester	Household goods (china & glass excepted)		
D[y] £5-1-3	wearing apparel, printed books & plate, in that part of the house only occupied by Thos. Marshall & communicating with		
	the first named, brick & slated	3/-	25
	All brick & slated & there are seven stoves in said workshops viz.		£3000
1886790 C[d]	Two with about two yards each of perpendicular pipe, one with about 5 yards of horizontal pipe, one with about 2 yards of perpendicular & 7 yards of horizontal pipe, one with about 2 yards of perpendicular & 4 yards of horizontal pipe, one with about 2 yards of perpendicular & 8 yards of horizontal pipe, & another stove, all well secured & used for warmth only		

N.B. There are two more stoves in the
aforesaid viz: one in first named
warehouse & one in second mentioned
warehouse each with more than 3ft of
pipe, well secured and used for warmth

Charles Dickens, Publisher

Sun Fire Office

GLDH Ms 11936/719

	12th September 1860		
1932853	Messrs Charles Dickens & William Henry Wills of no.26 Wellington Street, Strand, Publishers		
10/-	On their Household Goods, Wearing Apparel,		
Mids 1861	Printed Books & Plate (Office Furniture		
Triquet	included) in their House only situate as		
Camberwell	aforesaid. Brick		100
Duty	Stock, Utensils, Fixtures therein only		400
15/-		2/-	£500
1895909 Canc[d]			

The Prince of Wales

Sun Fire Office

GLDH Ms 11937/516

13th August 1862			
1995003	His Royal Highness the Prince of Wales House & Offices all communicating at Mere		
18/9	in Wilts, in tenure of Thomas Jupe, called		
Mids 1863	*Burton Farm*	1/6	450
Goodman	Stable, gighouse & Granary over. Cowhouse,		
Warminster	shedding Root house, Barn, wagon house &		
Dy £1-5-6	Carthouse, stable, all adjoining, near	3/-	400
Wilts			£850
Farm Outbgs	All brick or stone & tiled or slated		

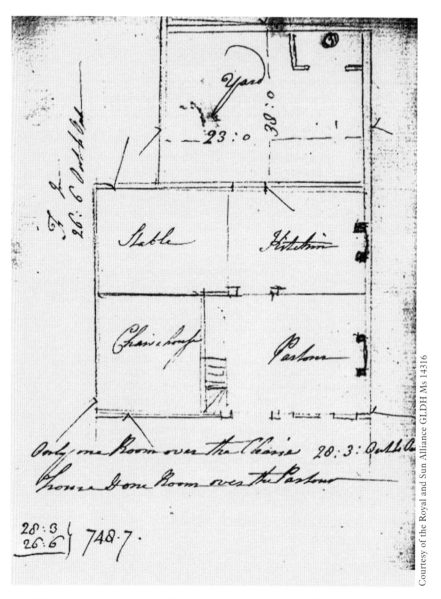

This page and opposite: London Assurance Corporation. Two pages from a surveyor' Plan Book dated 29th April 1747 showing the plan of a house.

Mr Jos. Wright On a Timber
house & Chaise house & Stable
Situate on the West side of Mile
End Old Town Bounding North
on Mr Prick Orchard

Surv. April 29th 1747

℀ Thos Stibbs

204

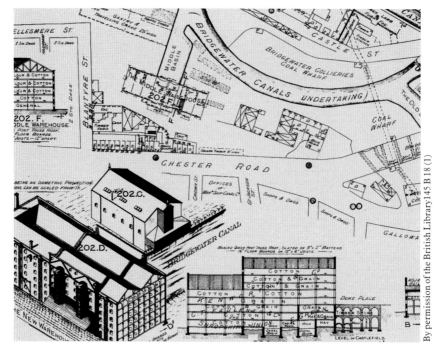

Above: Part of a Goad plan for Manchester

*Below: A Goad Insurance Plan, showing the location of the fire at Carter
Paterson & Co, London, 1897*

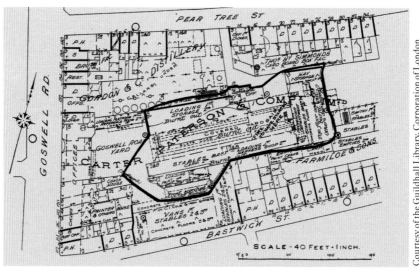

Chapter 15

Fire Insurance Maps and Plans

Fire insurance companies carried out their own surveys of property to be insured and drew up 'Fire Insurance maps and Plans'. These record in some detail the location and type of establishment, together with a detailed survey of the buildings to be insured and the work carried out in them. The construction of buildings was recorded. A brick and slated or tiled building was of lesser risk than a timber framed building with a thatched roof. The proximity of one building to another, and whether linked or detached was obviously of interest. Terraced houses without partitioned walls in the roofs were of higher risk and those with tradesmens' workshops, such as blacksmiths, wheelwrights and tin-smiths, were noted. The location of domestic dwellings to nearby factories, railways, canals and rivers involved a higher risk for the homeowners and therefore a higher premium rate was applied. Reference to individual building plans is often found written into insurance policies though, regrettably, relatively few of these plans survive. The insurance company plans which do survive are given in Appendix 2.

The cost of insuring factories and other industrial buildings took into account the building's construction and the type of heating systems installed as well as such equipment as boilers, forges, furnaces, plating baths, etc. The content of warehouses was recorded: cotton, wool, coal, timber, grain. acids, etc.

In 1886 Charles E. Goad began to produce fire insurance plans for many large towns and cities in Britain and his company continued updating these regularly (about every five or six years) until the 1960s. Since then Chas. E. Goad Ltd. has been producing plans of the shopping centres throughout Britain. The scale used was usually 1 inch to 40 feet, i.e. 1/480. Goad's plans show such detail as the type of building construction and also give the sizes of buildings and their use:

e.g.
PH   = public house
D   = dwelling
GRO   = grocer
TENS = tenements
OFFS = offices

Left: A rare example of a house doorway showing the original number 6 as well as the current number 12

Below: A London Assurance Corporation fire mark on a building. This particular design was issued in the 1720s

Colour codes give the materials used in the construction of buildings:

e.g.   pink   = brick, stone or concrete
                    yellow = wood
                    blue   = skylights
                    grey   = metals
                    orange = timber piled

Other codes identify lifts, roof construction is coded, and includes asbestos, corrugated iron, slates, tiles, etc. The location of steam boilers, fire alarms, hydrants and sprinklers are noted and street numbers of all buildings are also included.

House numbering was changed in the early 20th century. Until then the numbers of houses ran down one side of a street; 1, 2, 3, 4, 5, etc., and back up the other side. In order to aid postal delivery the numbering was changed so that odd numbers appeared on one side of the street and even numbers on the opposite side. Many family historians have been misled by the house number given in a census return or early directory. They have found a house today with that number and assumed it to be the residence of their ancestor. This is probably not the case. Goad's plans (where they exist) may help solve that problem. It is also possible where a continuous series of street directories or rate books is available, to identify changes in the numbering by following through householders year by year and noting the house number changes. Although the numbers of dwellings and other small buildings such as shops or public houses are shown on Goad's plans they do not give the names of owners or occupiers. References to street directories, however, will identify these persons.

A collection of Goad's plans is held in the Map Department of the British Library and another by the National Library of Scotland. Some are also held at the London Metropolitan Archives and in the Print Room of the Guildhall Library. Such plans relating to particular towns and cities are also held in many county record offices. Goad was a Canadian; over one thousand of his British plans are also held in the National Map Collection of Canada.

Insurance companies financed Goad's production costs by paying for a 'subscription to borrow' service. Access to these plans was limited to the subscribing companies and copying was not allowed.

These plans will be of particular interest to local historians who study the social and economic development of an area, and to some extent it architectural history. Fire Insurance Plans were produced by Goad for the following towns and cities:

1. Bath	10. Cambridge	19. Croydon
2. Batley	11. Campbeltown	20. Dewsbury
3. Bedford	12. Canterbury	21. Dover
4. Belfast (2)	13. Cardiff	22. Dublin (2)
5. Birmingham (2)	14. Chatham	23. Dundee (2)
6. Bradford (2)	15. Chelmsford	24. Edinburgh
7. Brighton	16. Colchester	25. Exeter
8. Bristol (2)	17. Cork	26. Folkestone
9. Bury St Edmunds	18. Coventry	27. Glasgow (6)

28. Gloucester
29. Goole
30. Greenock
31. Grimsby
32. Guildford
33. Halifax
34. Hartlepool Docks
35. Huddersfield
36. Hull (2)
37. Ipswich
38. Kidderminster
39. Kings Lynn
40. Leeds (2)
41. Leicester (3)
42. Leith
43. Limerick
44. Lincoln
45. Liverpool (6)
46. London, including Marylebone and Shoreditch
47. Londonderry
48. Long Eaton
49. Loughborough
50. Lowestoft
51. Luton
52. Maidstone
53. Manchester (6)
54. Margate
55. Newcastle
56. Newport
57. Northampton
58. Norwich
59. Nottingham (3)
60. Paisley
61. Peterborough
62. Plymouth
63. Ramsgate
64. Reading
65. Sheffield
66. Southampton
67. Sunderland
68. Swansea
69. Thames Valley (2)
70. River Tyne
71. Wellingborough
72. Yarmouth

Note: Where a place is covered by more than one plan the number of plans is given in brackets.

Appendix 1

Fire Insurance Companies and
Societies, 1680 to 1920
(Arranged chronologically by date
established)

List No	Name of Company or Society	Date Established	Places Covered	Records			Appendix
				Policy Registers	Other Records	Location	
1	The Fire Office Re-named the Phenix Office in 1705. (Wound up in 1722). Do not confuse with the Phoenix, List no 22	1680	London			none known	
2	The Society for Insuring Houses from Loss by Fire. Re-named The Friendly Society Appears to have been wound up after c1740)	1683	London			none known	
3	Contributors for Insuring Houses, Chambers or Rooms from Loss by Fire, by Amicable Contributions Re-named Hand-in-Hand Fire Office in1713. Re-named Hand-in-Hand Fire and Life Insurance Society in 1836. (Passed to the Commercial Union Assurance in 1905)	1696	London and Great Britain from 1806 (initially houses only)	yes	yes	Guildhall AVIVA	**2.13** **4.1.20**

List No	Name of Company or Society	Date Established	Places	Records			
				Policy	Other Covered	Location Registers	Appendix Records
4	Sun Fire Office. Re-named Sun Insurance Office in 1891. Amalgamated with Alliance Assurance Insurance Company. Company in 1959 to become Sun Alliance Insurance Company. Amalgamated with the Royal Insurance Company in 1997 to become the Royal and Sun Alliance Company	1710	Great Britain and overseas from 1838	yes	yes	Guildhall Bucks RO Cambridge CRO Cornwall RO Derby RO Devon RO Ex Essex RO Chelms Gloucester RO Hants RO Lancs RO Westmr Arch Notts Arch Surrey HC E Sussex RO W Sussex RO Wilts RO Hull Uni Lib	2.42 3.1.4 3.1.5 3.1.7 3.1.9 3.1.10 3.1.13 3.1.14 3.1.15 3.1.20 3.1.23 3.1.28 3.1.35 3.1.36 3.1.37 3.1.40 3.1.42
5	Union (or Double Hand-in-Hand) Fire Office. Re-named Union Assurance Society in 1813 (Taken over by Commercial Union Assurance Company in 1907	1714	London (initially goods only)	no	yes	Guildhall AVIVA	2.43 4.1.21

List No	Name of Company or Society	Date Established	Places Covered	Records			
				Policy Registers	Other Records	Location	Appendix
6	Westminster Fire Office (Passed to the Alliance Assurance Company in 1906)	1717	London and Great Britain from c1850 (initially houses only)	yes	yes	Westmr Arch Hants RO Surrey HC	**3.1.23** **3.1.15** **3.1.35**
7	Bristol Crown Fire Office (Taken over by the Sun Fire Office in 1837)	1718	Bristol	no	yes	Bristol RO	**3.1.3**
8	Edinburgh Friendly Insurance Against Losses by Fire (Passed to the Phoenix Fire Assurance Company in 1811)	1720	Edinburgh area	no	yes	Standard Life	**4.11.1**
9	The Friendly Society of Glasgow (Passed to the Phoenix Fire Assurance Company in 1811)	1720	Glasgow			none known	

| List No | Name of Company or Society | Date Established | Places Covered | Records | | | |
				Policy Registers	Other Records	Location	Appendix
10	London Assurance Corporation (Amalgamated with the Sun Alliance Insurance in 1965)	1720	Great Britain, Ireland and overseas	yes	yes	Guildhall Berks RO	2.29 3.1.2
11	Royal Exchange Assurance (Amalgamated with Guardian Assurance Company in 1968)	1720	Gt Britain and overseas	yes	yes	Guildhall N Devon RO Dorset RO Waltham F Arch Hants RO Sevenoaks Library	2.39 3.1.10 3.1.11 3.1.13 3.1.15 3.1.19
12	Bath Fire Office (Taken over by the Sun Fire Office in 1827)	1767	Bath, Bristol & Chippenham areas			none known	
13	New Bristol Fire Office (Taken over by the Imperial Fire Insurance Company in 1840)	1769	Bristol area			none known	

List No	Name of Company or Society	Date Established	Places Covered	Records			
				Policy Registers	Other Records	Location	Appendix
14	Hibernian Insurance Company (Taken over by the Sun Fire Office in 1839)	1771	Dublin area			none known	
15	Manchester Fire Office (Passed to the Phoenix Assurance in 1788)	1771	Manchester			none known	
16	Bristol Universal Fire Office (Wound up in 1778)	1774	Bristol			none known	
17	Bath Sun Fire Office (Amalgamated with the Sun Fire Office in 1838)	1776	Bath area	no	yes	Guildhall	2.3
18	Liverpool Fire Office (Taken over by the Phoenix Assurance Company in 1794)	1776	Liverpool			none known	
19	General Insurance Company of Ireland. Re-named the Phoenix Insurance Company of Ireland c1805 (Wound up in 1825)	1777	Dublin area			none known	

List No	Name of Company or Society	Date Established	Places Covered	Records				
				Policy Registers	Other Records	Location	Appendix	
20	Leeds Fire Office (Taken over by the Sun Fire Office in 1782)	1777	Leeds			none known		
21	Salop Fire Office (Taken over by the Alliance Assurance Company in 1890)	1780	Shropshire	yes	yes	Shropshire RO	**3.1.31**	
22	New Fire Office Re-named Phœnix Fire Office in1785 Re-named Phœnix Assurance Company in 1901	1781	Great Britain and overseas	yes	yes	Guildhall Cambridge RO Devon RO Ex Essex RO Colch Herts Arch Hunts CRO Lincs Arch Grims Lincs Arch Linc Nthbland RO Surrey HC W Sussex RO Pembroke RO Cambridge Uni Lib	2.32 **3.1.5** **3.1.10** **3.1.13** **3.1.17** **3.1.18** **3.1.22** **3.1.22** **3.1.27** **3.1.35** **3.1.37** **3.2.2** **5.1**	
23	Dublin Insurance Company (Taken over by the Phoenix Fire Office in 1817)	1782	Ireland			none known		

List No	Name of Company or Society	Date Established	Places Covered	Records			
				Policy Registers	Other Records	Location	Appendix
24	Dundee Assurance Company Against Losses by Fire (Wound up in 1832)	1782	Scotland			none known	
25	Newcastle upon Tyne Fire Office (Passed to the North British Insurance Company in 1859)	1783	Newcastle area	no	yes	Gateshead Library	3.1.12
26	Royal Exchange Assurance Company of Ireland (Company dissolved in 1823; assets transferred to the National Assurance Company of Ireland in 1853)	1784	Ireland			none known	
27	Wiltshire and Western Assurance Society Re-named the Salamander Fire Office in 1802. Re-named Salamander and Western Fire Assurance Society in 1831 (Taken over by the Sun Fire Office in1835)	1790	South West England	no	yes	Guildhall	2.45

				Records			
List No	Name of Company or Society	Date Established	Places Covered	Policy Registers	Other Records	Location	Appendix
28	Worcester Fire Office (Passed to the Phoenix Assurance Company in 1818)	1790	Worcester-shire			none known	
29	Norwich General Assurance Company (Amalgamated with the Norwich Union Fire Insurance Society in 1821)	1792	Norfolk and Suffolk			none known	
30	Norwich Union Fire Insurance Society	1797	Norfolk and Suffolk and Great Britain from c1805	yes	yes	Devon RO Ex Norfolk RO Northants RO Wolv Arch E Sussex RO Wilts RO AVIVA	**3.1.10** **3.1.25** **3.1.26** **3.1.33** **3.1.36** **3.1.40** **4.1.1**
31	British Fire Office (Amalgamated with the Sun Fire Office in 1804)	1799	London; and Great Britain and Ireland from c1801			none known	

List No	Name of Company or Society	Date Established	Places Covered	Records				
				Policy Registers	Other Records	Location		Appendix
32	Commercial Insurance Company of Dublin (Taken over by Guardian Assurance Company in 1827	1799	Ireland			none known		
33	Sun Insurance Company of Dublin (Amalgamated with the British Fire Office in 1804)	1800	Ireland			none known		
34	Aberdeen Fire Assurance Company (Wound up in 1823)	1801	Aberdeen			none known		
35	Essex Equitable Insurance Society Re-named Essex and Suffolk Equitable Insurance Society in 1806 (Became a subsidiary of Atlas Assurance Company in 1911)	1802	Essex and Suffolk	yes	yes	Guildhall Essex RO Chelms		2.15 3.1.13
36	Kent Fire Office (Taken over by the Royal Insurance Company in 1901)	1802	Kent	yes	yes	R&SA		4.10.1

| | | Records | | | |
List No	Name of Company or Society	Date Established	Places Covered	Policy Registers	Other Records	Location	Appendix
37	Suffolk Fire Office. Also known as the Suffolk and General Insurance Company (Taken over by the Alliance, British and Foreign Fire and Life Insurance Company in 1849 to become the Suffolk Alliance Life and Fire Assurance Company)	1802	Suffolk	yes	yes	Bury St Ed RO Ipswich RO	**3.1.34** **3.1.34**
38	Glasgow Fire Insurance Company (Fire business taken over by the Phoenix Fire Office in 1811)	1803	Glasgow	no	yes	Glas Uni Arch	**3.3.6**
39	Globe Insurance Company (Amalgamated with the Liverpool and London Fire and Life Insurance Company in 1864 to become the Liverpool and London and Globe Insurance Company)	1803	Great Britain and overseas	yes	yes	Guildhall Liverpool RO	**2.19** **3.1.20**

List No	Name of Company or Society	Date Established	Places Covered	Records				
				Policy Registers	Other Records	Location	Appendix	
40	Hampshire, Sussex and Dorset Fire Office (Taken over by the Alliance, British and Foreign Fire and Life Insurance Company in 1864)	1803	Hampshire Sussex and Dorset			none known		
41	Imperial Fire Insurance Company (Taken over by the Alliance Assurance Company in 1902)	1803	Great Britain and overseas	yes	yes	Guildhall PRO N Ireland	**2.21** **3.4.1**	
42	Albion Fire and Life Insurance Company (Fire business passed to the Protector Fire Insurance Company in 1828)	1805	Great Britain and overseas	no	yes	Zurich	**4.2.1**	
43	Birmingham Fire Office (Passed to the Lancashire Insurance Company in 1867)	1805	Birmingham			none known		

List No	Name of Company or Society	Date Established	Places Covered	Records			
				Policy Registers	Other Records	Location	Appendix
44	Caledonian Insurance Company (Became a subsidiary of the Guardian Asslrance Company in 1957)	1805	Scotland and England from 1813, and Ireland from 1834	yes	yes	Guildhall Nat Arch Scot	2.10 3.3.1
45	Fife Fire Insurance Company (Wound up c1828)	1806	Cupar area, Fife			none known	
46	County Fire Office (Became a subsidiary of the Alliance Assurance Company in 1906)	1807	Great Britain (private property only)	yes	yes	Guildhall N Devon RO Dorset RO Herts Arch Lincs Arch Linc Surrey HC Warwick CRO Wilts RO Doncaster Arch Sheffield Arch W York Arch Kirk	2.14 3.1.10 3.1.11 3.1.17 3.1.22 3.1.35 3.1.38 3.1.40 3.1.43 3.1.43 3.1.43

List No	Name of Company or Society	Date Established	Places Covered	Records			
				Policy Registers	Other Records	Location	Appendix
47	Eagle Insurance Company (Amalgamated with the British Dominions Insurance Company in 1917 to become the Eagle and British Dominions Insurance Company)	1807 (fire insurance until 1826)	England	no	yes	Zurich	4.2.2
48	Hope Fire and Life Assurance Company (Passed to the Imperial Life Insurance Company in 1844)	1807 (fire insurance until 1826)	London			none known	
49	West of England Fire and Life Insurance Company (Taken over by the Commercial Union Assurance Company in 1894)	1807	Mainly West of England, but spread as far as Ireland	yes	yes	Cornwall RO Devon RO Ex PRO N Ireland	3.1.7 3.1.10 3.4.1
50	Anchor Fire Office (Passed to the Norwich General Assurance Office in 1811)	1808	Norwich			none known	

List No	Name of Company or Society	Date Established	Places Covered	Records			
				Policy Registers	Other Records	Location	Appendix
51	Atlas Assurance Company (Taken over by the Royal Exchange Assurance in 1959)	1808	Great Britain	yes	yes	Guildhall Devon RO Ex Dorset RO	2.2 3.1.10 3.1.1
52	Sheffield Fire Office (Taken over by the Alliance, British and Foreign Fire and Life Insurance Company in 1863)	1808	Sheffield	no	yes	Sheffield Arch	3.1.43
53	Hercules Fire Insurance Company* (Taken over by the Scottish Union Insurance Company in 1849) *Do not confuse with the Hercules Insurance Company, List No 118	1809	Scotland	no	yes	AVIVA	4.1.2
54	North British Insurance Company (Amalgamated with the Mercantile Fire Insurance Company in 1862 to become the North British and Mercantile Insurance Company)	1809	Great Britain and overseas	yes	yes	Guildhall Herts Arch Nthbland RO Mitch Lib Glasgow AVIVA	2.33 3.1.17 3.1.27 3.3.4 4.1.3

List No	Name of Company or Society	Date Established	Places Covered	Records			
				Policy Registers	Other Records	Location	Appendix
55	Bristol Union Fire and Life Insurance Company (Wound up in 1844)	1818	Bristol			none known	
56	British Commercial Life and Fire Insurance Company (Amalgamated with the British National Insurance Company in 1860)	1820	London			none known	
57	Beacon Fire Insurance Company* (Taken over by the Protector Fire PInsurance Company in 1827) *Do not confuse with the Beacon Insurance Company, List No 143	1821	London			none known	
58	Guardian Fire and Life Assurance Company Re-named Guardian Assurance Comppany in 1902 (Amalgamated with the Royal Exchange Assurance in 1968)	1821	Great Britain and overseas	yes	yes	Guildhall Hunts CRO	**2.20** 3.1.18

List No	Name of Company or Society	Date Established	Places Covered	Records				
				Policy Registers	Other Records	Location		Appendix
59	Insurance Company of Scotland (Taken over by the Alliance, British and Foreign Fire and Life Insurance Company in 1847)	1821	Scotland	yes	yes	Nat Lib Scot		3.3.2
60	National Assurance Company of Ireland (Taken over by the Yorkshire Insurance Company in 1904)	1822	Ireland			none known		
61	Reading Insurance Company (Taken over by the Phoenix Assurance Company in 1841)	1822	Reading area, Berkshire			none known		
62	Royal Irish Assurance Company (Taken over by the Phoenix Assurance Company in 1827	1823	Ireland			none known		
63	West of Scotland Insurance Company Re-named the Metellus Insurance Company in 1837 (Taken over by the Phoenix Assurance Company in 1839)	1823	Scotland and overseas	no	yes	Mitch Lib Glasgow		3.3.4

List No	Name of Company or Society	Date Established	Places Covered	Records			
				Policy Registers	Other Records	Location	Appendix
64	Alliance, British and Foreign Fire and Life Insurance Company Re-named Alliance Assurance Company in 1905. (Amalgamated with the Sun Insurance Office in 1959 to become the Sun Alliance)	1824	Great Britain and overseas	yes	yes	Guildhall Devon RO Ex Dorset RO Hants RO Surrey HC E Sussex RO W Sussex RO W York Arch Kirk Pembroke RO	2.1 3.1.10 3.1.11 3.1.15 3.1.35 3.1.36 3.1.37 3.1.43 3.2.2
65	Berkshire, Gloucestershire and Provincial Life and Fire Assurance Company (Taken over by the Phoenix Assurance Company in 1831)	1824	Berkshire and Gloucestershire			none known	
66	East Kent and Canterbury Economic Fire Assurance Association (Taken over by the Phoenix Assurance Company in 1828)	1824	Kent			none known	

List No	Name of Company or Society	Date Established	Places Covered	Records			
				Policy Registers	Other Records	Location	Appendix
67	Essex Economic Fire Office (Taken over by the Manchester Fire and Life Assurance Company in 1858)	1824	unknown			none known	
68	Hertfordshire, Cambridgeshire and Country Fire Office (Taken over by the Phoenix Assurance Company in 1831)	1824	Hertfordshire and Cambridge-shire			none known	
69	Irish Alliance Insurance Company (Taken over by the National Assurance Company of Ireland)	1824	Ireland			none known	
70	Leeds and Yorkshire Fire and Life Insurance Company (Taken over by the Liverpool and London Fire and Life Insurance Company in 1864)	1824	Yorkshire	no	yes	W. York Arch Lds	3.1.43

List No	Name of Company or Society	Date Established	Places Covered	Records				Appendix
				Policy Registers	Other Records	Location		
71	Manchester Fire and Life Assurance Company. Re-named the Manchester Assurance Company in 1846. (Taken over by the Atlas Assurance Company in 1904)	1824	Great Britain	no	yes	Guildhall Lancs RO Liverpool RO Blackburn Lib E Sussex RO		2.30 3.1.20 3.1.20 3.1.20 3.1.36
72	Palladium Life and Fire Assurance Society (Fire insurance taken over by the Phoenix Assurance Company in 1829; the company was taken over by the Eagle Fire and Life Insurance Company in 1856)	1824	Great Britain	no	yes	Zurich		4.2.3
73	Patriotic Assurance Company of Ireland (Taken over by the Sun Alliance in 1972)	1824	Ireland			none known		
74	Saint Patrick Insurance Company of Ireland (Wound up c1829)	1824	Ireland			none known		

List No	Name of Company or Society	Date Established	Places Covered	Records			
				Policy Registers	Other Records	Location	Appendix
75	Scottish Union Insurance Company (Amalgamated with the Scottish and National Insurance Company in 1878 to form the Scottish Union and National Insurance Company)	1824	Scotland; and England from 1828; and Ireland from 1837	yes	yes	Portsmouth RO AVIVA	**3.1.15** **4.1.4**
76	Shamrock Assurance Company of Ireland (Wound up c1829)	1824	Ireland			none known	
77	Yorkshire Fire and Life Insurance Company Re-named Yorkshire Insurance Company in 1908. (Amalgamated with the General Accident Fire and Life Assurance Corporation in 1967)	1824	Great Britain	yes	yes	AVIVA	**4.1.5**
78	Aberdeen Fire and Life Assurance Company Re-named Scottish Provincial Assurance Company in 1852. (Taken over by the North British Mercantile Insurance Company in 1889)	1825	Scotland	yes	yes	Mitch Lib Glasgow AVIVA	**3.3.4** **4.1.6**

List No	Name of Company or Society	Date Established	Places Covered	Policy Registers	Other Records	Location	Appendix
						Records	
79	Aegis Fire and Life Insurance Company (Taken over by the English and Cambrian Life Insurance Company in 1850)	1825	Great Britain			none known	
80	Protector Fire Insurance Company (Amalgamated with the Phoenix Assurance Company in 1836)	1825	Great Britain	no	yes	Cambridge Uni Lib	5.2
81	Royal Irish Insurance Company (Wound up in 1827)	1825	Ireland	no	yes	Guildhall	2.40
82	Surrey and Sussex Fire and Life Assurance Company	1825	Brighton			none known	
83	Sussex County and General Fire and Life Assurance Company (Wound up c1825)	1825	Brighton			none known	
84	Nottinghamshire and Derbyshire Fire and Life Assurance Company (Taken over by the Imperial Life Insurance Company in 1869)	1832	Nottingham-shire, Derbyshire, Lincolnshire and Staffordshire	no	yes	Guildhall	2.35

List No	Name of Company or Society	Date Established	Places Covered	Records				
				Policy Registers	Other Records	Location	Appendix
85	District Fire Office (Taken over by the Alliance, British and Foreign Fire and Life Insurance Company in 1864)	1834	England	yes	yes	Birmingham Lib	**3.1.38**
86	Leicester Fire Office (Taken over by the Sun Fire Office in 1843)	1834	Leicestershire			none known	
87	York and North of England Fire and Life Insurance Company. Re-named the York and London Fire and Life Insurance Company in 1838 (Fire business taken over by Imperial Insurance in 1842)	1834	Yorkshire	no	yes	W York Arch Lds	**3.1.43**

List No	Name of Company or Society	Date Established	Places Covered	Records			
				Policy Registers	Other Records	Location	Appendix
88	Licensed Victuallers and General Insurance Company Re-named the Monarch Fire and Life Assurance Company in 1836. (Taken over by the Liverpool and London Fire and Life Insurance Company in 1857)	1835	Great Britain and overseas	no	yes	Guildhall	2.24
89	Liverpool Fire and Life Insurance Company. Re-named the Liverpool and London Insurance Company in 1847 Amalgamated with the Globe Insurance Company in 1864 to become the Liverpool and London and Globe Insurance Company (Taken over by the Royal Insurance Company in 1919)	1836	Great Britain and overseas	yes	yes	Guildhall Cumb RO Whit Liverpool RO W York Arch Cald W York Arch Hud W York Arch Lds	2.26 3.1.8 3.1.20 3.1.43 3.1.43 3.1.43

List No	Name of Company or Society	Date Established	Places Covered	Policy Registers	Other Records	Location	Appendix
						Records	
90	North of Scotland Fire and Life Assurance Company Re-named Northern Assurance Company in 1898 (Became a subsidiary of the Commercial Union Assurance Company in 1968)	1836	Great Britain	yes	yes	Guildhall Dundee Uni AVIVA	**2.34** **3.3.3** **4.1.7**
91	Shropshire and North Wales Assurance Company (Amalgamated with the Alliance, British and Foreign Fire and Life Insurance Company in 1890)	1837	Shropshire and North Wales	no	yes	Shropshire RO	**3.1.31**
92	General Life and Fire Assurance Company (Fire business purchased by the London and Lancashire Fire Insurance Company in 1892)	1837	Great Britain			none known	
93	English and Scottish Law Life Assurance Association (Amalgamated with the Eagle Star Insurance Company in 1918)	1839 (fire insurance until 1843)	Great Britain	yes	yes	Zurich	**4.2.4**

List No	Name of Company or Society	Date Established	Places Covered	Records				Appendix
				Policy Registers	Other Records	Location		
94	Church of England Life and Fire Assurance Trust and Annuity Institution Re-named England Assurance Institution in 1893 (Taken over by the Imperial Life Insurance Company in 1893)	1840	Great Britain	no	yes	Guildhall		2.11
95	Farmers and General Insurance Company Re-named the Royal Farmers and General Fire, Life and Hail Insurance Company in 1843 (Taken over by the Alliance British and Foreign Fire and Life Insurance Company in 1888)	1840	Great Britain	yes	yes	Guildhall Warwick CRO		2.16 3.1.38
96	Hampshire and South of England Insurance Society. Also known as South of England Insurance Society (Fire business transferred to the Sun Fire Office in 1847)	1841	Southern England			none known		

List No	Name of Company or Society	Date Established	Places Covered	Records			
				Policy Registers	Other Records	Location	Appendix
97	Scottish National Insurance Company (Amalgamated with the Scottish Union Insurance Company n 1878 to form ithe Scottish Union and National Insurance Company)	1841	Scotland, England and Ireland	no	yes	AVIVA	**4.1.8**
98	North of England Fire and Life Insurance Company (Amalgamated with the Liverpool and London Insurance Company in 1858)	1844	Great Britain	no	yes	Liverpool RO	**3.1.20**
99	Western Fire and Life Insurance Company (Amalgamated with the Northern Assurance Company in 1347)	1844	Glasgow	no	yes	Mitch Lib Glasgow	**3.3.4**
100	Bon Accord Life and Fire Insurance Guarantee Reversionary and Annuity Company. (Amalgamated with the Northern Assurance Company in 1849)	1845	Aberdeen	no	yes	Nat Arch Scot	**3.3.1**

List No	Name of Company or Society	Date Established	Places Covered	Records			
				Policy Registers	Other Records	Location	Appendix
101	Law Fire Insurance Society (Became a subsidiary of the Alliance Assurance Company in 1907)	1845	Great Britain	yes	yes	Guildhall Devon RO Ex Shakespeare BT Worcester RO Pembroke RO	**2.22** **3.1.10** **3.1.38** **3.1.41** **3.2.2**
102	Royal Insurance Company (Amalgamated with the Sun Alliance Insurance Company in 1997 to form the Royal and Sun Alliance Insurance Company)	1845	Great Britain	yes	yes	Liverpool RO Hunts CRO	**3.1.20** **3.1.18**
103	Star Insurance Company (Taken over by Manchester Assurance Company in 1853)	1845 (fire insurance until 1853)	Great Britain	yes	yes	Zurich	**4.2.5**
104	Sheffield and Rotherham Fire Insurance Company (Amalgamated with the Liverpool and London Fire and Life Insurance Company in 1858)	1845	Sheffield	no	yes	Liverpool RO	**3.1.20**

List No	Name of Company or Society	Date Established	Places Covered	Records			Appendix
				Policy Registers	Other Records	Location	
105	Architects, Civil Engineers, Builders and General Fire Insurance Company (Taken over by the Lancashire Insurance Company in 1853)	1847	Great Britain	no	yes	Liverpool RO	3.1.20
106	Anchor Fire and Life Insurance Company (Amalgamated with the Bank of London Insurance Company in 1857)	1849	Great Britain and overseas			none known	
107	Midland Counties Insurance Company (Amalgamated with the Royal Insurance Company in 1892)	1851	Great Britain	no	yes	Liverpool RO	3.1.20
108	Lancashire Insurance Company (Taken over by the Royal Insurance Company in 1901)	1852	Great Britain and overseas	no	yes	Liverpool RO	3.1.20
109	Provincial Welsh Fire and Life Insurance Company (Fire business taken over by the Alliance Assurance Company in 1874)	1852	Wales	no	yes	Denbigh RO	3.2.1

List No	Name of Company or Society	Date Established	Places Covered	Records			
				Policy Registers	Other Records	Location	Appendix
110	Achilles Insurance Company (Taken over by the City of London Life Assurance Society in 1858)	1853	London	no	yes	Zurich	4.2.6
111	British Equitable Assurance Company (Became a subsidiary of the Royal Exchange Assurance Company in 1924)	1854 (fire insurance from 1905)	Great Britain	no	yes	Guildhall	2.6
112	Law Union Fire and Life Insurance Company Re-named the Law Union and Crown Insurance Company in 1892. Re-named the Law Union and Rock Insurance Company in 1909 (Amalgamated with the London and Lancashire Insurance Company in 1919)	1854	Great Britain	yes	yes	Guildhall Devon RO Ex Hereford RO	2.23 3.1.10 3.1.16
113	Queen Insurance Company (Amalgamated with the Royal Insurance Company in 1891)	1857 (fire insurance from 1859)	Great Britain	yes	yes	Gloucester RO Liverpool RO	3.1.14 3.1.20

List No	Name of Company or Society	Date Established	Places Covered	Records			
				Policy Registers	Other Records	Location	Appendix
114	Commercial Union Assurance Company (Amalgamated with Norwich Union in 2000)	1861	Great Britain and overseas	yes	yes	Guildhall N Devon RO Shropshire RO Warwick CRO AVIVA	**2.12** **3.1.10** **3.1.31** **3.1.38** **4.1.22**
115	London and Lancashire Fire and Life Insurance Company. Re-named the London and Lancashire Fire Insurance Company in 1867. Re-named the London and Lancashire Insurance Company in 1919 (Amalgamated with the Royal Insurance Company in 1961)	1861	Great Britain and overseas	yes	yes	Guildhall Hunts CRO Liverpool RO	**2.28** **3.1.18** **3.1.20**
116	Mercantile Fire Insurance Company (Taken over by the North British Insurance Company in 1862 to become the North British and Mercantile Insurance Company) (This company linked with the Union Assurance Company in 1961)	1861	London (warehouses)	no	yes	Guildhall	**2.31**

List No	Name of Company or Society	Date Established	Places Covered	Records				
				Policy Registers	Other Records	Location	Appendix	
117	Prince Fire Insurance Company (Wound up in 1866)	1862	Great Britain	no	yes	Prudential Arch, London	**4.4.1**	
118	Hercules Fire and Life Insurance Company* (Wound up in 1869) * Do not confuse with the Hercules Fire Insurance Company, List No 53	1863	Great Britain	no	yes	Prudential Arch, London	**4.4.2**	
119	Western Fire Insurance Company (Taken over by the Alliance, British and Foreign Fire and Life Insurance Company in 1868)	1863	Great Britain			none known		
120	Albert Fire Insurance Company (Wound up in 1866)							
121	Birmingham Alliance Insurance Company (Amalgamated with Lancashire Insurance Company in 1870)	1864	Birmingham	yes	yes	Liverpool RO Wolv Arch	**3.1.20** **3.1.33**	
122	Scottish Commercial Fire and Life Insurance Company (Taken over by the Lancashire Insurance Company in 1880)	1865	Scotland			none known		

List No	Name of Company or Society	Date Established	Places Covered	Records			
				Policy Registers	Other Records	Location	Appendix
123	Scottish Imperial Fire and Life Insurance Company (Fire business acquired by Alliance in 1883)	1865 (fire insurance until 1883)	Great Britain	yes	yes	AVIVA	**4.1.9**
124	Etna Fire Insurance Company (Taken over by the United Ports and General Insurance Company in 1868)		Great Britain and Ireland			none known	
125	Primitive Methodist Insurance Company (Amalgamated with the Methodist Insurance Company in 1933)	1866	Great Britain	yes	yes	Gtr Man RO	**3.1.20**
126	Co-operative Insurance Society	1867	Great Britain	yes	yes	CIS Manchester	**4.3.1**
127	Britannia Fire Association (Taken over by the Anglo-French Fire Insurance Company n 1879)	1868	Great Britain			none known	

List No	Name of Company or Society	Date Established	Places Covered	Records			Appendix
				Policy Registers	Other Records	Location	
128	United Ports and General Insurance Company (Taken over by the English Fire and Life Insurance Company in 1869)	1868	Great Britain			none known	
129	London Guarantee and Accident Company (Amalgamated with the Guarantee Association of Scotland in 1873)	1869	Great Britain and overseas	no	yes	Cambridge Uni Lib	5.3
130	Mutual Fire Insurance Corporation (Taken over by the Palatine Insurance Company in 1890)	1869	Lancashire and Yorkshire			none known	
131	Ocean Railway and General Travellers Assurance Company Re-named the Ocean Accident and Guarantee Corporation in 1890. (Amalgamated with the Commercial Union Assurance Company in 1910)	1871 (fire insurance from 1906)	Great Britain	no	yes	Guildhall AVIVA	2.36 4.1.10

List No	Name of Company or Society	Date Established	Places Covered	Records				
				Policy Registers	Other Records	Location	Appendix	
132	Wesleyan Methodist Trust Assurance Company Re-named the Methodist Insurance Company (Amalgamated with the Primitive Methodist Insurance Company in 1869)	1871	Great Britain	no	yes	Gtr Man RO	3.1.20	
133	Morley Mutual Insurance Society (Amalgamated with the London and Lancashire Fire Insurance Company in 1915)	1872	Yorkshire	no	yes	W York Arch Lds	3.1.43	
134	Bute Insurance Company (Amalgamated with the State Fire Insurance Company in 1898)	1873	Isle of Bute	yes	no	Argyll and Bute District Arch	3.3.5	
135	Equitable Fire Insurance Company (Taken over by the London and Lancashire Fire Insurance Company in 1901)	1873	Great Britain			none known		
136	Great National Fire Insurance Company (Wound up in 1875)	1874	Northern Ireland	no	yes	PRO N Ireland	3.4.1	

List No	Name of Company or Society	Date Established	Places Covered	Records			
				Policy Registers	Other Records	Location	Appendix
137	Middlesex Fire Insurance Company (Wound up in 1877)	1874	London area			none known	
138	Licensed Victuallers and General Fire and Plate Glass Insurance Company (Wound up in 1879)	1875	Great Britain			none known	
139	Provident Clerks and General Accident Insurance Company Re-named the Provident Clerks and General Guarantee and Accident Company in 1907. (Amalgamated with White Cross Insurance Company to become Provident Accident and White Cross Insurance Company in 1925)	1876 (fire insurance from c1907)	Scotland	no	yes	Guidhall Nat Arch Scot	2.38 3.3.1
140	National Fire Insurance Corporation (Taken over by the Royal Insurance Company in 1888)	1878	Great Britain			none known	

List No	Name of Company or Society	Date Established	Places Covered	Records			
				Policy Registers	Other Records	Location	Appendix
141	Lion Fire Insurance Company (Taken over by the Yorkshire Fire and Life Insurance Company in 1902)	1879	Great Britain and overseas	no	yes	AVIVA	**4**.1.19
142	Fire Insurance Association Re-named the Albion Fire Insurance Association in 1893	1880	Great Britain	no	yes	Guildhall	**2**.18
143	Blue Ribbon Life, Accident, Mutual and Industrial Insurance Company Re-named the Abstainers and General Insurance Company in 1890 Re-named the Beacon Insurance Company in 1933	1883	Great Britain	no	yes	Birmingham Lib	**3**.1.38
144	Palatine Insurance Company (Amalgamated with the City of London Fire Insurance iCompany in 1892)	1886	Great Britain and overseas	no	yes	Guildhall AVIVA	**2**.37 **4**.1.11

List No	Name of Company or Society	Date Established	Places Covered	Records				
				Policy Registers	Other Records	Location	Appendix	
145	Welsh Calvanistic Methodist Assurance Trust	1886	Wales	no	yes	Nat Lib Wales	**3.2.3**
146	West of Scotland Fire Office Re-named the West of Scotland Insurance Office (Became a subsidiary of Commercial Union in 1924)	1886	Great Britain	no	yes	Nat Lib Scot AVIVA	**3.3.2** **4.1.12**
147	British Law Fire Insurance Company Re-named the British Law Insurance Company in 1918	1888	Great Britain	yes	yes	Guildhall N Devon RO Nat Arch Scot	**2.9** **3.1.10** **3.3.1**
148	Free Church of Scotland Fire Insurance Trust Re-named the United Free Church of Scotland Fire Insurance Trust in 1901. Re-named the Church of Scotland Insurance Company in 1982	1888	Scotland	yes	yes	Nat Arch Scot	**3.3.1**

List No	Name of Company or Society	Date Established	Places Covered	Records				
				Policy Registers	Other Records	Location	Appendix	
149	Fine Art and General Insurance Company (Became a subsidiary of the North British and Mercantile Insurance Company from 1917)	1890	Great Britain	no	yes	Guildhall Gloucester RO AVIVA	**2.17** **3.1.14** **4.1.13**	
150	Licenses and General Insurance Corporation and Guarantee Fund. Re-named the Licenses and General Insurance Company in 1917. (Became a subsidiary of the Guardian Assurance Company in 1956)	1890	Great Britain	no	yes	Guildhall	**2.25**	
151	Congregational Fire Insurance Company Renamed the Congregational and General Insurance Company in 1908	1891	Great Britain	yes	yes	Currer House, Bradford	**4.5.1**	

List No	Name of Company or Society	Date Established	Places Covered	Records				
				Policy Registers	Other Records	Location	Appendix	
152	State Fire Insurance Company Renamed the State Assurance Company in 1910 (Became a subsidiary of the Royal Exchange Assurance in 1924)	1891	Great Britain	yes	yes	Guildhall	**2.41**	
153	National Insurance Company of Great Britain (Became a subsidiary of the Commercial Union Assurance Company in 1917)	1897	Great Britain	no	yes	AVIVA	**4.1.14**	
154	Birmingham Mutual Fire and General Insurance Association. Re-named the Central Insurance Company in 1902. (Taken over by the Liverpool and London and Globe Insurance Company in 1907)	1899	Great Britain	no	yes	Guildhall W York Arch Lds	**2.4** **3.1.43**	
155	Mutual Property Recovery and Accident Company Re-named the Mutual Property Insurance Company in 1902 Re-named the Crusader Insurance Company in 1946	1899	Great Britain	no	yes	unknown	*see footnote*	

Note: Accounts, Board Minutes, Shareholders Records and Staff Association Minutes recorded in *The British Insurance Business* by Cockerell and Green

List No	Name of Company or Society	Date Established	Places Covered	Records			Appendix
				Policy Registers	Other Records	Location	
156	North Western Insurance Company (Taken over by the British Dominions General Insurance Company in 1914)	1899	Liverpool and Manchester	no	yes	Zurich	**4.2.7**
157	Municipal Mutual Insurance (Taken over by Zurich Insurance in 1993)	1903	Great Britain	yes	yes	Zurich	**4.2.8**
158	Provincial Fire Insurance Company (Amalgamated with the Drapers and General Insurance Company in 1909)	1903	Great Britain	no	yes	Cumb RO Kendal	**3.1.39**
159	British Dominions Marine Insurance Company Re-named the Eagle Star and British Dominions Insurance Company in 1917 Re-named the Eagle Star Insurance Company in 1937	1904	Great Britain and overseas	yes	yes	Devon RO Ex N Devon RO W York Arch Hud W York Arch Kirk Zurich	**3.1.10** **3.1.10** **3.1.43** **3.1.43** **4.2.9**

List No	Name of Company or Society	Date Established	Places Covered	Policy Registers	Other Records	Records		Appendix
						Location		
160	British General Insurance Company (Became a subsidiary of the Commercial Union Assurance Company in 1926)	1904	Great Britain and overseas	yes	yes	Guildhall W York Arch Hud W York Arch Kirk AVIVA		2.8 3.1.43 3.1.434 4.1.15
161	Theatres Mutual Insurance Company (Became a subsidiary of the Eagle Star Insurance Company in 1920)	1904	Great Britain	no	yes	Zurich		4.2.10
162	Baptist Fire Insurance Company Re-named the Baptist Insurance Company in 1926)	1905	Great Britain	no	yes	Baptist Insurance, London		4.6.1
163	Cornhill Insurance Company	1905 (fire insurance from 1918)	Great Britain	yes	yes	Cornhill Insurance, Guildford		4.7.1
164	White Cross Insurance Association Renamed the Provident Accident and White Cross Insurance Company in 1925 (Amalgamated with the Provident Accident and Guarantee Company in 1925). See also List No 139	1906 (fire insurance from 1925)	Great Britain	no	yes	Guildhall AVIVA		2.38 4.1.17

List No	Name of Company or Society	Date Established	Places Covered	Records				
				Policy Registers	Other Records	Location	Appendix	
165	Liverpool Victoria Insurance Corporation (Taken over by the Commercial Union Assurance Company in 1913)	1907	Great Britain	no	yes	Guildhall AVIVA	**2.27** **4.1.17**	
166	Royal Scottish Insurance Company (Became a subsidiary of the Northern Assurance Company in 1914)	1907	Scotland and North England	no	yes	Mitch Lib Glasgow	**3.3.4**	
167	British Fire Insurance Company (Became a subsidiary of the London and Lancashire Insurance Company in 1923)	1908	Great Britain	no	yes	Guildhall	**2.7**	
168	British Commercial Fire Insurance Company (Wound up in 1959)	1908	Great Britain	no	yes	Guildhall	**2.5**	
169	Drapers Mutual Fire and General Insurance Company Re-named Monument Insurance Company in 1944	1909	Great Britain	no	yes	Cumb RO Kendal	**3.1.39**	

List No	Name of Company or Society	Date Established	Places Covered	Records				
				Policy Registers	Other Records	Location	Appendix	
170	Welsh Insurance Corporation (Became a subsidiary of the London and Scottish Assurance Corporation in 1911).	1909	Great Britain	no	yes	AVIVA	**4.1.18**	
171	Gresham Fire and Accident Insurance Company (Became a subsidiary of Legal and General Assurance Society in 1934)	1910	Great Britain and overseas	no	yes	Legal & General	**4.8.1**	
172	National Farmers Union Mutual Insurance Society	1910	Great Britain	no	yes	Hereford RO	**3.1.16**	
173	Royal London Auxiliary Insurance Company (Amalgamated with the Royal London Mutual Insurance Society in 1921)	1910	Great Britain	no	yes	RLM Colchester	**4.9.1**	
174	National Employers Mutual Insurance Association (Wound up in 1990)	1914	Great Britain	yes	yes	unknown	*see footnote*	
							-	

Note: Board and Shareholders Minutes and Policy Registers recorded in *The British Insurance Business* by Cockerell and Green

List No	Name of Company or Society	Date Established	Places Covered	Records				
				Policy Registers	Other Records	Location	Appendix
175	United British Insurance Company (Became a subsidiary of the Royal Exchange Assurance in 1927)	1915	Great Britain	no	yes	Guildhall	**2**.44
176	Olympic Fire and General Reinsurance Company (Amalgamated with the Tariff Reinsurances in 1924)	1919	Great Britain	no	yes	Cambridge Uni Lib	5.4
177	Tariff Reinsurances (Became a subsidiary of the Phoenix Assurance Company in 1933)	1919	Great Britain	no	yes	Cambridge Uni Lib	5.5

Appendix 2

Records at the Guildhall Library, London

The following lists those records of particular interest to family and local historians held at the Guildhall Library, London, arranged in alphabetical order of company name. Each company name given in this list is the original name of the company. The alternative names are given in brackets. It does not include companies which dealt only with life insurance.

The list numbers in brackets are the list numbers given in Appendix 1.

Albion Fire Insurance Association – see *Fire Insurance Association*

2.1 *Alliance British and Foreign Fire and Life Insurance Company* (List no 64)

Fire Insurance Policy number 3537348	1899	Ms 14979
Policy to no. 29 St Swithins Lane	1825	Ms 23469
Fire and General Committee Minutes	1910 to 1923	Ms 18255
Board and Committee Minutes (34 volumes)	1824 to 1926	Ms 12162A

2.2 *Atlas Assurance Company* (List no 51)

Register of Agents (7 volumes)	1897 to 1912	Ms 16,176
Miscellaneous policies	1886 to 1926	Ms 16,808
Board and Committee Minutes (29 volumes)	1807 to 1939	Ms 16170

2.3 *Bath Sun Fire Office* (List no 17)

Directors' Minutes	1836 to 1869	Ms 18815

2.4 *Birmingham Mutual Fire & General Insurance Association* (Central Insurance Company)(List no 154)

Board and Committee Minutes	1899 to 1909	Ms 11700

2.5 *British Commercial Fire Insurance Company* (List no 168)

Board and Shareholders Minutes	1910 to 1934	Ms 24897

2.6 *British Equitable Assurance Company* (List no 111)

Board Minutes	1925 to 1942	Ms 16181

2.7 *British Fire Insurance Company* (List no 167)
Board and Committee Minutes (1 volume)   1916 to 1925   Ms 21315

2.8 *British General Insurance Company* (List no 160)
Register of Total Losses (marine)   1927 to 1942   Ms 23684

2.9 *British Law Fire Insurance Company* (*British Law Insurance Company*) (List no 147)
Board Minutes (12 volumes)   1888 to 1918   Ms 12162D
Fire and General Purpose Committee
Minutes (16 volumes)   1888 to 1926   Ms 112162E

2.10 *Caledonian Insurance Company* (List no 44)
Board and Committee Minutes
(20 volumes)   1890 to 1938   Ms 16184

Central Insurance Company – see *Birmingham Mutual Fire and General*

2.11 *Church of England Life and Fire Assurance Trust and Annuity Institution* (*England Assurance Institution*) (List no 94)
Board Minutes (12 volumes)   1844 to 1893   Ms 12160D

2.12 *Commercial Union Assurance Company* (List no 114)
Committee Minutes
(Fire and Accidents) (38 volumes)   1861 to 1938   Ms 14026

2.13 *Contributors for Insuring Houses, Chambers or Rooms from Loss by Fire, by Amicable Contributions* (*Hand-in-Hand Fire Office*)(List no 3)
General Minute Books
(34 volumes, some gaps)   1697 to 1833   Ms 8666
Policy Registers (with name indices)
(150 volumes, some gaps)   1696 to 1865   Ms 8674
Policy Registers (3 volumes)   1805 to 1816   Ms 8675
Policy Registers (with name indices)
(4 volumes)   1803 to 1830   Ms 8676
Policy Registers (with name indices)
(3 volumes)   1830 to 1866   Ms 8677
Numerical Indices to policy numbers
1 to 105428   Ms 8678
Indices of names to:

Ms 8676 volumes 3 and 4	1820 to 1830	} Ms 8679
Ms 8677 volumes 1 and 2	1830 to 1859	
Ms 8674 volumes 148 and 149	1823 to 1846	
Ms 8674 volumes 146 to 149	1815 to 1846	Ms 8681
Ms 8674 volumes 143 to 147	1807 to 1823	} Ms 8680
Ms 8675 volumes 1 to 3	1805 to 1816	
Ms 8676 volumes 1 to 3	1806 to 1824	

Topographical Indices to:

Ms 8674 vols 147 to 149	1819 to 1846	} Ms 8682
Ms 8676 vols 2 to 4	1814 to 1830	
Ms 8677 vols 1 and 2	1830 to 1859	

Topographical Indices to:

Ms 8674 vols 144 to 148	1810 to 1831	} Ms 8683
Ms 8675 vols 1 to 3	1805 to 1816	

Topographical Index to London area

Ms 8674 vols 144 to 148	1810 to 1831	
Ms 8675 vol 3	1812 to 1816	} Ms 8684
Ms 8677 vols 1 and 2	1830 to 1859	
Pewterers' Company, policies for	1718 to 1853	Ms 22254
Property in Lime Street		
Parish Property, St. Bride Fleet Street;		
policies	1840 to 1842	Ms 6636
Parish Property, St Christophers Le Stocks	1672 to 1772	Ms 21626
Policy numbers 77791 and 77793		
Parish Property, St.John the Baptist, Walbrook	1785	Ms 581
St.Michael Queenhithe, property in Huggin Lane	1766	Ms 22838
and Thomas Street		
Vintner's Company, policy	1722	Ms 15494
Surveyor's Estimate Book	1806 to 1830	Ms 8686

2.14 *County Fire Office* (List no 46)

Agent's Register (Mr James Cox)	1856 to 1867	Ms 18816
Stow-on-theWold		
Endorsement Register (1 volume)	1859 to 1903	Ms 18817

Double Hand-in-Hand Fire Office – see *Union*

England Assurance Institution – see *Church of England Life and Fire*

Essex and Suffolk Equitable Insurance Society – see *Essex Equitable*

2.15 *Essex Equitable Insurance Company* (*Essex and Suffolk Equitable Insurance Society*)
(List no 35)

Board Minutes (11 volumes)	1802 to 1941	Ms 16206

2.16 *Farmers and General Insurance Company*
(*Royal Farmers and General Fire, Life and Hail Insurance Company*)(List no 95)

Hail and Glass Register	1906 to 1930	Ms 14996
Agents Instructions (5 volumes)	1858 to 1886	Ms 14997
Board Minutes (21 volumes)	1839 to 1887	Ms 14989
Papers re Steam Traction (1 bundle)	1879 to 1901	Ms 14999
List of Agents (by County)	late 19th century	Ms 14998

2.17 *Fine Art and General Insurance Company* (List no 149)

Board and Committee Minutes	1890 to 1933	Ms 14044
(5 volumes)		

2.18 *Fire Insurance Association* (*Albion Fire Insurance Association*)(List no 142)

Board Minutes (1 volume)	1890 to 1894	Ms 16153

2.19 *Globe Insurance Company* (List no 39)

Board and Committee Minutes	1803 to 1864	Ms 11657
(5 volumes)		
Agent's Policy Register	1823 to 1827	Ms 11679
(policy numbers 82971 to 93780)		
Policies relating to property in	1804 to 1899	Ms 8079
Upper Thames Street (includes policies		
for the Hand-in-Hand and the Globe)		

Register of Agents Securities
(arranged topographically) (1 volume)   c1830 to c1850   Ms 11685

Office Ledgers (3 volumes)   1803 to 1850   Ms 11674
Journals (3 volumes)   1803 to 1850   Ms 11675

2.20 *Guardian Fire and Life Assurance Company* (List no 58)
Board and Committee Minutes (36 volumes)   1821 to 1941   Ms 14281
Fire Committee Minute Book (12 volumes)   1872 to 1932   Ms 14282
Fire Department General Ledger   1821 to 1867   Ms 18106
Fire Department Journal (includes details of
losses with namesand addresses of claimants)   1821 to 1832   Ms 18107
Register of Local Agents (1 volume)   1821 to 1862   Ms 18111

Hand-in-Hand Fire Office – see Contributors for Insuring Houses, Chambers or Rooms
from Loss by Fire

2.21 *Imperial Fire Insurance Company* (List no 41)
Board Minutes (29 volumes)   1803 to 1902   Ms 12160A
St.Sepulchre, Holborn; Parish Estates   1862 to 1907   Ms 7245
Policy Register (Order Book)   1864 to 1877   Ms 14100
Herstmonceux, Sussex, Agency

2.22 *Law Fire Insurance Society* (List no 101)
Board and Committee Minutes (44 volumes)   1845 to 1927   Ms 15010
Salaries (names etc.) (1 volume)   1883 to 1914   Ms 15018
Salaries (names etc.) (1 volume)   1883 to 1910   Ms 15019
Ledgers (4 volumes)   1845 to 1920   Ms 15016

2.23 *Law Union Fire and Life Insurance Company* (*Law Union and Crown; Law Union and
Rock*) (List no 112)
Board and Committee Minutes (23 volumes)   1858 to 1952   Ms 21258
Register of Salaries   1896 to 1902   Ms 21276
Register of Salaries – Head Office (7 volumes) 1902 to 1948 ⎫
Register of Salaries at Branches   1902 to 1957 ⎬ Ms 21277
Staff Registers-Head Office and   c1905 to 1931   Ms 21278
Branches (2 volumes)
Branch Office Staff Serving in   c1915   Ms 21279
Armed Forces
Head Office Staff Serving in   c1915   Ms 21280
Armed Forces
First five fire policies all relating   1854   Ms 21269
to Plymouth
Farming Stock Fire Policy Registers (2 volumes) 1854 to 1867   Ms 21270
Fire Policy Endorsement Book (2 volumes)   1857 to 1861   Ms 21271

2.24 *Licensed Victuallers and General Insurance Company* (*Monarch Fire and Life Assurance
Company*) (List no 88)
Board Minutes (7 volumes)   1835 to 1857   Ms 11661

2.25 *Licenses and General Insurance Company* (List no 150)
Board Minutes (21 volumes)   1890 to 1937   Ms 16213

2.26 *Liverpoool Fire and Life Insurance Company* (*Liverpool and London and Globe Insurance Company*) (List no 89)

Fire Committee Agenda Books	1871 to 1908	Ms 11665
Fire and Accident Committee Minutes		Ms 11666

2.27 *Liverpool Victoria Insurance Corporation* (List no 165)

General Meetings Minutes	1913 to 1921	Ms 14060

2.28 *London and Lancashire Insurance Company* (List no 115)

Board and Committee Minutes	1861 to 1950	Ms 21296
Staff Agreements (in volume1)	1869 to 1875	Ms 21310
(4 volumes; volumes 2, 3 & 4 include leases, agreements and deeds)		
Policy Register; Number 1	1862 to 1863	Ms 21306
Policy Register	1862 to 1867	Ms 21307
Policy Register – Town Agents, No 1	1863	Ms 21308
Register of Fire Claims	1862 to 1865	Ms 21309

2.29 *London Assurance Corporation* (List no 10)

Directors' Minutes (58 volumes)	1722 to 1926	Ms 8728
Policy Register (all Irish)	1845 to 1881	Ms 8747D
(policy numbers 132455 to 599520 – not all numbers used)		
Fire Committee Minutes (68 volumes)	1725 to 1924	Ms 8735
Register of Fire Renewal Policies	1721 to 1726	Ms 8740A
(gives names of policy holders but places not given)		
Policy Registers (4 volumes, gaps in dates)	1722 to 1826	Ms 8747
Policy Registers (3 volumes, all Jersey)	1856 to 1898	Ms 8747A
Policy Registers – Worcester Branch (10 volumes)	1893 to 1934	Ms 17598
Index to volume 10 only		Ms 17598A
Premium Registers	1721 to 1727	Ms 8748
(2 volumes, gives names and places).		
Volume 3, Agents Ledger	1721 to 1728	
Fire Charter Journals (4 volumes)	1721 to 1835	Ms 8744
Plan Book (52 plans of houses and trade property in London and Home Counties)	1746 to 1747	Ms 14316
Survey Book. Plans for London area	1882 to 1884	Ms14656
Certificates of Burials	1751 to 1829	Ms 8759
Register of Probates	1720 to 1843	Ms 8757
(6 volumes; volume 6 is index to the other 5 volumes)		

2.30 *Manchester Fire and Life Assurance Company* (*Manchester Assurance Company*)(List no 71)

Board and Committee Minutes	1825 to 1904	Ms 16222
(18 volumes)		
Losses and Claims (2 volumes)	1901 to 1903	Ms 16227

2.31 *Mercantile Fire Insurance Company* (List no 116)

Board Minutes	1861 to 1862	Ms 14038

Monarch Fire and Life Assurance Company – see *Lincensed Victualers*

2.32 *New Fire Office (Phoenix Fire Office)* (List no 22)
Policy for William Rust for

numbers 60 and 61 Aldermanbury	1824	Ms 14573
Policy for St. Andrew, Holborn	1853	Ms 4262

2.33 *North British Insurance Company (North British and Mercantile Insurance Company)*
(List no 54)

Board and Committee Minutes	1862 to 1927	Ms 14040
Wharf and Warehouse Plans, London	1863 to 1903	Ms 15627
Wharf and Warehouse Plans, London	1863 to 1923	Ms 15628

2.34 *North of Scotland Fire and Life Assurance Company (Northern Assurance Company)*
(List no 90)

Court Minutes (2 volumes)	1865 to 1931	Ms 14062

Northern Assurance Company – see *North of Scotland Fire and Life*

2.35 *Nottinghamshire and Derbyshire Fire and Life Assurance Company* (List no 84)

Board Minutes – Chesterfield (1 volume)	1858 to 1869	Ms 18311
Agents Instructions	1836 to 1865	Ms 18275
(and list of shareholders)		

2.36 *Ocean Railway and General Travellers Assurance Company* (List no 131)

Board Minutes (2 volumes)	1877 to 1892	Ms 14032
Accident Department Minutes (18 volumes)	1891 to 1940	Ms 14033

2.37 *Palatine Insurance Company* (List no 144)

Board and Court Minutes (4 volumes)	1893 to 1935	Ms 14057

Phoenix Fire Office – see *New Fire Office*

2.38 *Provident Clerks and General Accident Insurance Company (White Cross Insurance
Association)* (List no 139 and List no 164)

General Meetings Minutes (1 volume)	1911 to 1958	Ms 16831

2.39 *Royal Exchange Assurance* (List no 11)

Fire Committee Minute Books,indexed	1825 to 1888	Ms 16237
(10 volumes)		
Fire Policy Registers – First Series (7 volumes)	1753 to 1759	Ms 7252
Fire Policy Registers – Second Series	1773 to 1833	Ms 7253
(97 volumes)		
Fire Insurance Registers (37 volumes)	1803 to 1883	Ms 7254
Head Office, London		
Fire Policy Registers (32 volumes)	1809 to 1870	Ms 7255
Supplementary Agents Series		

Royal Farmers and General – see *Farmers and General*

2.40 *Royal Irish Insurance Company* (List no 81)

Policy List (Deeds of Agreement)	1827 to 1834	Ms 8761

Salamander Fire Office – see *Wiltshire and Western*

2.41 *State Fire Insurance Company* (List no 152)
Board Minutes (5 volumes)   1891 to 1944   Ms 16259

2.42 *Sun Fire Office* (List no 4)
Management Committee   1725 to 1902   Ms 11932
Minute Books (46 volumes)
Country Committee   1730 to 1897   Ms 11935
Minute Books (32 volumes)
General Committee Minute Books (19 volumes)   1709 to 1896   Ms 11931
(indexed)
Town Committee (23 volumes)   1730 to 1896   Ms 11934
General Cash Books (40 volumes)   1750 to 1890   Ms 12019
Policy Registers (old series)   1710 to 1863   Ms 11936
(733 volumes)
Policy Registers, Craigs Court   1726 to 1732   Ms11936A
(2 volumes)
Policy Abstract Books
volume 1   1854 to 1855   Ms11936C
volume 2 (mostly London and Home Counties)   1861
volume 3   1862 to 1863
Plans of Insured Property (London)   1802 to 1806   Ms 11936D
Abstract Books of Fire Policies from   Ms 21376
Ms 11936/196-9
Policy Registers – Country Dept   1793 to 1863   Ms 11937
(527 volumes)
Register of Country Losses (5 volumes)   ⎫
(alphabetical names)   ⎬   1803 to 1864   Ms 11937A
                                         ⎭
Indices to Policy Registers (4 parts)   1711 to 1712 ⎫
to Ms 11936/2 & 4   1714 to 1715 ⎬   Ms 17816
                                                                ⎭
Card Index to Ms 11936/4 to 33   ⎫
(by Alan Redstone)   ⎬   1714 to 1731   Ms 17817
(alphabetical names with counties)   ⎭
Numerical Index to policies 29001 to   1752 to 1846   Ms 21595
134000   and Ms 21596
Endorsement Books (incomplete)   1728 to 1865   Ms 12160
(137 volumes)
New Policy Endorsement Books   1819 to 1861   Ms 12161
(11 volumes)
Register of Town Losses (London)   1851 to 1866   Ms 11934B
Papers Relating to Fires (12 sheets)   ⎫
Statement by Ann Leslie, coffee woman,   ⎪
Princes Street, Leicester Fields on   ⎪
11 Feb 1777 with inventory (4 bundles)   ⎪
Statement by Samuel Worrell; fire at 3   ⎪
Lincolns Inn, New Square on 13 Dec1782   ⎪
with inventory   ⎪
Statement by Captain Joseph Richards;   ⎬   Ms 15040
fire in warehouse of Hudson Bay Co   ⎪
in Narrow Street, Limehouse on 16 Dec   ⎪
1779 (policy number 395480)   ⎪
Thomas Harridge payment for work   ⎪
repairing dwelling house at Leigh, Essex ⎪
damaged by fire 28 Dec1773   ⎪
(policy number 327775)   ⎭

Memoranda of Wills (2 volumes) with burial certificates	1755 to 1833	Ms 12025
Fire Insurance Policy number 182691 to William Davis chandler and dealer in coals, at corner of Great Poultney Street and Silver Street 18 May 1761; with endorsement		Ms 15816
Claims upon loss of, or damage to property and stock arranged alphabetically within various counties, with index of claimants	1770 to 1788	Ms 31688
Miscellaneous Claims, London	1771 to 1788	Ms 21075
Firemens' Bonds	1788 to 1824	Ms 15046
Special Report Book	1804 to 1889	Ms11935A
Receipt Books	1807 to 1828	Ms 14107

2.43 *Union* (or *Double Hand-in-Hand*) *Fire Office* (*Union Assurance Society*) (List no 5)

Board and Committee Minutes (68 volumes)	1714 to 1893 and 1904 to 1906	Ms14022
Board and Committee Minutes (17 volumes)	1907 to 1939	Ms14022A
Fire Committee Minutes (1 volume)	1903 to 1905	Ms 16834

2.44 *United British Insurance Company* (List no 175)

Board Minutes (1 volume)	1929 to 1939	Ms 16260

White Cross Insurance Association – see *Provident Clerks and General Accident*

2.45 *Wiltshire and Western Assurance Society* (*Salamander Fire Office*) (List no 27)

Take-over papers only (by the *Sun*)	Ms 11935E

Appendix 3

Records in County Record Offices and other Local Archives

The list numbers in brackets are the list numbers given in Appendix 1.

3.1   **England** (Arranged by Historic County)

3.1.1   **Bedfordshire**

3.1.2   **Berkshire**
Berkshire Record Office
9 Coley Avenue
Reading
Berkshire RG1 6AF

London Assurance Corporation (List no 10)

Policy Registers – Reading Agency	1863 to 1889	D/EX 113/1 to 4

3.1.3   **Bristol**
Bristol Record Office
'B' Bond Warehouse
Smeaton Road
Bristol BS1 6XN

Bristol Crown Fire Office (List no 7)

Various individual policies and related material	5535/1- 66
Correspondence etc. re history	37165/4/3/1

3.1.4   **Buckinghamshire**
Buckinghamshire Record Office
County Hall
Aylesbury
Buckinghamshire HP20 1UA

Sun Fire Office (List no 4)

Policy Register: Stony Stratford Agency	1842 to 1889	D100/50
Alliance Assurance Company		
Policy Register: Aylesbury Agency	1875 to 1953	AR 18/91

3.1.5   **Cambridgeshire**
County Record Office
Shire Hall
Cambridge CB3 OAP

Phoenix Fire Office (List no 22)
Policy Register: St. Ives (Hunts) Agency   1895 to 1904   micro-film
Policy Register: Royston (Herts) Agency   1900 to 1906   micro-film

Sun Fire Office (List no 4)
Policy Register: Cambridge Agency   1951 to 1956   R97/13

3.1.6   **Cheshire and Chester**
none

3.1.7   **Cornwall**
Cornwall Record Office
County Hall
Truro
Cornwall TR1 3AY

Company not given (William Salter, agent)*
Policy Register: Truro Agency   1841 to 1864   AD 81/45

* Kelly's Cornwall Directory for 1856 lists William Salter as agent for the *Sun Fire and Life Office* (List no 4)

West of England Fire and Life Insurance Company (List no 49)
Policies and Receipts
Mevagissey Property   1870 to 1924   X 331/45-51

See also Devon Record Office, Exeter (3.1.10) for Accounts and collections for
Cornwall

3.1.8   **Cumberland**
Cumbria Record Office
Scotch Street
Whitehaven
Cumbria CA28 7BJ

Liverpool and London and Globe Insurance Company (List no 89)
Account Book   1904 to 1911   D/BT/4/2

3.1.9   **Derbyshire**
Derbyshire Record Office
County Hall
Matlock
Derbyshire DE4 3AG

Sun Fire Office (List no 4)
Policy Register: Wirksworth Agency   1860 to 1924   D161 B/9/1

3.1.10 **Devonshire**
Devon Record Office
Castle Street
Exeter
EX4 3PU

Phoenix Fire Office (List no 22)
Business Register: Ashburton Agency	1837 to 1861	924B/B9/1

Alliance British and Foreign Fire and Life Insurance Company (List no 64)
Policy Register: Bampton Agency	1898 to 1903	1044B add/23

Law Union and Rock Insurance Company (List no 112)
Policy Register: Chagford Agency	1944 to 1952	3963M/B 516

Sun Fire Office (List no 4)
Fire Office Ledger: Chumleigh Agency,	1887 to 1891	4283
Policy Renewal Register: Exeter Agency	1908 to 1910	3842 M/BA5

West of England Fire and Life Insurance Company (List no 49)
Accounts and Collection Book Cornwall	1867 to 1884	4253B/Z5
Policy Registers: Crediton Agency	1808 to 1847	4293B/R1-3
Policy Register	1813 to 1861	4293B add 2/R12
Policy Registers:	1808 to 1821	
Exeter and Exmouth Agencies	1868 to 1877	
	1877 to 1883	4196B/A1-4
	1883 to 1889	
Policy Registers: Honiton Agency	1920 to 1929	337B add2/misc
volumes 1 & 4		
Agent's Diary: Thorverton	1843	1044B/M/F33
Policy Register: Tiverton Agency	c1860	R4/1/PP8

Atlas Assurance Company (List no 51)
Agent's Account Book: Cullompton	1828 to 1840	74B/Z7
Agency (fragment of)		

Norwich Union Fire Insurance Society (List no 30)
Policy Register: Cullompton Agency	1863 to 1889	1044Badd/Z2
Account and Renewal Books:	1913 to 1936	867B/MZ11/1-9
Totnes Agency		
Policy Register	20th century	1004B add/Z1

Law Fire Insurance Society (List no 101)
Prospectus and other papers; Devon	1845 to 1874	58/9 Box 52/4
Account Books: Totnes Agency	1918 to 1925	867B/MZ 12/1-2

Eagle Star and British Dominions Insurance Company
(British Dominions Marine Insurance Company)(List no 159)
Account Books: Totnes Agency   1934 to 1951   867B/MZ 13

Various Insurance Companies
Policy Registers etc: Crediton Agency   1902 to 1955   3177B/G1-4,6-8
Fire Policy Order Book   1934 to 1967   4950B add/A206

North Devon Record Office
Tuly Street
Barnstaple
EX31 1EL

Commercial Union Assurance Company (List no 114)
Policy Register: Bideford Agency   1890 to1960   2239B/22/9

British Law Insurance Company (List no 147)
Policy Register: Bideford Agency   1910 to 1920   2239B/22/1

County Fire Office (List no 46)
Policy Register: Bideford Agency   1900 to 1955   2239B/22/8

Eagle Star and British Dominions Insurance Company (List no 159)
Policy Register: Bideford Agency   1920 to 1927   2239B/22/2

Royal Exchange Assurance (List no 11)
Policy Register: Bideford Agency   1896 to 1924   2239B/22/4

3.1.11   **Dorsetshire**
         Dorset Record Office
         Bridport Road
         Dorchester
         Dorset DT1 1RP

County Fire Office (List no 46)
Policy Register: Lyme Regis Agency   1825 to 1864   D.654/1

Royal Exchange Assurance (List no 11)
Policy Register: Wareham Agency   1839 to 1863   D/WLC:Z31-32

Atlas Assurance Company (List no 51)
Policy Books: Wimborne Minster Agency 1827 to 1950   D/CRL:C1/1/1-4

Alliance Assurance Company (List no 64)
Policy Order Book:
Wimborne Minster Agency   c1920 to 1950   D/CRL:C2/1/1-2
and Office Ledger

3.1.12 **Durham**
Gateshead Central Library
Gateshead
NE8 4LN

Newcastle Upon Tyne Fire Office (List no 25)
Accounts   1807 to 1821

3.1.13 **Essex**
Essex Record Office
Wharf Road
Chelmsford
Essex CM2 6YT

Sun Fire Office (List no 4)
Policy Registers: Braintree Agency   (dates not given)   Acc.A5407(D/F69)

Essex Equitable Insurance Company (List no 35)
Policy Register: Chelmsford Agency   1802 to 1805   D/F 21/1

Essex and Suffolk Equitable Insurance Society (List no 35)
Instructions Book: Maldon Agency   1816 to c1916   D/F 21/2-31

Unidentified Company
Policy Record Book:
Great Dunmow Agency   c1930 to 1964   D/F 159

Essex Record Office
Stanwell House
Stanwell Street
Colchester
Essex CO2 7DL

Phoenix Assurance Company (List no 22)

Policy Registers: Colchester Agency	1850 to 1963	D/F 129/1/1-4
Colchester Agency	1890 to 1969	D/F 129/1/11-19
Endorsement Books: Colchester Agency	1892 to 1961	D/F 129/1/5-6
Index to Endorsement Books: Colchester Agency }	1850 to 1896	D/F 129/1/7
Premium Account Books: Colchester Agency	1889 to 1924	D/F 129/1/8-10

Waltham Forest Archives
Vestry House Museum
Vestry Road
Walthamstow
London E17 9NH

Royal Exchange Assurance (List no 11)
Fire Order Books: Leytonstone Agency   1865 to 1888   L 28/REA 1-3

3.1.14 **Gloucestershire**
Gloucestershire Record Office
Clarence Row
Alvin Street
Gloucester GL1 3DW

Queen Insurance Company (List no 113)
Policy Registers: Cheltenham Agency   1895 to 1906   D 5672 1/1-2

Sun Fire Office (List no 4)
Policy Registers: Fairford Agency   1840 to 1877   D 1070 V/1-3
                 Tewkesbury Agency   1824 to 1924   D 2079 V/11-24
                 Pershore Agency   1902 to 1936   D 2079 V/19

Fine Art and General Insurance Company (List no 149)
Policy Registers: Tewkesbury Agency   1911 to 1943   D 2079 V/22-3

3.1.15 **Hampshire**
Hampshire Record Office
Sussex Street
Winchester
Hampshire SO23 8TH

Royal Exchange Assurance (List no 11)
Fire Books and Policies: Bishops Waltham 1873 to 1917   45M69/222
Papers for Highclere Esate   1838 to 1857   15M52/520

Alliance British and Foreign Fire and Life Insurance Company (List no 64)
Registers of Insurances: Hambledon area 1893 to 1903   70M78/B1-B3

Sun Fire Office (List no 4)
Registers of Insurances:
Southampton area   1873 to 1880   70M78/B4

Westminster Fire Office (List no 6)
Register of Insurances:
Southampton area   1892 to 1950   70M78/B5

Portsmouth City Record Office
Museum Road
Portsmouth PO1 2LJ

Scottish Union and National Insurance Company (List no 75)
Renewal Register:
Bishops Waltham Agency   1911 to 1930   3A/4

3.1.16 **Herefordshire**
        Herefordshire Record Office
        The Old Barracks
        Harold Street
        Hereford HR1 2QX

        Law Union Fire and Life Insurance Company (List no 112)
        Policy Register: Hereford Agency   1872 to 1883   BB89/1

        National Farmers Union Mutual Insurance Society (List no 172)
        Miscellaneous Receipts   BE94/3-8

3.1.17 **Hertfordshire**
        Hertfordshire Archives and Local Studies
        County Hall
        Hertford SG13 8DE

        North British and Mercantile Insurance Company (List no 54)
        Policy Register: Barnet Agency   1902 to 1927   D/Ebt B38

        County Fire Office (List no 46)
        Policy Registers, Endorsement Books, etc. 1828 to 1945   D/Z 97/1-20

        Phoenix Assurance Company (List no 22)
        Policy Registers: Ware Agency   1851 to 1950   D/Ecn B59-63

        See also Cambridgeshire

3.1.18 **Huntingdonshire**
        Cambridgeshire County Record Office (Huntingdon)
        Grammar School Walk
        Huntingdon PE29 3LF

        Guardian Assurance (List no 58)
        Instruction Books   1937 to 1950   Accession 3035
        Renewal Register   c1930s
        Policy Registers: St Neots Agency   1854 to 1938
        (18 volumes)

        Phoenix Assurance Company (List no 22)
        Renewal Register: St Neots Agency   1927 to 1928

        Royal Insurance (List no 102)
        Policy Register: St Neots Agency   1927 to 1931

        London and Lancashire Insurance Company (List no 115)
        Policy Register: St Neots   not dated

        See also Cambridgeshire

3.1.19 Kent
Sevenoaks Library
Buckhurst Lane
Sevenoaks
Kent TN13 1LQ

Royal Exchange Assurance (List no 11)
Policy Register: Westerham Agency   1869 to 1916   WU5/Z1

3.1.20 Lancashire
Lancashire Record Office
Bow Lane
Preston PR1 2RE

Sun Fire Office (List no 4)
Policy Registers: Oldham Agency   1877 to 1911   DDRE/1/26
                 Carnforth Agency   c1910   DDX 831/1/1
Renewal List: Carnforth Agency   c1910   DDX 831/1/2

Manchester Fire and Life Assurance Company (List no 71)
Policies and Endorsements:
Blackburn Agency   1830 to 1843

Greater Manchester Record Office
56 Marshall Street
New Cross
Manchester M4 5FU

Primitive Methodist Insurance Company (List no 125)
Board Minutes and Correspondence   1866 to 1933
Policy Register   1866 to 1894

Wesleyan Methodist Trust Assurance Company (*Methodist Insurance Company*)
(List no 132)
Board and Committee Minutes   1872 to 1971
Policy Specimens   1900 to 1970

Liverpool Record Office
Central Library
William Brown Street
Liverpool L3 8EW

Birmingham Alliance Fire Insurance Company (List no 121)
Board and Committee Minutes   1864 to 1872

Globe Insurance Company (List no 39)
Board Minutes   1815 to 1833

Liverpool Fire and Life Insurance Company (*Liverpool and London and Globe*)
(List no 89)

Board Minutes	1846 to 1872	368 ROY
Committee Minutes – various	1836 to 1891	
(9 volumes)		
Ledgers (15 volumes)	1836 to 1859	

London and Lancashire Insurance Company (List no 115)

Journals	1862 to 1888
Ledgers	1861 to 1886

Midland Counties Insurance Company (List no 107)

Fire Journals	1855 to 1892
Fire Ledger	1855 to 1892

North of England Fire and Life Insurance Company (List no 98)

Board Minutes	1848 to 1852

Queen Insurance Company (List no 113)

Board Minutes (5 volumes)	1857 to 1891

Sheffield and Rotherham Fire Insurance Company (List no 104)

Board Minutes	1844 to 1848

Manchester Fire and Life Assurance Company (List no 71)
Policies and Endorsement:

Blackburn Agency	1830 to 1843	B368

Royal Insurance Company (List no 102)

Agency Book	1865 to 1866
Fire Policies	1847 to 1898
List of Agents	1858

Lancashire Insurance Company (List no 108)

Board Minutes	1852 to 1902

Birmingham Alliance Fire Insurance Company (List no 121)

Board Minutes	1864 to 1872

Sheffield and Rotherham Fire Insurance Company (List no 104)

Board Minutes	1844 to 1848

Architects, Civil Engineers, Builders and General Fire Insurance Company (List no 105)

Shareholders' Minutes	1848 to 1850

Blackburn Central Library
Blackburn
BB2 1AG

Manchester Fire and Life Assurance Company (List no 71)
Policies and Endorsements:
Blackburn Agency   1830 to 1843   micro-film
                                             (orig. at Lancs RO)

3.1.21   Leicestershire
none

3.1.22   Lincolnshire
North East Lincolnshire Archives
Town Hall
Grimsby DN31 1HX

Phoenix Assurance Company (List no 22)
Policy Renewal Register: Grimsby   1930s   242/6

Lincolnshire Archives
St Rumbold Street
Lincoln LN2 5AB

Phoenix Assurance Company (List no 22)
Account Book: Barton on Humber   1845 to 1871   BH 9

County Fire Office (List no 46)
Correspondence: Market Deeping   1875 to 1895   SW 1/3

3.1.23   Middlesex
Westminster City Archives
10 St Anns Street
London SW1P 2DE

Westminster Fire Office (List no 6)
Minutes, etc.   1717 to 1943   Acc 343
Minutes   1717 to 1787   ⎫
                                             1907 to 1961   ⎬ Acc 1971
Registers of Shareholders, Agents, etc.   1871 to 1924   ⎪
Policy Register   1717 to 1721   ⎭

Sun Insurance Office (List no 4)
Scrap Book   1884 to 1917   ⎫ Acc 447
Photograph Album   1932 to 1969   ⎭

3.1.24   Monmouthshire
none

3.1.25   Norfolk
Norfolk Record Office
Gildengate Square
Upper Green Lane
Norwich NR3 1AX

Norwich Union Fire Insurance Society (List no 30)

Policy Register: Norfolk area	1874 to 1889	Damaged ref.lost
Account Book: Northwold Agency	1912 to 1921	MC 62/85,86

3.1.26 Northamptonshire
Northamptonshire Record Office
Wootton Hall Park
Northampton NN4 8BQ

Norwich Union Fire Insurance Society (List no 30)

Policy Registers: Northampton Agency	1811 to 1821	ZA 3314
Northampton Agency	1863 to 1892	ZA 3318
Northampton Agency	1874 to 1921	ZA 3319 to
(8 volumes – continuous series)	}	ZA 3326

General Hailstorm Assurance Society
(This company covered property damage from hailstorms only and not against fire.
It is therefore not included in Appendix 1)

Policy Register: Northampton Agency	1890 to 1928	ZA 3328

3.1.27 Northumberland
Northumberland Record Office
Melton Park
North Gosforth
Newcastle-upon-Tyne NE3 5QX

North British and Mercantile Insurance Company (List no 54)

Policy Registers: Bedlington Agency	1862 to 1949	NRO 2279/1-4
(4 volumes)		
Agents' Letter Books	1878 to 1906	(A) ZBL 1

Phoenix Assurance Company (List no 22)
Office Manual,

Petty Cash Book, etc.: Alnwick Agency	1920s to 1960s	NRO 2619
Insurance Books, Policies & Accounts	1886 to 1931	(A) ZSA 46

3.1.28 Nottinghamshire
Nottinghamshire Archives
County House
Castle Meadow Road
Nottingham NG2 1AG

Sun Fire Office (List no 4)

Policy Registers: Newark Agency	1797 to 1892	DDH 155/102-106

3.1.29 Oxfordshire
none

3.1.30 Rutland
none

3.1.31 Shropshire
Shropshire Records and Research Centre
Castle Gates
Shrewsbury SY1 2AQ

Commercial Union Assurance Company (List no 114)
Policy Register and Expiry Register   1925   2359

Salop Fire Office (List no 21)
Policy Registers   1780 to 1904   ⎫   SRO 3008
Board Minutes   1780 to 1794   ⎭

Shropshire and North Wales Assurance Company (List no 91)
Board Minutes   1836 to 1889
Endorsements   1837 to 1890

3.1.32 Somerset
none

3.1.33 Staffordshire
Wolverhampton Archives & Local Studies
42-50 Snow Hill
Wolverhampton WV2 4AG

Norwich Union Fire Insurance Society (List no 30)
Policy Register   1863 to 1877   D/SSW/XIX

Birmingham Alliance Fire Insurance Company (List no 121)
Policy Register   1864 to 1870   DX/159

3.1.34 Suffolk
Bury St. Edmunds Record Office
77 Raingate Street
Bury St. Edmunds
Suffolk IP33 2AR

Suffolk Alliance Life and Fire Assurance Company (*Suffolk Fire Office*) (List no 37)
Policy Register: West Suffolk   late 19th century   HD 1105/12

Ipswich Record Office
Gatacre Road
Ipswich
Suffolk IP1 2LQ

Suffolk Fire Office (*Suffolk Alliance Life and Fire Assurance Company*) (List no 37)
Minutes, Policy Registers,etc.   1802 to 1960   HH 401

3.1.35 **Surrey**
Surrey History Centre
130 Goldsworth Road
Woking
Surrey GU21 1ND

Westminster Fire Office (List no 6)

Policy Registers: Reigate Agency		1853 to 1954	2173/1/1-17,21-32
	Redhill Agency	1903 to 1928	2173/1/18-20,33

Phoenix Assurance Company (List no 22)

Policy Registers: Chertsey Agency		1788 to 1812	6200/657
	Bagshot Agency	1854 to 1864	361/81//3

Sun Fire Office (List no 4)

Policy Registers: Chertsey Agency	1902 to 1960s ⎫	
Endorsement Books: Chertsey Agency	1900 to 1942 ⎬	6200/704, 706,710

County Fire Office (List no 46)

Policy Register: Chertsey Agency	1950s to 1960s	6200/709

Alliance Assurance Company (List no 64)

Policy Register: Chertsey Agency	1950s to 1960s	6200/707

3.1.36 **Sussex, East**
East Sussex Record Office
The Maltings
Castle Precincts
Lewes
East Sussex BN7 1YT

Sun Fire Office (List no 4)

Policy Register: Hailsham Agency	1863 to 1873	AMS 5628/9/1

Alliance British and Foreign Fire and Life Insurance Company (*Alliance Assurance Company*) (List no 64)

Policy Registers: Hastings Agency		1820s to 1878	AMS 5704
	Hastings Agency	1909 to 1932	AMS 6195/6

Manchester Assurance Company (List no 71)

Collection Legder: Brighton Agency	1899 to 1915	AMS 6329/3

Norwich Union Fire Insurance Society (List no 30)

Policy Register: Hailsham Agency	1905 to 1924	AMS 6160/11/3

3.1.37 **Sussex, West**
West Sussex Record Office
Sherburne House
3 Orchard Street
Chichester PO19 1RN

Sun Fire Office (List no 4)

Policy Registers: Chichester Agency	1834 to 1866	Raper Mss 166-168
Instruction Book: Chichester Agency	1839 to 1860	Raper Mss 169
(Includes policy holders' and details of property insured)		
Endorsement Registers:		
Chichester Agency	1834 to 1879	Raper Mss 170-174
Letters from Head Office	1861 to 1875	Raper Mss 177-189
to Chichester Agency		
General Correspondence from	1882 to1885	Raper Mss 190-201
Head Office to Chichester Agency		

Alliance, British and Foreign Fire and Life Insurance Company (*Alliance Assurance Company*)(List no 64)

Record Book: Chichester Agency	1872 to 1965	Add Mss 19363
(Gives details of property insured and their owners)		
Letter Books: Chichester Agency	1937 to 1948	Mss1257-1283
Holmes, Campbell & Co		

Phoenix Fire Office (List no 22)

Accounts: Chichester Agency	1785 to 1818)	Add Mss 17007-17011
Index of Parishes (photocopies)		Add Mss 17012

3.1.38 **Warwickshire**
Warwick County Record Office
Priory Park
Cape Road
Warwick CV34 4JS

County Fire Office (List no 46)

Policy Registers: Kineton Agency	1837 to 1840, 1849	CR 1295

Commercial Union Assurance Company (List no 114)

Policy Register: Kineton Agency	1897 to 1910	CR 908

New Fire Office/Phoenix Fire Office (List no. 22)

Agents' Registers: Atherstone District	1784 to 1899	CR 1039/1-9
Account Books: Atherstone District	1865 to 1899	CR 1039/10-12

Royal Farmers and General Fire, Life and Hail Insurance Company (List no 95)

Policy Register:		
Shipston-on-Stour, cattle plague	1866 to 1867	CR 609/16

The Shakespeare Birthplace Trust
Henley Street
Stratford-Upon-Avon
CV37 6QW

Law Fire Insurance Society (List no 101)
Policy Register: Stratford-upon-Avon   1913 to 1933   DR 325/I/375

County Fire Office (List no 46)
Policy Regiser: Stratford-Upon-Avon   1945   DR 325/714

Birmingham Central Library
Chamberlain Square
Birmingham B3 3HQ

Blue Ribbon Life, Accident, Mutual and Industrial Insurance Company
(Abstainers and General Insurance Company)(Beacon Insurance Company) (List no 143)
Executive Committee Minutes   1883 to 1933   MS 1605/2/1-5
Registers of Claims refused   1885 to 1936   MS 1605/8/1 & 2
Registers of Head Office Salaries   1904 to 1927   MS 1605/9/4 & 5
Staff appointments, resignations ⎫
dismissals, salary increases, etc. ⎭   1925 to 1945   MS 1605/10/1-5

District Fire Office (List no 85)
Board Minutes   1852
Claims Register   1864
Policy Register   1849 to 1850
Wages Book   1870

3.1.39 **Westmorland**
Cumbria Record Office
Kendal
Cumbria LA9 4RQ

Drapers Mutual Fire and General Insurance Company (Monument Insurance Company)
(List no 169)
Board Minutes   1920 to 1954

Provincial Fire Insurance Company (List no 158)
Board and Committee Minutes   1921 to 1963
Claims Registers   1904 to 1920

3.1.40 **Wiltshire**
Wiltshire and Swindon Record Office
County Hall
Trowbridge
Wiltshire BA14 8BS

Sun Fire Office (List no 4)
Policy Register: Salisbury Agency   1832 to 1843   682/7
Policy Register: Westbury Agency   1879 to 1919   2221 bx1

Policy and Renewal Registers:
Trowbridge Agency   1835 to 1935   Acc 1910
Registers (12 Volumes, some indexed)   Boxes A & B

Endorsement Registers: 1850 to 1909   (Box B)

County Fire Office (List no 46)
Policy and Renewal Registers: 1867 to 1954   Acc 1910
Trowbridge Agency   Boxes A & C
(8 volumes, some indexed)

Norwich Union Fire Insurance Society (List no 30)
Policy Register: Trowbridge Agency   1818 to 1830   Acc 1919 Box A
Policy Order Book: Trowbridge Agency   1906 to 1921   Acc 1919 Box C
Policy Order Book: Trowbridge Agency   1917 to 1952

3.1.41   **Worcestershire**
         Worcestershire Record Office
         County Hall
         Spetchley Road
         Worcester WR5 2NP

         Law Fire Insurance Society (List no 101)
         Policy Orders: Evesham (3 volumes)   1846 to 1891   899:251 BA5044/7
         Account Book: Evesham   1886 to 1889

3.1.42   **Yorkshire – East Riding**
         The University of Hull
         Brynmor Jones Library
         Hull HU6 7RX

         Sun Fire Office (List no 4)
         Policy Registers: Hull Agency   1804 to 1924   DX/43/1-17
         (17 volumes)
         Premium Book: Hull Agency   1867 to 1915   DX/43/18

3.1.43   **Yorkshire – West Riding**
         Doncaster Archives
         King Edward Road
         Doncaster DN4 0NA

         County Fire Office (List no 46)
         Policy Registers: Thorne Agency   1818 to 1920   DY/CFO
         (14 volumes)

         West Yorkshire Archive Service, Calderdale
         Northgate House
         Northgate
         Halifax HX1 1UN

Liverpool and London and Globe Insurance Company (List no 89)
Policy Registers(14 volumes): Elland   c1865 to c1953   HGA/6-19
Account and Claims Register: Elland   1865 to 1925   HGA/1
Claims Registers (8 volumes): Elland   1920 to 1962   HGA/48-54
Renewal Register: Elland   1908 to 1913
HGA/58

Sheffield Archives
52 Shoreham Street
Sheffield S1 4SP

County Fire Office (List no 46)
Policy Registers: Thorne   1818 to 1920   134/B1/1-14 (film)

Sheffield Fire Office (List no 52)
Ledger: Sheffield   1826 to 1838   SC 1087

West Yorkshire Archive Service, Kirklees
Hudderfield Central Library
Princess Alexandra Walk
Huddersfield HD1 2SU

Liverpool and London and Globe (List no 89),
Alliance Assurance (List no 64), *British General* (List no 160), *County Fire Office*
(List no 46), *Eagle Star* (List no 159), etc (mixed)
Policy Registers: Batley
(9 vols; all indexed)   1865 to 1956
KC71

West Yorkshire Archive Service, Leeds
Chapeltown Road
Sheepscar
Leeds LS7 3AP

York and North of England Fire and Life Insurance Company (*York and London Fire and
Life Insurance Company*) (List no 87)
Cash Book
1834 to 1850   LSE/23

Leeds and Yorkshire Fire and Life Insurance Company (List no 70)
Letter Book
1824 to 1829   Acc.3393
Board Minutes (3 volumes)   1843 to 1875

Liverpool and London and Globe Insurance Company (List no 89)
Minute Books – Leeds and Yorkshire   1864 to 1875 (2 volumes)
Rough Minute Books (9 volumes)   1864 to 1880

Morley Mutual Insurance Society (List no 133)
Board Minute Book   1872 to 1909

Central Insurance Company (List no 154)
Board Minute Books (2 volumes)   1903 to 1943

3.2   **Wales**

The only relevant records located in Wales are the following:

3.2.1   Denbighshire Record Office
46 Clwyd Street
Ruthin LL15 1HP

Provincial Welsh Fire and Life Insurance Company (List no 109)
Board and Committee Minutes   1852 to 1890
Staff Register   1852 to 1906

3.2.2   Pembrokeshire Record Office
The Castle
Haverfordwest
Pembrokeshire SA61 2EF

Phoenix Fire Office (List no 22)
Policy Register   1881 to 1965   D/RKL/1391

Law Fire Insurance Society (List no 101)
Policy Register: Milford Haven   1874 to 1880   D/RTM/13/19
Receipts and Premiums Due   1917 to 1927   D/RTM/13/22

Alliance Assurance Company (List no 64)
Policy Register   1937 to 1951   D/RTM/13/28

3.2.3   National Library of Wales
Manuscript Department
Aberystwyth
Dyfed SY23 3BU

Welsh Calvanistic Methodist Assurance Trust (List no 145)
Board and Assembly Minutes   1929 to 1951
Correspondence   1913,1935 to 1951

3.3   **Scotland**

3.3.1   The National Archives of Scotland
HM General Register House
Edinburgh EH1 3YY

Bon Accord Life and Fire Insurance Guarantee Reversionary and Annuity Company
(List no 100)
Board Minutes   1845 to 1849   1448

British Law Fire Insurance Company (List no 147)
Board Minutes   1889 to 1921

> *Caledonian Insurance Company* (List no 44)
> Committee Minutes   1839 to 1931
> Claims Registers   1888 to 1931
> Policy Register   1805 to 1807
>
> *Free Church of Scotland Fire Insurance Trust* (*United Free Church of Scotland Fire Insurance Trust*)(List no 148)
> Policy Registers   1888 to 1949   GD1/681/6-13
> Endorsation Books   1898 to 1948   GD 1/681/14-16
>
> *Provident Clerks and General Accident Insurance Company* (List no 139)
> Board Minutes   1876 to 1907

3.3.2   The National Library of Scotland
            Edinburgh EH1 1EW

> *Insurance Company of Scotland* (List no 59)
> Policy and Endorsement Register:
> Glasgow Agency   1836 to 1848   NLS, Acc5252
>
> *West of Scotland Fire Office* (List no 146)
> Board Minutes   1886 to 1937

3.3.3   University of Dundee
            Department of Archives and Manuscripts
            Dundee DD1 4HN

> *North of Scotland Fire and Life Assurance Company* (*Northern Assurance Company*) (List no 90)
> Policy Registers (2 volumes)   1887 to 1934   MS 48/8&9
> Premiums Register   1922 to 1947   MS 48/10

3.3.4   The Mitchell Library
            North Street
            Glasgow G3 7DN

> *Aberdeen Fire and Life Assurance Company* (*Scottish Provincial Assurance Company*)(List no 78)
> Board Minutes   1840 to 1873   TD 446/1
>
> *North British Insurance Company* (*North British and Mercantile Insurance Company*)(List no 54)
> Board Minutes: Glasgow   1841 to 1922   TD 446/5
> Branch Minutes: Glasgow   1922 to 1954

Minutes: Edinburgh	1809 to 1926	
Committee Meetings	1861 to 1939	
Fire Ledgers	1826 to 1843	
Fire Ledger: Edinburgh	1882 to 1956	
Fire and Agency Sub-committee	1934 to 1946	

Royal Scottish Insurance Company (List no 166)

Diretcors' Minutes	1908 to 1919	TD 446/8

Western Fire and Life Insurance Company (List no 99)

Board Minutes	1844 to 1859

West of Scotland Insurance Company (*Metellus Insurance Company*)(List no 63)

Board Minutes	1823 to 1837

3.3.5   Argyll and Bute District Archives
Kilmoray
Lochgilphead
Argyll PA31 8RT

Bute Insurance Company (List no 134)

Policy Register	1873 to 1882

3.3.6   Glasgow University Archives
13 Thurso Street
Glasgow G11 6PE

Glasgow Fire Insurance Society (List no 38)

Miscellaneous Records	1803 to 1811	UGD71/1/1-6

3.4   **Ireland**

The only relevant records located in Ireland are:

3.4.1   The Public Record Office of Northern Ireland
66 Balmoral Avenue
Belfast BT9 6NY

Imperial Fire Insurance Company (List no 41)

Endorsement Registers: Belfast	1851 to 1867	T 1367

West of England Fire and Life Insurance Company (List no 49)

Policy Register: Londonderry	1858 to 1867	T 2775
Declaration Book: Londonderry, etc.	1821 to 1857	

Great National Fire Insurance Company (List no 136)

Correspondence	1874 to 1875

Appendix 4

Records held by Insurance Companies

4.1   AVIVA[formerly CGNU/Norwich Union]
Surrey Street
Norwich NR1 3DR

The list numbers in brackets are the list numbers given in Appendix 1.

4.1.1.   *Norwich Union Fire Insurance Society* (List no 30)

Policy Order Book: Faversham		1839 to 1843	54/2/2
Policy Order Book : Folkestone		1842 to 1859	54/2/2
Policy Order Book: Oxfordshire		1886 to 1889	54/2/2
Policy Order Book: Oxfordshire		1864 to 1866	54/2/2
Policy Order Book: Essex		1843 to 1866	
		1840 to 1900	54/2/2
		1903 to 1941	
Policy Order Book: Surrey [?]		not dated	54/2/2
Policy Order Book: Whitehaven		1821 to 1848	54/2/2
Policy Register number 3		1863 to 1882	38/3/1
Policy Register: Charing, Kent		1883	54/2/2
Agency Expenses		1818 to 1821	38/4/1
Agency Expenses		1818 to 1821	38/6/1
Agency Register: Charing, Kent		1817 to 1859	10/2/1
Agency Register: East Starling[?]		1954	57/2/1
Agency Register		19th century	57/2/1
Agents' Balances		1879	38/1/1
Agents' Expenses		1888	38/1/1
Proprietors' Registers		1879 to 1908	33/4/1
Accounts: Newcastle		1889 to 1894	38/4/1
Accounts		1877,1885	61/4/2
Agency File: South Africa			44/1/2
Appendix Ledgers		1856 to 1879	10/2/1
Appendix Ledgers		1880 to 1896	10/2/1
Applications for Employment		1882 to 1893	38/2/3
Apprenticeship Indenture for John R. Cramb		1905	38/6/1
Clerks' Attendance Book		1876 to 1877	38/4/1

Clerkship Examination paper [blank]	1900	38/6/1
Copy Policies: Portugal	1895,1912	57/2/1
Correspondence, Staff Matters: Dublin	1912	38/2/3
Correspondence, Ernest Felce, clerk	1887	38/6/1
Correspondence, Charles Arthur Bathurst Bignold, Management structure: Midlands	1909 to 1910	60/4/3
Correspondence, Staff Matters	1884	38/6/1
Losses: Ireland	1818 to 1821	38/1/1
Losses: London	1818 to 1821	38/1/1
Disbursements: Liverpool, Exeter, Birmingham, Bristol, Ireland	1818 to 1821	38/4/1
Board Minutes (extracts)	1853	17/2/3
Board Minutes (extracts)	1843	17/2/3
Fire Ledger, number 3	1829 to 1850	33/4/2
Staff List, Fire Office	1871 to 1872	38/6/1
Fire Committee Reports	1906	4/3/1
Foreign Agents Expenses	1880	38/2/3
Career Papers: Frank Dalton	1860 to 1910	38/2/3
Incendiary Losses	1881	38/4/1
Ledger	1856 to 1874	33/4/2
Correspondence, fraudulent claims Samuel Bignold	1819	17/2/3
Correspondence, Samuel Bignold, William Freeman of Lavenden	1813	38/1/2
List of Agents	1806	57/2/1
Losses and Premiums	1874 to 1883	38/1/1
Losses	Sept. 1891	38/1/1
Motor Insurance Register	1933 to 1970	58/1/1
Notebook	1797 to 1814	38/6/1
Notebook belonging to C.E.Bignold	1849	39/5/1
Notebook belonging to G.O.Clark	1899	38/6/1
Notebook: interviews with policy holders	1947	39/5/1
Note re Staff Pensions	1933	38/6/1
Outstanding Losses	1979	38/4/1
Picture of Fireman John Lang, Exeter	1865	2/1/3
Various Policies	19th & 20th centuries	38/2/1 38/2/2 38/2/3 38/3/1 38/4/1 38/6/1
Policy: Greenwich	1860	17/2/4
Policy Order Book	1880 to 1882	54/2/1
Premium and Commission Account	1879	38/4/1
Premium Receipt	1823	17/2/4
Premium Receipts	19th century	39/5/1
Premium Receipts	19th & 20th century	33/2/4
Premiums and Commission	1880	38/2/3
Proprietors' Journal	1840 to 1979	44/2
Register of Staff Birthdays	1871,1878	38/6/1
Salary Book	1886 to 1889	38/4/1
Salary Details	1932 to 1950	53/2/1

284

An advertisement for the North British and Mercantile Insurance Company

Schedule of Losses	1818 to 1821	38/4/1
Staff Record Cards	1937 to 1964	38/6/1
Staff List	1958	38/2/3
Unpaid Losses	1875, 1876	38/2/3
Policy Ledger: Isle of Man & Ireland	1838 to 1869	30/4/2

4.1.2   *Hercules Fire Insurance Company* (List no 53)
Board Minutes   1847 to 1848

4.1.3.   *North British Insurance Company* (List no 54)
Board and Committee Minutes   1902 to 1966
Policy Register   1844 to 1845

4.1.4   *Scottish Union Insurance Company* (List no 75)
Board and Committee Minutes   1824 to 1968
Policy Registers   1861 to 1957

4.1.5   *Yorkshire Fire and Life Assurance Company* (List no 77)
Board Minutes   1902 to 1968
Claims Records   1884 to 1900
Policy Registers   1824 to 1945

4.1.6   *Aberdeen Fire and Life Assurance Company*
(Scottish Provincial Assurance Company) (List no 78)
Policy Register   1854 to 1882

4.1.7   *North of Scotland Fire and Life Assurance Company*
(Northern Assurance Company) (List no 90)
Agency Appointments   1852 to 1967
Board and Committee Minutes   1934 to 1964

4.1.8   *Scottish National Insurance Company* (List no 97)
Board Minutes   1841 to 1847, 1862
                              to 1866,1870 to 1878

4.1.9   *Scottish Imperial Fire and Life Insurance Company* (List no 123)
Policy Registers   1866 to 1902
Claims Records   1911 to 1945

4.1.10   *Ocean Railway and General Travellers Assurance Company* (List no 131)
Board and Committee Minutes   1940 to 1965

4.1.11   *Palatine Insurance Company* (List no 144)
Board and Committee Minutes   1935 to 1966

4.1.12   *West of Scotland Fire Office* (List no 146)
Board Minutes   1938 to 1984

4.1.13   *Fine Art and General Insurance Company* (List no 149)
Board and Committee Minutes   1933 to 1966

4.1.14   *National Insurance Company of Great Britain* (List no 153)
Board Minutes   1938 to 1984

4.1.15   *British General Insurance Company* (List no 160)
Board Minutes   1940 to 1984

4.1.16   *White Cross Insurance Association (Provident Accident and White Cross Insurance Company)* (List no 164)
Board Minutes   1925 to 1984

4.1.17   *Liverpool Victoria Insurance Corporation* (List no 165)
Board Minutes   1914 to 1950

4.1.18   *Welsh Insurance Corporation* (List no 170)
Board Minutes   1919 to 1984

4.1.19   *Lion Fire Insurance Company* (List no 141)
The records of this company were held by *General Accident Fire and Life Assurance Corporation*, Perth. This company was taken over by CGNU (now AVIVA) where the records are now held.
Staff Salaries   1891 to 1903

The following records were previously held by *Commercial Union Assurance Company* and are now with AVIVA (formerly CGNU/Norwich Union):

4.1.20   *Hand-in-Hand Fire and Life Insurance Society* (List no 3)
Board Minutes   1903 to 1967
Amalgamation Papers   1905
Policy Notebook   1815 to 1831

4.1.21   *Union* (or *Double Hand-in-Hand*) *Fire Office* (*Union Assurance Society*) (List no 5)
Board and Committee Minutes   1714 to 1893
and 1904 to 1906

4.1.22   *Commercial Union Assurance Company* (List no 114)
Board and Committee Minutes   1861 to 1988
Correspondence   1865 to 1867
Claims (marine)   1863 to 1960
Policy Records (marine)   1863 to 1961
Staff Salaries   1895 to 1915

4.2   *Zurich* (previously *Eagle Star*)
Montpellier Drive,
Cheltenham,
Gloucestershire GL53 7LQ

4.2.1   *Albion Fire and Life Insurance Company* (List no 42)
Amalgamation Papers only   1858

4.2.2   *Eagle Insurance Company* (List no 47)
Board Minutes   1807 to 1976

4.2.3   *Palladium Life and Fire Assurance Society* (List no 72)
Claims: Swansea Agency   1835 to 1852
Policy Papers   1824 to 1856

4.2.4   *English and Scottish Law Life Assurance Association* (List no 93)
              Board Minutes   1842 to 1934
              Policy Registers   from 1840

4.2.5   *Star Life and Fire Assurance Society* (List no 103)
              Board Minutes   1845 to 1967
              Policy Registers   from 1864

4.2.6   *Achilles Insurance Company* (List no 110)
              Policies   1858

4.2.7   *North Western Insurance Company* (List no 156)
              Accounts   1910 to 1915

4.2.8   *Municipal Mutual Insurance* (List no 157)
              Board Minutes   1903 to 1914
              Claims Registers   1908 to 1923
              Policy Registers   from 1903
              Staff Managers' Register   1903 to 1925

4.2.9   *British Dominions Marine Insurance Company* (*Eagle Star Insurance Company*)
              (List no 159)
              Board Minutes   1934 to 1963
              Claims Records   1926 to 1933

4.2.10   *Theatres Mutual Insurance Company* (List no 161)
              Board Minutes   1904 to 1960

4.3   *Co-operative Insurance Society*
              Miller Street
              Manchester M60 0AL

4.3.1   *Co-operative Insurance Society* (List no 126)
              Agents' Records   1922 to 1926
              Board Minutes (Scotland)   1900 to 1917
              Policy Records   1886 to 1919

4.4   *Prudential plc*
              Laurence Pountney Hill
              London EC4R 0HH

4.4.1   *Prince Fire Fire Insurance Company* (List no 117)
              Board Minutes   1862 to 1869

4.4.2   *Hercules Insurance Company* (List no 118)
              Board Minutes   (Extracts only)

4.5   *Congregational and General Insurance Company*
              Currer House
              13 Currer Street
              Bradford BD1 5BA

4.5.1   *Congregational Fire Insurance Company* (List no 151)
               Board Minutes   1938 to 1973
               Claims Records and Photographs   1927 to 1963
               Policy Registers   1891 to 1966

4.6   *Baptist Insurance Company*
               19 Billiter Street
               London EC3

4.6.1   *Baptist Fire Insurance Company* (List no 162)
               Board Minutes   from 1914

4.7   *Cornhill Insurance plc*
               57 Ladymead
               Guildford
               Surrey GU1 1DB

4.7.1   *Cornhill Insurance Company* (List no 163)
               Board Minutes   1905 to 1972
               Policy Register   1905 to 1912

4.8   *Legal and General Group*
               Temple Court
               11 Queen Victoria Street
               London EC4N 4TP

4.8.1   *Gresham Fire and Accident Insurance Company* (List no 171)
               Board Minutes   1926 to 1961
               Claims Records   1957 to 1964
               Staff Records   1911 to 9146

4.9   *Royal London Mutual Insurance Society*
               27 Middleborough
               Colchester
               Essex CO1 1RA

4.9.1   *Royal London Auxiliary Insurance Company* (List no 173)
               Board Minutes   1910 to 1920

4.10   *Royal & Sun Alliance*
               Leadenhall Court
               1 Leadenhall Street
               London EC3V 1PP

4.10.1   *Kent Fire Office* (List no 36)
               Board and Committee Minutes   1802 to 1819
               Policy Registers   1804 to 1830
               Surveys   1814 to 1824

4.11   *Standard Life Assurance Company*
               30 Lothian Road
               Edinburgh EH1 2DH

4.11.1   *Edinburgh Friendly Insurance Against Losses by Fire* (List no 8)
               Board Minutes   1846 to 1850

Appendix 5

Fire Insurance records held at Cambridge University Library

Cambridge University Library,
West Road,
Cambridge
CB3 9DR

The list numbers in brackets are the list numbers given in Appendix 1.

5.1 *New Fire Office*, established 1781 (List no 22)
Re-named *Phoenix Fire Office* 1785
Re-named *Phoenix Assurance Company* 1901

Policy Renewal Register: Brighton Branch	1936 to 1966	PX 958
Letter Book, with Accounts:		
Beith, Ayrshire	1840 to 1864	PX 959
Policy Order Register: Bedford,	1847 to 1858	PX 961
Policy Order Register: Bedford	1865 to 1874	PX 962
Policy Order Register: Bewdley,		
Worcestershire	1854 to 1940	PX 963
Policy Order Registers (4 volumes):	1821 to 1880	PX 964
Shipston, Worcestershire		to
		PX 967
Policy Order Registers (4 volumes):	1880 to 1913	PX 968
Shipston, Worcestershire		to
		PX 97
Endorsement Register:		
Birmingham Branch	1906 to 1968	PX 972
Policy Order Registers:		
Chichester, Sussex	1785 to 1818	PX 973
(4 volumes)		to
		PX 976
Policy Order Register: Devon	1783 to 1785	PX 977
Policy Order Register: Elgin,		
Elginshire	1789 to 1880	PX 978
Policy Order Register: Ely, Cambridgeshire	1831 to 1840	PX 979

Policy Order Register: Ely, Cambridgeshire (3 volumes)	1857 to 1880	PX 980 to PX 982
Policy Order Register: Guildford	1785 to 1838	PX 983
Policy Order Register: Guildford	1847 to 1865	PX 984
Policy Order Register: Hampshire	1836 to 1856	PX 985
Policy Order Register: Kidwelly, Carmarthen	1838 to 1841	PX 986
Policy Order Register: Lancaster	1797 to 1806	PX 987
Policy Order Register: Linton, Cambridgeshire	1831 to 1840	PX 988
Policy Order Register: Liverpool	1848 to 1856	PX 989
Policy Order Registers (2 volumes): Monmouth	1836 to 1927	PX 990 and PX 991
Policy Order Register: Peterborough	1811 to 1827	PX 992
Policy Order Register: Portsmouth	1830 to 1851	PX 993
Policy Order Register: Chertsey, Surrey	1812 to 1836	PX 994
Policy Order Register: Shifnal, Shropshire	1820 to 1845	PX 995
Policy Order Registers (3 volumes): Swansea	1785 to 1841	PX 996 to PX 998
Policy Order Register: Southampton	1783 to 1859	PX 999
Policy Order Register: Wootton-under-Edge, Gloucestershire	1805 to 1857	PX 1000
Policy Order Register: Yarmouth, Norfolk	1787 to 1833	PX 1001
Policy Order Register: Wellingborough, Northamptonshire	1827 to 1870	PX 1002
Policy Order Register: Worcester	1854 to 1893	PX 1003
Endorsements, Fire Policies, London	1843	PX 960
Endorsement Register: Upton on Severn Agency	1850 to 1852	PX 1004
List of Loss Registers, alphabetical B and C	1794 to 1825	PX 1255
(The registers to which these refer do not survive)		

5.2 *Protector Fire Insurance Company* (List no 80)
Board and Amalgamation Papers   1825 to 1837

5.3 *London Guarantee and Accident Company* (List no 129)
Board and Committee Minutes   from 1872

5.4 *Olympic Fire and General Reinsurance Company* (List no 176)
Board Minutes   1919 to 1924

5.5 *Tariff Reinsurances* (List no 177)
Staff Minute Book   1936 to 1970
Staff Salaries   1948 to 1959

Appendix 6

Index of Craftsmen and Traders, with Abstracts of their Policies in the Sun Fire Office Policy Registers, 1710 to 1840

This index currently (1n 2003) covers the following years:

Town Department GLDH Ms 11936
1710 to1768, 1770 to1774, 1776(part) to 1778(part), 1780 to 1782(part), 1785(part) to 1787(part), 1789(part) to 1802(part), 1808(part) to 1816(part),1818(part) to 1821(part), 1824(part) to 1827(part), 1828 to 1830 (part), 1834 (part), to 1836 (part), 1838 (part) to 1840 (part).

It should be noted that the Town Department policy series was originally contained in 733 volumes of which 60 are missing.

Country Department GLDH Ms 11937
1793 to 1800, 1803 (part), 1804 (part) to 1806 (part), 1809 (part) to 1811 (part), 1814 (part) to 1816 (part), 1819 (part) to 1821 (part), 1824 (part) to 1825 (part), 1834 (part) to 1835 (part), 1840 (part).

This period is included in 37 volumes of which 3 are missing
(1 volume missing for the year 1794 and 2 volumes missing for 1796/97)

The index is held in four sections:–
1. M/L = At the Museum of London. (This covers policies for Greater London only except where otherwise stated). Card indices; alphabetical for trades and surnames.
2. Mari = At the National Maritime Museum, Greenwich.
   Card indices; alphabetical for trades and for surnames. National coverage.
3. T/L = At the Royal Armouries, Leeds. (Originally the Tower of London).
   Card index alphabetical for surnames. National coverage.
4. Tex = Textiles Department*
   Furn = Furniture Department*
   Metals = Metals Department
   Prints = Prints Department
   These are departments at the Victoria and Albert Museum, London.
   Card indices; alphabetical for trades and for surnames. National coverage. (London and Provincial)

* These two departments have been amalgamated to form the Textiles, Furniture and Fashion Department

CHAMPION   JAMES   GUN SMITH

1192675   of The City of Chichester   21st January 1835

On a house only in New Town of the said city
in tenure of Wm Humphrey Carpenter £300. Out-
building near used as a kitchen £50. Carpenters
workshop near no pitch nor tar heated nor
stove therein £50

SUN INSURANCE 11937 VOL 217 PAGE   Total £400

SUBMITTED BY _Bally Audley_ EN5 3JD

FIELD   John Perring   gun maker

1226610   7 July 1836

of No 61 Leman K Goodmans Fields

On household goods wearing apparel plate & books in his
dwelling house brick & timber   £350

China & glass   50

Stock & utensils & goods in trust therein   600
& in manufactory & house communicating therewith
in Johnson Court Lambeth St Goodman Fields
a forge therein brick & timber   3000

Total £4000

SUN INSURANCE 1936 VOL 546 PAGE —

SUBMITTED BY _Acklam_

FIELD, JOHN PERRING   Gun Maker   17/8/1836

1225585 of 61 Leman Street, Goodmans Fields

Utensils, stock, goods in trust in his manufactory
& house adjoining & communicating situated
in Johnsons Court, Lambeth Street,
Goodmans Fields, a forge therein £1500

Total £1500

SUN INSURANCE 1936 VOL 547 PAGE

SUBMITTED BY _r.P.P.illo_

Three sample cards from the Craftsmen and Traders Index

Accoutrement Maker	Tex	Brewer	M/L
Anchor Maker/Smith	Mari	Brick Maker	M/L
Annato Maker (red dye)	Tex	Brightsmith	M/L
Armourer	T/L	Brimstone Refiner	M/L
Army Taylor	Tex	Broom Maker	M/L
Arras Maker	Tex	Brush Maker	M/L
Arras Weaver	Tex	Buckle Cutter (silver only)	M/L
Artificial Flower Maker	M/L	Buckle Maker	Tex
Artist	M/L	Buckram Stiffener	Tex
Auger Maker	M/L	Button Maker	M/L
Awl Blade Maker	M/L	Button Mould Turner	M/L
Back Maker	M/L	Cabinet Maker	Furn
Baize (Bay) Maker	Tex	Cage Maker	M/L
Balance Wheel Cutter	Metals	Calenderer	Tex
Ballast Heaver	Mari	Calico Boiler	Tex
Bandbox Maker	Tex	Calico Printer	Tex
Barge Builder	Mari	Capilaire Maker	Tex
Barrel Forger	T/L	Cap Maker	Tex
Barrel Filer	T/L	Cape Maker	Tex
Barometer Case Maker	Furn	Card Maker	M/L
Barometer Maker	Mari	Carpet Maker & Weaver	Tex
Basket Maker	M/L	Carver & Guilder	Furn
Bay Factor or Maker	Tex	Caster (gold & silver)	Metals
Bed Lace Maker	Tex	Castor Maker	Furn
Bedstead Maker	Furn	Caulker	Mari
Bell Founder	M/L	Caul Maker	M/L
Bellows Maker	M/L	Chair Maker	Furn
Bird Cage Maker	M/L	Charcoal Man	M/L
Bitt Maker	M/L	Chaser (watch)	Metals
Blacking Maker	M/L	Children's Milliner	Tex
Blacksmith	M/L	Child's Coat Maker	Tex
Blanket Maker	Tex	China Painter	M/L
Blind Maker	Tex	China Maker	M/L
Bleacher	Tex	Chinaman	M/L
Block Maker		China Rivetter	M/L
(see Mast Maker)	Mari	Chronometer Maker	Mari
Blue Maker	Tex	Cloth Worker	Tex
Boat Builder	Mari	Clothier	Tex
Bookbinder	M/L	Clock Maker	Metals
Boot Maker	Tex	Clock Case Maker	Furn
Boot & Shoe Maker	Tex	Cloth Drawer	Tex
Bobbin Maker	Tex	Clog Maker	M/L
Bombazine Maker	Tex	Coach Body Maker	M/L
Bottle Merchant	M/L	Coach Engraver	M/L
Bow String Maker	T/L	Coach Lace Maker	Tex
Bowyer	T/L	Coach Harness Maker	M/L
Box Maker, writing	Furn	Coach Maker (not master)	M/L
Box Maker, knife	Furn	Coach Painter	M/L
Box Maker	Furn	Coach Spring Maker	M/L
Brass Wire Founder	M/L	Coach Trimming Maker	Tex
Brass Wire Drawer	M/L	Coach Tyre Smith	M/L
Brass Worker	M/L	Coach Wheel Maker	M/L
Brazier	M/L	Coach Wheelwright	M/L
Breeches Maker	Tex	Coat Maker	Tex

Collar Maker	M/L	Felt Maker or Monger	Tex
Colourman or Maker	M/L	Ferret Lace Weaver	Tex
Comb Maker	M/L	Figure Maker	M/L
Compass Maker	Mari	File Cutter	M/L
Compound Distiller	M/L	Fine Drawer	Tex
Cooper	M/L	Fire Smith	M/L
Copperplate Maker	Prints	Firkinman	M/L
Copperplate Chaser	Prints	Fish Hook Maker	M/L
Copperplate Engraver	Prints	Fisherman	Mari
Copperplate Printer	Prints	Fishing Tackle Maker	Mari
Coppersmith	M/L	Flannel Maker	Tex
Cord Maker	M/L	Flax Dresser	Tex
Cork Cutter	M/L	Flax Spinner	Tex
Corver	Mari	Flock Dresser	M/L
Cotton Printer	Tex	Floorcloth Printer/	
Cotton Spinner	Tex	Painter/Maker	Tex
Counterpane Weaver	Tex	Flute Maker	M/L
Crepe Maker	Tex	Foil Beater	M/L
Cruel Man or Seller	Tex	Founder	M/L
		Frame Maker	Tex
Dealer in Marine Stores	Mari	Framework Knitter	Tex
Diamond Cutter	Metals	French Box Maker	M/L
Diamond Polisher	Metals	French Trimming Maker	Tex
Dice Maker	M/L	Fringe Maker	Tex
Die Sinker	M/L	Fustian Maker & Dyer	Tex
Distiller	M/L	Fustian Weaver	Tex
Doll Carver	M/L		
Dowlas Maker	Tex	Garter Maker	Tex
Drapers (all kinds)	Tex	Gauze Dresser	Tex
Drawing Master	Prints	Gilder	Furn
Dressmaker	Tex	Glazier	M/L
Dry Cooper	M/L	Glass Blower	M/L
Drugget Maker	Tex	Glass Cutter	M/L
Drum Maker	M/L	Glass Engraver all country	M/L
Duffel/ Duffle Maker	Tex	Glass Grinder	M/L
Dyer	Tex	Glass Maker	M/L
		Glass Seller	M/L
Earthenware Maker	M/L	Glover	Tex
Edgetool Maker	M/L	Glue Maker	M/L
Embosser	M/L	Gold & Silver Button Maker	Metals
Embroiderer	Tex	Gold & Silver Lace Maker	Tex
Emery Maker	M/L	Gold & Silver Refiner	Metals
Enameller	Metals	Gold & Silver Smith	Metals
Engineer	M/L	Gold & Silver Spinner	Metals
Engine Maker	M/L	Gold & Silver Wire Drawer	Metals
Engine Turner	M/L	Gold & Silver Worker	Metals
Engraver	Prints	Gold Beater	M/L
Etcher	Prints	Goldsmith	Metals
		Gownsman	Tex
Face Painter	M/L	Grinder	M/L
Fan Maker	Tex	Gun Barrel Maker	T/L
Fancy Dress Maker	Tex	Gun Finisher	T/L
Feather Dealer & Maker	M/L	Gun Lock Hardener	T/L
Feather Dresser	Tex	Gun Lock Maker	T/L
Felmonger	Tex	Gun Maker	T/L

Gun Smith	T/L	Lace Bed Weaver	Tex
Gun Stock Maker	T/L	Lace Ferret Weaver	Tex
		Lace Fringe Weaver	Tex
Haberdasher	Tex	Lace Orris Weaver	Tex
Habit Maker	Tex	Lace Worsted Weaver	Tex
Haft Maker	Metals	Lapidary	M/L
Hairdresser	Tex	Last Maker	M/L
Hairman & Dealer in Flock	Tex	Lath Render	M/L
Hair Merchant	Tex	Lead Caster	M/L
Hair Throwster	Tex	Lead Maker	M/L
Handkerchief Printer	Tex	Leather Cutter	M/L
Harness Maker	M/L	Leather Drawer	M/L
Harp Maker	M/L	Leather Dresser	M/L
Harpsichord Maker	Furn	Leather Gilder	M/L
Hartshorn Dealer	M/L	Lighterman	Mari
Hatter or Hat Maker	Tex	Lighter Builder	Mari
Hat - miscellaneous	Tex	Lincloth Maker	Tex
Hat Presser	Tex	Linen Dyer	Tex
Herald Painter	M/L	Linen Weaver	Tex
Heel Maker	Tex	Link Maker	M/L
Hemp Dresser	Tex	Locksmith	M/L
Herbalist	M/L	Looking Glass Maker	M/L
Hoop Bender	M/L	Loom Maker & Broker	Tex
Horn Maker (wind & brass)	M/L		
Horner	M/L	Machine Ruler	M/L
Horn Turner	M/L	Machinery Maker	M/L
Horsehair Maker	Tex	Mackler (seller of weavers'	
Hosier	Tex	goods)	Tex
Hot Presser	Tex	Mahogany Dealer	M/L
		Manchester Warehouseman	Tex
Indian Gownman	Tex	Mangle Maker	M/L
Indigo Maker	Tex	Mantua Maker	Tex
Ink Maker	M/L	Map Maker	M/L
Inlayer	Furn	Map & Print Colourer	M/L
Instrument Maker	M/L	Marble Merchant	M/L
Iron Founder	M/L	Marble Polisher	M/L
Ironmaster	M/L	Mast Maker & Block Maker	Mari
Ironmonger	M/L	Marine Stores Dealer	Mari
Iron Plate Worker	M/L	Mariner	Mari
Italian Merchant	M/L	Mason	M/L
Ivory Turner	M/L	Master Mariner	Mari
		Match Maker	M/L
Jack Maker	M/L	Mathematical Instrument	
Japanner	Metals	Maker	Mari
Japanned Leather Hat		Mathematician	M/L
Bleacher	Tex	Mat Maker	M/L
Jersey Comber	Tex	Mattress Maker	M/L
Jersey Weaver	Tex	Men's Mercer	Tex
Jeweller	M/L	Mercer	Tex
Joiner/Joyner (c1730 only)	Furn	Merchant Tailor	Tex
		Metal Worker	M/L
Knife Case or Box Maker	Furn	Mezzotinter	Prints
Knot Maker	M/L	Mezzotinto Scraper	Prints
		Milliner	Tex
Laceman/woman	Tex	Mill Washer	M/L

Millwright	M/L	Picture Frame Maker	Furn
Miniature Painter	M/L	Pilot	Mari
Mop Maker	M/L	Pinker	Tex
Mop Stick Maker	M/L	Pin Maker	M/L
Mop Yarn Maker	M/L	Pipe Maker	M/L
Muff & Tippet Maker	Tex	Plane Maker	M/L
Musical Instrument Maker	M/L	Plaster of Paris Maker	M/L
Musician	M/L	Plate Glass Maker	M/L
Music Master	M/L	Plate Worker	M/L
Music Printer	M/L	Pocket Book Maker	M/L
Muslin Manufacterer	Tex	Porcelain Trades & Dealers	M/L
Mustard Maker	M/L	Potash Maker	M/L
		Potter	M/L
Nautical Instrument Maker	Mari	Pottery Trades & Dealers	M/L
Necklace Maker	M/L	(all country)	
Needle Maker	M/L	Powder Flask Maker	T/L
Net Maker	Mari	Press Maker	M/L
Nightgown Maker	Tex	Print Cutter	M/L
		Printed Paper	
Oar Maker	Mari	Hangings Maker	M/L
Oil & Colourman	M/L	Printer	M/L
Oilman	M/L	Print Maker	Prints
Operator of the Teeth	M/L	Print Publisher	Prints
Optical Glass Maker	M/L	Pump Maker	M/L
Optician	M/L	Purse Maker	M/L
Orchell Weaver	Tex		
Organ Builder	Furn	Quadrant Maker	Mari
Ornamental Paper Artist	M/L	Quarterman	Mari
Orris Lace Maker	Tex	Quill Maker	M/L
Orris Weaver	Tex	Quill & Feather Merchant	M/L
Ostrich Feather Dealer	Tex	Quilter	Tex
Oil/Oyle Cooper	M/L	Quilt Warehouseman	Tex
Pack Thread Spinner	M/L	Razor Maker	M/L
Painter (Artist only)	M/L	Razor Strop Maker	M/L
Painting Brush Maker	M/L	Reed Maker	Tex
Paper Hanging		Refiner	M/L
Manufacturer	M/L	Refiner (Brimstone)	M/L
Paper Maker	M/L	Repeating Watch Motion	
Paper Stainer	M/L	Maker	Metals
Papier Mâché Maker	M/L	Ribbon Dresser	Tex
Parasol Maker	M/L	Ribbon Maker	Tex
Pasteboard Maker	M/L	Ribbon Weaver	Tex
Patent Pearl Maker	M/L	Rigger	Mari
Patten Maker	Tex	Robe Maker	Tex
Pattern Drawer	Tex	Rope Maker	Mari
Pearl Bead Maker	M/L	Roper	Mari
Pencil Maker	M/L	Rug Maker	Tex
Pen Cutter	M/L		
Perfumer	M/L	Sack Weaver	Tex
Perriwig Maker	Tex	Sacking Weaver	Tex
Peruke Maker	Tex	Saddle Tree Maker	M/L
Petticoat Maker	Tex	Saddle Tree Riveter	M/L
Pewterer	Metals	Sail Maker	Mari
Piano Maker	Furn	Sailcloth Weaver & Maker	Tex

Saltpetre Refiner	M/L	Silk Manufacturer	Tex
(Patent) Sash Line Maker	M/L	Silk Mercer	Tex
Satin Dresser	Tex	Silk Merchant	Tex
Satin Weaver	Tex	Silk Printer	Tex
Saw Maker	M/L	Silk & Satin Dresser	Tex
Sawyer	M/L	Silk Throwster	Tex
Say Maker	Tex	Silk Twister	Tex
Scale Beam Maker	M/L	Silk Weaver	Tex
Scale Maker	M/L	Silver Buckle Maker	Metals
Scavelman	Mari	Silver Caster	Metals
Scissors Maker	M/L	Silver Chaser	Metals
Scourer	Tex	Silver Foil Maker	M/L
Screen Maker	M/L	Silver – miscellaneous	Metals
Screen Ink Maker	M/L	Silversmith	Metals
Screw Maker	M/L	Silver Turner	Metals
Sculptor	M/L	Size Boiler	M/L
Scumbag Maker	M/L	Size Whiting Maker	M/L
Sea Biscuit Maker	Mari	Skin Dyer	Tex
Seal Engraver	M/L	Slea Maker	Tex
Sealing Wax Maker	M/L	Smith	M/L
Secret Springer	Metals	Snuff Maker	M/L
Sedan Chair Maker	Furn	Soap Boiler	M/L
Serge Maker	Tex	Soap Maker	M/L
Serge Weaver	Tex	Soda Water Maker	M/L
Sewing & Indian Cotton	Tex	Sofa Maker	Furn
Manufacturer		Spanish Leather Dresser	M/L
Sextant Maker	Mari	Spangle Maker	Tex
Shag Weaver	Tex	Spectacle Maker	M/L
Shagreen Case Maker	Furn	Spermaceti Candle Maker	M/L
Shaloon Weaver	Tex	Spinning Wheel Maker	Furn
Shawl Cutter	Tex	Spoon Maker	M/L
Shawl Designer	Tex	Spur Maker	T/L
Shawl Fringer	Tex	Spurrier	T/L
Shawl Maker/Manufacturer	Tex	Staffordshire Ware Trades	M/L
Shawl Presser	Tex	(All country)	
Shawl Printer	Tex	Starch Maker	M/L
Shawl Weaver	Tex	Statuary	M/L
Ship Agent	Mari	Stay Maker	Tex
Ship Breaker	Mari	Steel Worker	M/L
Ship Builder	Mari	Sticking Plaster Maker	M/L
Ship Carpenter	Mari	Stockinger	Tex
Ship Carver	Mari	Stocking Framework Knitter	Tex
Ship Caulker	Mari	Stocking Legger	Tex
Ship Chandler	Mari	Stocking Maker/Trimmer	Tex
Ship Master	Mari	Stocking Presser	Tex
Ship Merchant	Mari	Stocking Scourer	Tex
Ship Owner	Mari	Stocking Weaver	Tex
Shipwright	Mari	Stone Carver	M/L
Shoemaker	Tex	Straw, Chip, Leghorn &	Tex
Shot Maker	T/L	Willow Bleacher	
Shovel Maker	M/L	Straw Bonnet Maker	Tex
Shroud Maker	M/L	Straw Hat Maker	Tex
Silk Dresser	Tex	Strong Waterman	M/L
Silk Dyer	Tex	Stuff Mercer	Tex
Silkman	Tex	Sugar Baker	M/L

Sugar Boiler	M/L	Veneer Manufacturer	Furn
Sugar Cooper	M/L	Vest Manufacturer	Tex
Sugar Refiner	M/L	Vinegar Maker & Merchant	M/L
Surgical Instrument Maker	M/L	Violin Maker (including	M/L
Surgical Spirit Maker	M/L	accessories)	
Sweep Washer	M/L	Violin String Maker	M/L
Sword Cutler	T/L		
Sword Guilder	T/L	Waistcoat & Vest Maker	Tex
Silvester Maker (red dye)	Tex	Warehouse Keeper	M/L
		Warehouseman (all kinds)	M/L
Tabby Waterer	Tex	Warper	Tex
Tambour Worker	Tex	Watchcase Maker	Metals
Tapestry Worker	Tex	Watch Chain Maker	Metals
Tarpaulin Maker	M/L	Watch Chaser	Metals
Tailor/Taylor	Tex	Watch Engraver	Metals
Telescope Maker	Mari	Watch Finisher	Metals
Textile Paper (for weavers)	Tex	Watch Gilder	Metals
Thimble Maker	M/L	Watch Glass Maker	Metals
Thread Maker	Tex	Watch Maker	Metals
Thread Twister	Tex	Watch Piercer	Metals
Throwster	Tex	Watch Spring Maker	Metals
Thermometer Maker	M/L	Water Colour Maker	M/L
Timber Merchant	M/L	Water Gilder	M/L
Tide Surveyor	Mari	Waterman	Mari
Tide Waiter	Mari	Waterproof Hat Maker	Tex
Tinman	M/L	Weaver	Tex
Tin Manufacturer	M/L	Weaver, Fustian	Tex
Tinplate Worker	M/L	Weaver, Ferret Lace	Tex
Tire/Tyre Smith	M/L	Weaver, Orched	Tex
Tobacco Cutter	M/L	Weaver, Sailcloth	Tex
Tobacco Pipe Maker	M/L	Weaver, Satin	Tex
Tobacco & Snuff Maker	M/L	Weaver, Serge	Tex
Tool Maker	M/L	Weaver, Shag	Tex
Tool Seller	M/L	Weaver, Shaloon	Tex
Tortoiseshell Box Maker	Furn	Weaver, Silk	Tex
Toy Maker	M/L	Weaver (any other)	Tex
Toyman	M/L	Wedge Maker	M/L
Trimming Maker	Tex	Whalebone Cutter	M/L
Trunk Maker	M/L	Whalebone Merchant	M/L
Truss Maker	M/L	Whalebone Warehouseman	M/L
Tucker	Tex	Wharfinger	Mari
Turner	M/L	Wheelwright	M/L
Turpentine Maker	M/L	Wheeldrawer	M/L
Twine Spinner	M/L	White Lead Manufacturer	M/L
Twisterer	Tex	Whitesmith	M/L
		Whiting Maker	M/L
Upholder	Furn	Wind & Brass Instrument	M/L
Upholsterer	Furn	Maker	
Umbrella Maker	Tex	Wire Drawer	M/L
Undertaker	M/L	Wire Drawer (gold & silver)	Metals
		Wire Maker	M/L
Vellum Binder	Prints	Wire Worker	M/L
Velvet Dyer	Tex	Women's Cloak Maker	Tex
Velvet Weaver	Tex	Woollen Manufacturer	Tex
Venetian Blind Maker	Tex	Woollen Printer	Tex

Woollen Weaver	Tex
Wool Scribbler	Tex
Woollen Spinner	Tex
Worsted Lace Maker	Tex
Worsted Maker	Tex
Whitster (bleacher)	Tex
Wine Cooper	M/L
Writing Box Maker	Furn
Yarn Maker	Tex
Yeast Manufacturer	M/L
Zinc Manufacturer	M/L

Appendix 7

An explanation of the pre-decimal Monetary System (Pounds, shillings and pence) used in Fire Insurance records.

£1	=	one pound
1s	=	one shilling
1d	=	one penny
$\frac{1}{2}$d	=	half a penny
$\frac{1}{4}$d	=	quarter of a penny, or farthing

20 shillings	=	one pound
12 pence	=	one shilling
240 pennies	=	one pound

Examples:-

2d	=	two pennies (tuppence)
3d	=	three pennies (thruppence)
6$\frac{1}{2}$d	=	sixpence and a half penny (sixpence ha'penny)
10s or 10/-	=	ten shillings
12s-6d or 12/6 or 12-6	=	twelve shillings and sixpence
£2-11-5$\frac{1}{2}$	=	two pounds, eleven shillings and five pence ha'penny

Sovereign	=	one pound
Guinea	=	one pound and one shilling
Crown	=	five shilling
Half a crown	=	two shillings and sixpence
Florin	=	two shillings
Thruppence	=	three pence
Ha'penny	=	half a penny
Farthing	=	quarter of a penny

Personal Name Index

Place Name Index

Acknowledgements – Document Transcripts

Transcripts of the Sun Fire Office, Nottinghamshire and Derbyshire Fire and Life Assurance Company, Monarch Fire and Life Assurance Company, London Assurance Corporation, Law Union Fire and Life Insurance Company, County Fire Office, Church of England Life and Fire Assurance Trust, Globe Insurance Company, Farmers and General Insurance Company, Law Fire Insurance Society, Law Union and Crown Insurance Company and the London and Lancashire Insurance Company held at the Guildhall Library, London, are reproduced by permission of the Royal and Sun Alliance and the Keeper of Manuscripts at the Guildhall Library.

Transcripts of Phoenix Fire Office Records held at Cambridge University Library are reproduced by permission of the Syndics of Cambridge University Library. Transcripts of Phoenix Fire Office records held at the Warwickshire County Record Office are reproduced by permission of the Warwickshire County Archivist.

Transcripts of records from the Manchester Fire and Life Assurance Company, Essex and Suffolk Equitable Insurance Company, Royal Exchange Assurance and the Atlas Assurance Company are reproduced by permission of AXA Insurance.

Transcripts of records of the London Assurance Corporation held at the Berkshire Record Office are reproduced by permission of the Berkshire County Archivist and the Royal and Sun Alliance.

Transcripts of records of the Law Union Fire and Life Insurance Company held at the Herefordshire Record Office are reproduced by permission of the Hereford County Archivist and the Royal and Sun Alliance.

Transcripts of records of the Hand-in-Hand Fire Office, Norwich Union Fire Insurance Society and the West of England Fire and Life Insurance Company are reproduced by permission of AVIVA.

Transcripts of Admiralty records held at The National Archives (formerly the Public Record Office), London, are reproduced by permission of Her Majesty's Stationery Office.

Abstracts from the Aston Samford parish register are reproduced by permission of the Buckinghamshire County Archivist.

Select Bibliography

Anon, *After Fifty Years*, The London and Lancashire Fire Insurance Company
 London & Lancashire Insurance Co, 1912
Anon, *A History of the Caledonian Insurance Company*, Constable, London, 1905
Baumer, Edward, *The Early Days of the Sun Fire Office*, Sir Joseph Causton &
 Sons Ltd, London, 1910
Bulau, Alwin E., *Footprints of Assurance*, Macmillan, New York, 1953
Chapman, Stanley D., *The Devon Cloth Industry in the Eighteenth Century*, Devon
 & Cornwall Record Society. New Series Volume 23, 1978
Cockerell H.A.L. and Green, E., *The British Insurance Business 1547 to 1961*,
 Heinemann, London, 1976
Dickson, P.G.M., *The Sun Insurance Office*, Oxford University Press, London,
 1960
Drew, Bernard, *The Fire Office*, Curwin, London, 1952
Edmundson, Roger, *Staffordshire Potteries Insured with the Salop Fire Office,
 1780–1825*, Journal of The Northern Ceramics Society, Volume 6, 1987
Fothergill, George A., *British Fire Marks*, William Green, Edinburgh & London,
 1911
Golding, C. E., *A History of Re-insurance with Sidelights on Insurance*, Private
 Circulation (Printed by Walterlow & Sons Ltd), Birchin Lane, London, 1st
 Edition 1927, 2nd Edition 1931
Head, Victor, *The Story of the National Farmers Union Mutual Insurance Society
 Limited*, National Farmers Union, 1985
Henham, Brian, *Hand in Hand*, Commercial Union, London, 1996
Jones, E. L., Porter S., Turner M., *A Gazetteer of English Urban Fire Disasters
 1500-1900*, Historial Geography Research Series No.13, August 1984
Liveing, Edward, *A Century of Insurance. The Commercial Union Group of
 Companies 1861-1961*, Witherby, London, 1961
Noakes, Aubrey, *The County Fire Office*, Witherby, London, 1957
Raynes, H.E., *A History of British Insurance*, Pitman, London, 1964
Relton, F.B., *An Account of Insurance Companies during the 17th and 18th Centuries*,
 Swan Sonnenschein, London, 1893
Rowley, Gwyn, *British Fire Insurance Plans*, Chas. E. Goad, 1984
Ryan, R.J., *A History of the Norwich Union Fire and Life Societies from 1797 to 1914*,
 PhD Thesis, 1983
Schooling, Sir William, *Alliance Assurance*, Alliance, London, 1924
Shepherd, A.F, *Links with the Past. A History of the Eagle Insurance Company,
 Eagle Star, and British Dominions Insurance Company*, 1917
Supple, Barry, *The Royal Exchange Assurance*, Cambridge University Press, 1970

Supple, Barry, *Insurance in British History in the Historian and The Business of Insurance*, Manchester University Press, 1984

Syed, Isabel, *Eagle Star*, Eagle Star, Cheltenham, 1997

Trebilcock, Clive, *Phoenix Assurance and the Development of British Insurance*, Cambridge University Press, 1985

Westall, Oliver M., *The Provincial Insurance Company 1903 to 1938*, Manchester University Press, 1992

Williams, B., *Fire Marks and Insurance Office Fire Brigades*, Layton, London, 1927

Williams, B., *Specimens of British Fire Marks*, Layton, London, 1934

Wright, B.W., *The British Fire Mark 1680 to 1879*, Woodhead & Faulkner, 1982

Decorative heading to policy from Albion Fire and Life Insurance Company
Courtesy of Zurich